Light in the Valley of the Shadow of Death

GLOBAL LIBRARY

Light in the Valley of the Shadow of Death

Edited by
Roman Soloviy

GLOBAL LIBRARY

© 2025 Eastern European Institute of Theology

Published 2025 by Langham Global Library
An imprint of Langham Publishing
www.langhampublishing.org

Langham Publishing and its imprints are a ministry of Langham Partnership

Langham Partnership
PO Box 296, Carlisle, Cumbria, CA3 9WZ, UK
www.langham.org

ISBNs:
978-1-78641-197-6 Print
978-1-78641-261-4 ePub
978-1-78641-262-1 PDF

All rights reserved. No part of this publication may be reproduced, stored in a retrieval system or transmitted, in any form or by any means, electronic, mechanical, photocopying, recording or otherwise, without the prior written permission of the publisher or the Copyright Licensing Agency.

Requests to reuse content from Langham Publishing are processed through PLSclear. Please visit www.plsclear.com to complete your request.

All Scripture quotations, unless otherwise indicated, are taken from the Holy Bible, New International Version®, NIV®. Copyright ©1973, 1978, 1984, 2011 by Biblica, Inc.™ Used by permission of Zondervan.

Scripture quotations marked (ESV) are taken from The Holy Bible, English Standard Version® (ESV®), copyright © 2001 by Crossway, a publishing ministry of Good News Publishers. Used by permission. All rights reserved.

British Library Cataloguing-in-Publication Data
A catalogue record for this book is available from the British Library

ISBN: 978-1-78641-197-6

Cover & Book Design: projectluz.com
Illustrations © Katerina Sad / full name SADOVSHCHUK KATERYNA
Translated from Ukrainian by Marichka Androshchuk

Langham Partnership actively supports theological dialogue and an author's right to publish but does not necessarily endorse the views and opinions set forth here or in works referenced within this publication, nor can we guarantee technical and grammatical correctness. Langham Partnership does not accept any responsibility or liability to persons or property as a consequence of the reading, use or interpretation of its published content.

Contents

Foreword vii

1 Diary of a Theologian. 3
　Taras Dyatlik

2 Theological Education among the Ruins. 49
　Oleksandr Geychenko

3 Homeless God. 67
　Nadiyka Gerbish

4 Finding Yourself When You're Tossed in a Sea of Lost Faces. 79
　Kseniia Trofymchuk

5 Reclaiming Home. 97
　Pavlo Horbunov

6 It's Still Too Dark Here, but I'm No Longer Afraid 119
　Denis Gorenkov

7 I Will Follow You: Where Will You Lead Me? 143
　Yevhen Yazvinskyy

8 A Christian in the Army: An AFU Officer's Story. 183
　Illia Flisiuk

9 Loving Was Never Easy 217
　Andriy Polukhin

10 On Being the Wife of a Soldier Fighting on the Front Line 239
　Alla Shyrshyna

11 Faith in Spite of Everything. 259
　Daria Papushoi

12 Gospel in a Yellow Box 279
　Dmytro Tyshchenko

Foreword

War became the watershed of our lives, dividing them into "before" and "after." I remember well my thinking in February–March of 2022: we will never be able to go back to the life we had in Ukraine before Russia's full-scale invasion. Back then, that feeling of complete severance from the past and the impossibility of returning to the same old life was more of an emotional reaction to the trauma caused by this atrocious war. Today, that feeling, driven by horrifying statistics and personal stories, has settled into a firm understanding of a new reality. Many Ukrainians will not be able to just go back. Some served in the army and were killed in action or taken captive. Some have lost their houses to shelling or Russian occupation. According to UN statistics, as of August 2024, more than six million of our fellow citizens have become refugees abroad, and just as many have become internally displaced persons, trying to build a new life in parts of Ukraine farther from the front lines.

Not only did the war sever us from our past, but it continues to divide us, building walls aimed at separating civilians and soldiers, those who fled the country and those who decided to stay, those who still have their homes and families and those living in desolation and loneliness because of destruction and death. Families are suffering, forced apart by war and emigration. Such divisions lead to severe psychological trauma, alienation, and misunderstandings between various groups of Ukrainians. Yet, despite all these challenges, Ukrainian society shows incredible resilience. Volunteers, civil society organizations, and everyday citizens are persistently working to bridge these divides, support those in need, and keep unity for the sake of a future for all.

Churches, in general – and evangelical Protestants in particular – have been instrumental in the rally to defend our country, continue the healing of our bruised and broken Ukrainian society, and shape our future. Going against the stereotypes often associated with Ukrainian Protestants – such as distancing themselves from society and a tradition of pacifism – believers from these churches joined in the fight to save the country and its citizens, even in the first days of the invasion. How exactly did they do that? This book brings together twelve authors to tell their stories. Each one of them has joined in the fight against evil, the fight to preserve dignity and freedom. They made their choice back then and reaffirm it daily as they pass through this collective Gethsemane filled with fear, loss, and despair. Yet they have faith that after Calvary comes Resurrection. That's what these authors have in common. That's what they share with readers – their personal and profound experience of the last few years, an experience where faith is inextricably intertwined with doubts, fear is bound up with courage, and loneliness goes hand in hand with connection.

How do evangelical theologians perceive and process an impending war? How do they respond as it erupts, bringing challenges and losses? Taras Dyatlik, theologian and educator, takes a diary-entry approach to reflect on this experience during eleven days of February 2022. He touches on the foreboding of war, his return to Ukraine from his trip abroad, and the coordination of efforts among Ukrainian evangelical educational institutions as they poured all their resources and efforts into helping Ukrainians who were fleeing hostilities. The events of those few days highlight the trauma brought on by war but also the impact that faith, prayer, and love for God and neighbour can have on our ability not only to cope with our own struggles but to begin a ministry to serve the victims of war. The inability of Russian evangelicals to condemn this war and its root cause – the imperialist ideology of "Russki mir" – echoes throughout his reflections. Nonetheless, in the first days of the full-scale invasion, during the darkest hour of despair and uncertainty, Taras Dyatlik affirms the ultimate truth of our time, which is the main message of this book: "The light of Christ shines even in the darkest moments."

As theological educational institutions originally located in southern Ukraine sought refuge in safer parts of the country, seminaries in central and western Ukraine were transformed into volunteer hubs. Oleksandr Geychenko recounts the evacuation of the Odesa Theological Seminary from his perspective as its rector, sharing his experiences of those first few weeks and months of the full-scale war. Like many of us, he faced the phenomenon of a "delayed life" and had to come to terms with the dreadful reality that this war would last for quite some time and that our lives had changed forever. He describes how the war exposed the inability of traditional theological language to capture feelings of powerlessness and anger but, at the same time, also allowed him to turn to the imprecatory psalms and learn anew how to express his feelings to God, transforming pain into prayer and tears into faith that God will have the final say.

The next two authors raise the issue of losing a home and the need for a home. What they have in common with each other, and with millions of other Ukrainians, is that at the beginning of the full-scale invasion, they both had to leave Ukraine for a while. Nadiyka Gerbish, a writer, opens up about her painful experience during the first two weeks of the war – her exhausting move to another country, her separation from her husband, and her miscarriage. How many other Ukrainian women endured similar struggles because of the enormous stress brought on by the war? Perhaps we'll never know with certainty. Despite all this, Nadiyka aspires to foster hope, believing that the judgement on evil has already been pronounced and that light will ultimately prevail. While we're still trapped in time and have not yet been delivered into eternity, we must continue to shine the light, hold on to hope, and create a home every single day. How this can be possible today is the question raised by our next author and theologian, Kseniia Trofymchuk, who draws on concepts familiar to modern people: the experience of being "borderless" and seeing oneself as part of a "global village" without strong attachment to the idea of a "home." Referencing the literary works of Viktor Domontovych, Kseniia explores issues surrounding the identity of a modern person as the sense of belonging to a land and having connection to a past slowly dwindles. Ukrainian emigrants who remained in the West after World War II experienced this loss of connection to their homeland with a particularly vivid existential poignancy. Today, this distressing experience of being uprooted is the fate of millions of Ukrainian refugees – including Kseniia – scattered around the world by the ruthless forces of war. Yet, even in distant foreign lands, they do not feel entirely "homeless" as many countries – from Europe and North America to Japan and Australia – have opened their doors to welcome Ukrainian refugees. This miracle of hospitality may not restore a home, but it can certainly help heal the wounds and offer hope to press on.

What does "home" mean to a Christian who has joined the army? Pavlo Horbunov – a theology lecturer before the beginning of the war and a military chaplain since – ponders this question. Like some other contributors to this book, he was abroad when the full-scale invasion began; yet without hesitation, he returned to Ukraine and voluntarily enlisted in the Armed Forces of Ukraine. As a biblical theologian, Pavlo believes that the spiritual reason for this war – and all wars – is a lie, a deception that has characterized the works of the devil throughout the ages and is exemplified in present-day Russian propaganda. He asserts that every Christian must constantly be on guard, refusing to be deceived or to allow spiritual blindness, cowardice, or laziness to take root in their minds. He attempts to dispel illusions such as the hope for peace without justice, reconciliation without the perpetrators' repentance, and ending the war without returning home – both literally and theologically. He believes that all soldiers are wayfarers who lay down their heads wherever they are and give their all to stop evil so that refugees and exiles can return to their homes.

The journey to military service takes different roads for different Christians. Denis Gorenkov, a theologian and volunteer before the war began, shares his deeply personal experience. This is an incredibly raw and honest story of his path to God, the intense personal crisis the war caused, and his rediscovery of himself as he served in the army, where he could "finally see himself as he was meant to be." Amid the darkness and horrors of war, he still felt the path beneath his feet and saw the light leading him on. After serving for a year as a private, Denis received his credentials and became a chaplain; later, he became a lecturer at the Centre for Training of Military Chaplains in Kyiv. He defines an army chaplain's mission as, first and foremost, being a presence that is a sign of God's care and a source of spiritual support for soldiers. As such, it is important to feel the pain that others are going through and let this drive our efforts towards the future of the Ukraine that we all dream of and long to see.

The next three authors also voluntarily enlisted in the Armed Forces of Ukraine. Yevhen Yazvinskyy enlisted on the tenth day of the war. Why would a leader of Campus Crusade for Christ, with no prior military experience, become a sergeant in the Signal Corps? Just like many others, he was compelled by anger at the horrors of war but also by the realization that he faced a crucial moment of decision and had to choose whether to run, hide, or take responsibility for what happened to his country. According to Yevhen, God called him to step into the chaos and horrors of war. But to answer that call, he had to overcome his fear and follow wherever the Lord might lead, trusting even in the darkest hour. The war became Yevhen's Gethsemane – a time of intense spiritual trials and existential crises that prompted him to rethink his previously held theological beliefs. At the same time, the front lines brought a new revelation about the preciousness of God's creation and, consequently, the responsibility we carry for the world God has created, in addition to the right to enjoy the gifts God has given. The war breaks down the walls between Christian traditions: "Santa" (Yevhen's call sign) and his Orthodox friend created a makeshift chapel at the battalion's command post in partially besieged Sievierodonetsk just to provide spiritual support and care to their weary brothers-in-arms.

Illia Flisiuk, an officer of the Armed Forces of Ukraine, spent a full year helping people as a volunteer. Then, on the first anniversary of Russia's full-scale invasion, he enlisted. His story is a testimony of sacrifice, valour, and God's protection amid the fray of war. At the same time, it is a lament – an expression of pain over the fact that not all of his brothers and sisters share his ardour for volunteering or support his decision to enlist. Illia's story is reminiscent of the heroes of faith in the Old Testament, who, although they did sometimes flee from their enemies, courageously stood their ground against evil and chose to trust God even in seemingly hopeless situations.

For Andriy Polukhin, currently a Private First Class, protecting his country through serving in the Armed Forces of Ukraine is, first and foremost, an expression of his love for his homeland and his people. His fight for dignity and freedom for all began on the Maidan during the Revolution of Dignity and continued at the Donetsk Airport, where he was a chaplain-medic in one of the Ukrainian platoons that stood their ground at this landmark of Ukraine's defence from September 2014 to 23 January 2015. After that, Andriy served as a volunteer chaplain for some time before switching to ministering to youth in the city of Svitlodarsk, once again as a volunteer. He enlisted in the army at the beginning of March 2022. Initially, he was part of the medical corps but now serves as a Press Officer in one of the battalions. Andriy is brutally honest in writing about his incredible moral fatigue, the torment of missing his wife, and the heartbreak of losing his brothers-in-arms. Nevertheless, he continues to emphasize that love is a choice to act for the good of those you love. For this reason, he has resolved to follow this path through to the end.

Endless worries about a loved one, loneliness, and the weight of responsibility for children are just a few of the challenges faced by Christian women married to soldiers. Alla Shyrshyna shares her experience as the wife of a combatant officer who enlisted on the first day of the full-scale invasion. The cities in the Donetsk region where they met, got married, and began their life together are now under Russian occupation and mostly destroyed, and Alla's husband, Oleksandr, is at the front lines nearly all the time. Alla writes candidly about the constant worries that plague her and other military wives, the distress they feel due to the lack of understanding from other people – including the church community – and the dire need for ministries and programmes to support military families and provide a much-needed respite. Despite these challenges, she believes that even in the dreary, never-ending, and exhausting daily routine, God is there with her and knows her.

Faith against all odds is what Daria Papushoi, wife of a fallen hero, chooses. Their story began in 2020 in Mykolaiv, when she came there as a missionary. Daria met Pavlo during his leave from service in the Anti-Terrorist Operation (ATO). Their relationship developed quickly, and they were married just five months before the full-scale invasion. On the very next day following the announcement of mobilization, Pavlo enlisted in the Air Assault Forces. Daria prayed for him constantly. Drawing on her own experience, she shares advice for army wives who are called to motivate, inspire, support, and deeply love their husbands even – and especially – in this dark hour. After a year and eight months of war, Pavlo was killed in action by a Russian drone strike. A couple of months later, Daria gave birth to their son, Tymofii. Despite her grief and loss, she still believes in God's unconditional love and continues to pray and trust.

Volunteer efforts have become one of the most crucial Christian ministries during this war. Christians evacuate people from cities where the front lines have advanced too close, provide assistance and support to residents of liberated territories and internally displaced persons, organize humanitarian aid centres, and volunteer in military hospitals. Pastor Dmytro Tyshchenko describes the ministries of the mission Ukraine for Christ. Russia's brutal invasion of Ukraine forced him to ask: Can God be found amid war? Is it possible to feel God's presence in the midst of cruelty and atrocities? The answer came to him during his stay in Lviv. Dmytro felt that in times of national catastrophe, joy can only be found in serving others, in ministering to your neighbour. Therefore, this pastor and his crew launched a humanitarian aid project that continues its efforts to this day. A hallmark of their ministry is bright yellow food boxes. These kits give Christians an opportunity to engage with people in need on a personal level. Amid hopelessness, despair, and darkness, the colour yellow serves as a reminder of light and a new day that is most definitely coming.

As I conclude this foreword, I want to express my deepest gratitude to all the authors who dared to share their stories in this book. During this process, some of them had to face their fears again. For others, this act of recollection became almost therapeutic, bringing healing and relief. Some took this opportunity to express their pain and leave a testimony for future generations. All of them – just like the majority of Ukrainians – are deeply, and probably permanently, traumatized by the war. They have suffered irreplaceable losses and carry wounds that will only be healed in the Heavenly City. They are still walking through "the valley of the shadow of death" (Ps 23:4 ESV), yet they choose to keep believing, keep hoping, and keep loving.

Roman Soloviy

"These pages invite the reader to engage in a profound theological reflection on war, to reimagine our faith in light of suffering, and to act, compelled by love for God and our neighbour." Taras Dyatlik (p. 3)

1

Diary of a Theologian

Taras Dyatlik
Regional Director, Scholar Leaders; Theological Education Consultant, Mesa Global

Prologue

Diary of a Theologian is a chronicle of eleven days during February 2022 – the watershed of my personal life and the life of my country, Ukraine. These pages are a patchwork of my thoughts and experiences, pieced together from my personal diary, text messages in various apps, social media posts, and correspondence. Each line of this diary testifies to how quickly the world we know can be upended, turning a peaceful life into a trial that tests our faith, hope, and love in the face of war.

From the anxious foreboding of 18 February to the horrific events of full-scale invasion on 24 February, my notes go beyond recounting chronological events to capture the wrenching existential and theological questions that I was facing. This is a story of faith challenged by the brutal trials of war, a story of theology tasked with answering the perplexing questions and complex issues of human existence. This is a story about a search for God amid the chaos of destruction and an attempt to reframe events in the light of Scripture and Christian tradition.

Diary of a Theologian is not just my personal story. It is also a reflection on the nature of evil and suffering, the power of prayer and unity, and the role of the church in trying times. It is an attempt to capture the moment when faith meets its greatest challenge – a real war. It is just a glimpse of the story of the Christians of Ukraine, looking to God for strength to persevere as they face the stark reality of the invasion.

These pages invite the reader to engage in a profound theological reflection on war, to reimagine our faith in light of suffering, and to act, compelled by love for God and our neighbour. They remind us of the preciousness of peace and the power of unity in Christ. They also point to a hope that does not fade, even in the darkest hour, because our Lord is the God of hope and resurrection.

Faraway Clouds
Friday, 18 February 2022; location: Rivne

> When you see a cloud rising in the west, immediately you say, "It's going to rain," and it does.
>
> Luke 12:54

7:15 a.m. I woke up early. My heart was heavy. The news was far from encouraging: Putin had signed an executive order to call up reservists of the Russian army for training. This decision caused a great deal of anxiety, not just for me but for many Ukrainians. It indicated preparations for potential military action. Why does a human being, gifted with the ability to reason and the capacity for compassion, choose violence? These thoughts continue to haunt us, even though the Ukrainian government reassures us that everything is under control and that everything will be just fine. The people on the streets seem far more tense than usual. At a store, I noticed some customers stocking up on dry goods and water. Are people really getting ready for the worst?

9:30 a.m. I found out that the British Embassy is being temporarily relocated to Lviv because of the threat of Russian invasion. This only underscores the gravity of the situation. Our Ministry of Foreign Affairs has called on world leaders to address Russia's escalating actions and provocations. Ukrainian diplomats have been trying to garner international support to prevent more hostilities. Will that be enough?

11:45 a.m. Alarming news came in from the Donbas: since midnight, enemy forces opened fire fifty-three times. Escalation is clearly evident. I ponder the nature of human aggression and its consequences. Could it be that deep within the heart of every aggressor there is fear and insecurity, which they try to hide behind an appearance of strength? With every item I placed in my plastic Xiaomi travel bag in preparation for my trip to Chisinau, I keep thinking: "What if I have to come back urgently?" So, I decided to bring a bit more cash than usual.

2:20 p.m. I found out about a strange incident: a journalist from a restricted media outlet made his way to a broadcast of the Rada channel, the official TV channel of the Ukrainian government. And now he's reporting on some sort of special operation. It all feels surreal – as if we've stepped into a scene from some strange movie.

4:55 p.m. The vice president of the US, the secretary-general of NATO, and leaders of the Baltic countries have discussed the threat that Russia presents. This demonstrates the heightened international focus on the situation in Ukraine. President Biden is scheduled to deliver a statement regarding the Russian crisis. This is an important sign of support from the US and its preparedness to respond to hostile actions. And yet – will that be enough?

6:30 p.m. I'm meditating on the words of the apostle Matthew: "Blessed are the peacemakers, for they will be called children of God" (Matt 5:9). How can we, as Christians, be peacemakers in these trying times? I pray for the leaders and governments of our countries, for those whose decisions will influence the potential for lasting peace in our region. What else is there left to do? Oh Lord, give us wisdom and strength for these uncertain times. Help us be salt and light even as the clouds of war gather around us. May your peace reign in our hearts and spread to those around us.

8:10 p.m. I sent out a letter on behalf of the board of the Euro-Asian Accreditation Association (EAAA), calling for prayers for peace:

> "Blessed are the peacemakers, for they shall be called sons of God" (Matt 5:9).
>
> Dear partners, leaders, faculty, and students of educational institutions of the EAAA, peace be unto you! On behalf of the board of the EAAA, we want to call you to join us in prayer for the leaders and governments of our countries, whose decisions and actions have so much impact on the stability of peace in our region. Please, pray that the fear of the Lord would be upon those working to resolve current political tensions. We ask you to pray for stable and lasting peace in our region and for God, in his loving mercy, to keep leaders and authorities from engaging in military action. Also, we ask for your prayers that the Lord would renew our minds in Christ Jesus:
>
>> So that we, as citizens of many countries and people of many races and ethnicities, may display the unity of God's people in love

> So that we, being transformed by the renewal of our minds, may discern the will of God – which is good, acceptable, and perfect.
>
> So that in these difficult circumstances, God's people may be standing firm in one spirit, with one mind striving side by side for the faith of the gospel (Phil 1:27).

We are praying for all of you. May the God of love and peace be with us all (2 Cor 13:11). The council and partners of the EAAA.

9:45 p.m. On social media, I've been watching how people are reacting to the situation. Some are leaving Ukraine; others are staying. I can't judge those who decide to leave – everyone cares for the safety of their own family. Life is like a toothpaste tube: when pressed hard, whatever is inside our hearts spills out. I posted my thoughts about this on Facebook.

> It's a very painful subject . . . still, I can't help but share. As my grandma Tanya used to say, I really hate it when people get out of Ukraine (not in an orderly, planned emigration, but right now, in anticipation of the TIME OF WAR, so they can get away from it as far as possible should it come), and they write preachy posts on how fiery strong we ought to love Ukraine. They keep writing, calling, admonishing . . .
>
> Sure, every person cares for their own and their family's safety. Nothing's wrong with that. I don't blame those who are leaving, neither Ukrainians nor foreigners. That is not what I'm talking about . . . I'm talking about admonitions from "beyond the border." Life is like a tube of toothpaste: when pressed hard, out of it – out of our inmost parts – flows out whatever is deep in our hearts. And whatever comes out, at times, has very little to do with Christ, his mission, his cross, his peace . . .
>
> Speaking of which . . . The peace of Christ does not mean keeping silent in order to keep the peace. It's a dialogue between God and person, between person and God, where we're not afraid to speak our minds, where we don't deprecate or dehumanize one another. It's a dialogue with our neighbour, the other, the different, the enemy . . . yes, the enemy as well. For we were enemies of God, but there came one that, through his cross, destroyed the animosity between God and humanity through reconciliation

and acceptance of God's truth. Not through silence and concealment but through confession, that is, through calling things out for what they are, be it at the foot of the cross or from the heights of the cross of Christ.

I'm praying, watching, doing what I ought to do, and waiting for what might be possible to get done when the TIME OF WAR comes. Our eloquence in social media posts can display one thing, but when the TIME comes, it may turn out that my "tube" is filled with something altogether different: hatred, dismissiveness, dehumanization . . . So, we pray and keep being the salt and the light . . .

10:50 p.m. We briefly discussed a plan for the potential evacuation of the staff and faculty at Odesa Theological Seminary. They are located on the shores of the Black Sea, which is in the red danger zone since the waters are now completely under the control of the Russian Navy.

11:25 p.m. As darkness fell, the authorities of the so-called Donetsk People's Republic announced the evacuation of the city of Donetsk – but only for women and children. Men aged 18–55 were not given passage. Instead, they were mobilized. Ukrainians are concerned that the women and children being packed into buses right now could become soft targets for a terrorist act that could then legitimize an attack on Ukraine as a "response to the genocide of the Donbas people." Pastors in Donetsk have been begging members of their congregations, for their own safety, not to leave – and especially not to get on those buses. Should they decide to leave, they are being advised to stay away from the buses with women and children because those could very well be shot at or destroyed as a means of provocation. In downtown Donetsk, a van was blown up, spreading panic among the people. Many buildings have been rigged with explosives, ready to be blown to smithereens at a moment's notice. Why are innocent people being used as pawns in Russia's dirty games?

11:45 p.m. I'm going to bed with this thought: How can we, as God's people, stand firm in one spirit, with one mind, striving side by side for the faith of the gospel (Phil 1:27) in such perplexing circumstances? I pray, keep watch, do what I ought to do, and wait for whatever else can be done whenever the time comes . . .

First Gusts of the Wind
Saturday, 19 February 2022; location: Rivne, Kyiv

> Your thunder was heard in the whirlwind, your lightning lit up the world; the earth trembled and quaked.
>
> Psalm 77:18

7:30 a.m. I woke up with a heavy heart. I leave for Kyiv today, then go to Chisinau on business. News from the Donbas has been rather disheartening: the situation has grown increasingly tense with the rising rate of fire. Pro-Russia separatists have announced an "evacuation" of local civilians to Russia. I feel anxiety pounding in my chest like another heartbeat.

8:15 a.m. Over breakfast, I read through the news on Telegram. Every channel talks about the possibility of invasion. Natalia, my wife, looks at me without saying a word, but I can see the fear in her eyes and read her unspoken question: "Do you have to go?" I hug her and try to comfort her, even though I feel my own confidence wavering.

9:15 a.m. Today, I'm using BlaBlaCar, a ride-share service, to get from Rivne to the airport in Kyiv; after that, I will be flying out to Chisinau with a stop in Istanbul. Istanbul is where I will meet up with Evan Hunter, my colleague from Scholar Leaders. There is more disheartening news about Russia amassing its forces along the Ukrainian borders – both in Russia and Belarus. Many Ukrainians have already left the country, just as a precaution. Some of them continue to admonish the ones still staying on about the proper ways to love Ukraine. My feelings are a wild mix of worry and determination. It's hard to describe.

10:05 a.m. I sent out instructions in our family chat on what to do if we should come under fire. I pray that we'll never need to use them, but the Lord is the only one who knows what the future holds for us.

11:40 a.m. As I was travelling, the news came in: The Verkhovna Rada of Ukraine (our parliament) has adopted a new law: "On the approval of the Decree of the President of Ukraine 'On the Imposition of Martial Law in Ukraine.'" This law was supported by 300 out of 310 deputies registered to vote. That's almost unanimous. My heart is weighed down even more with worry for I don't know what kind of country I will be returning to from Moldova in two weeks' time.

1:30 p.m. A pit stop at a gas station. The checkout lines are longer than usual. People are stocking up on fuel, water, and snacks. The air is thick with tension.

I keep overhearing bits and pieces of conversations: "Have you packed a go-bag yet?" "Where are you going to go if it comes to that?" I try not to succumb to the widespread panic, but I can feel it creeping in.

2:20 p.m. Another stop, just for a break. I keep thinking about the latest events. The imposition of martial law is a serious matter that points to the country's preparation for a full scale war. But how will this impact our daily living, ministry, and work? I pray for wisdom for our leaders and protection for our people.

4:55 p.m. I arrived in Kyiv and checked into the Hotel Myr by the Holosiivska metro station, quite aware of the irony of the meaning of the hotel's name: peace. I'm looking at the latest updates on the coronavirus. Over the last twenty-four hours, the number of infections has increased by more than 31,000. There were 31,125 new cases, 260 people died, and 30,487 recovered. Over the entire period of the COVID-19 pandemic, there have been 4,703,323 reported infections, 3,926,496 recovered, and there were 104,366 deaths. These numbers remind us of yet another challenge we're facing at the same time as this prospect of war – seven days ago, on 12 February, we buried my Natalia's father, Petro Oleksiiovych. The coronavirus killed him in just two weeks – there was nothing the doctors could do. I feel surrounded by death – and it's closing in.

7:30 p.m. It's dinner time. On the campus of the Divitia Gratiae University in Chisinau, we will be working with six different institutions of higher theological education from Eastern Europe and Central Asia on the Vital Sustainability Initiative (VSI) under the auspices of Scholar Leaders. I'm trying to focus on what needs to be accomplished there, but my thoughts are preoccupied with the situation in Ukraine.

9:45 p.m. I have read my Bible and prayed. Now, I'm pondering the nature of prayer in such difficult times. This thinking transformed into a post on my blog. Does God hear us? Will he change the path of history in answer to our prayers? So many questions are swarming in my head, yet none of them have answers.

> An honest prayer is not just an expression of our desires but rather a meaningful dialogue with God. It's an opportunity to open your heart and share the innermost thoughts and yearnings, but at the same time, it's a path toward understanding and accepting the will of God. During prayer, we're often faced with a paradox: on the one hand, we seek justice, especially when we feel we've been wronged. We come before God, demanding his intervention and

restoration of justice. But, on the other hand, being fully aware of our own imperfections, we ask God for mercy and the forgiveness of our trespasses. This dichotomy – the desire for justice to be done to others and mercy to be extended to us – reflects the complexity of human nature and our continuous quest for the balance between justice and mercy. Real prayer teaches us not only to ask but to listen, not only to demand but to accept. It helps us see the situation from God's point of view. Through prayer, we learn to be merciful to others just like God was and is merciful to us; we learn to seek justice not just for ourselves but also for others.

11:10 p.m. I went for a walk before going to bed. Kyiv seems rather tense. There are fewer people than usual out on the streets. Those who are out walk in such a rush, as if they're trying to run away and hide from a looming invisible threat. My mind is still mulling over the subject of prayer. If we are praying sincerely, we will no doubt hear the question coming from the Sovereign Lord: Why do you beg for mercy for yourself and, in the same breath, demand just retribution for another? As we pray for the judgement of the Righteous Judge, are we ready to accept his justice, rather than his mercy, for ourselves? I don't know, Jesus . . . I'm just praying for your mercy for us all.

11:40 p.m. I went to bed with a question: How can we remain human and compassionate in such challenging times? How do we find that balance between justice and mercy? If a major war is inevitable, may God grant us wisdom and strength to go through these trials with honour. I fell asleep praying for my family.

Falling Barometer
Sunday, 20 February 2022; location: Kyiv, Istanbul, Chisinau

> Hypocrites! You know how to interpret the appearance of the earth and the sky. How is it that you don't know how to interpret this present time?
>
> Luke 12:56

7:15 a.m. I woke up with heavy thoughts. Today is my last day in Ukraine before I leave for Chisinau. I'm still plagued by anxiety. I spent some time emailing and trying to focus on my work, but my thoughts kept going back to the situation in my country.

9:00 a.m. During breakfast at the hotel, I notice the tension in the air. People are talking quietly and frequently checking their phones. I keep overhearing bits of conversations: discussions about possible evacuations and ways to contact your loved ones in case of an emergency. I feel their anxiety rubbing off on me . . .

11:30 a.m. I called for a taxi to get from my hotel to Kyiv's airport, Boryspil. The driver was awfully quiet, but once we started talking about what was happening, he shared his worries: "I don't even know if it's worth making plans for next month. Who knows what tomorrow will bring?"

The news is still disheartening: pro-Russian separatists claimed "a threat of an offensive" coming from Ukraine and announced "evacuation" of civilians from ORDLO[1] to Russia. The leadership of the so-called Donetsk People's Republic and Luhansk People's Republic declared martial law. I can feel the tensions rising with every passing hour. A series of explosions and provocations happen in the temporarily occupied territories. Russia shamelessly uses these incidents as a pretext for accusing Ukraine of "aggression."

I recall the words of Svetlana Alexievich: "War kills time, precious time for humans."[2] These words ring so true. Despite persistent worry, I try to focus on my work. How can one keep their wits about them and act sensibly in moments like these?

1:00 p.m. Kyiv Boryspil Airport. Security checks are done, luggage is checked in, and I sit and wait for boarding to begin, hoping that nothing goes wrong and that the flight won't be cancelled. I had already cancelled my railway ticket for a Kyiv–Odesa connection, which was my backup plan. My thoughts keep turning to the situation in Ukraine. The US and its allies report a continuous increase of Russian armed forces at Ukraine's border and a high likelihood of escalation. I remember my grandparents – they lived through World War II. Very rarely did they speak of those times, but their silence spoke volumes. I posted about this on my blog. Will our generation have to go through something like that? I pray not.

> Speaking about being human . . . When I went to school in 1980–1988, back in Rivne, it was a typical Soviet Secondary school of its time. Back then, a few WWII veterans were still alive – like

---

1. This refers to certain occupied territories of the Donetsk and Luhansk regions.
2. Svetlana Aleksievich et al., *The Unwomanly Face of War: An Oral History of Women in World War II*, First Edition (New York: Random House, 2017), 172.

Mykola Nikulin, whose book *Memories of the War* I'm re-reading right now. So, as students at School №10, we went out occasionally to visit with those veterans who rode out the storm of war. One of them lived near the Philharmonic music hall. He was a retired paratrooper. We visited him a few times. He'd always been very quiet, barely saying a word. I remember asking him in childish curiosity: what was the war like? His eyes welled up with tears ... He'd sit there, quietly. He'd offer us tea, ask us about our school and whatever else was new, and that was it. That was the extent of what was supposed to be an inspirational and patriotic teaching of youngsters through war stories. For all the years we'd visited him, all I found out was that a few times he had to parachute straight into hell ...

Both sets of my grandparents and their parents as well lived near the edge of a forest. The list of agents that plundered them is extensive: first a round of Soviets, then the Germans, then Red Army partisans, then the "boys from the forest" (but likely, just disguised NKVD[3] operatives, not Ukrainian Insurgent Army soldiers), then the retreating Germans, then the advancing Soviet Army, then the second round of Soviets (the first one lasted 1939–1941), then the "boys from the forest" again, then NKVD would ask around, then KGB would "make inquiries" ... Through it all, they had Jews from Germans, "boys from the forest" from the Soviets, partisans from Nazis, some "sensible" German soldiers of retreating German army from Ukrainian Insurgents, and gave food to the fleeing starving Wehrmacht soldiers ...

Nowadays, it'd be quite easy to convict them for all their crimes under martial law – by each of the three parties. The first would just shoot them for helping the "boys from the forest" (regardless of who those guys really were), the second would have them shot for rescuing and hiding Jews, the third – for feeding Germans, the fourth – for harbouring the partisans. Too easy to dismiss, dehumanize, and execute as traitors of all three regimes ... Either

---

3. People's Commissariat for Internal Affairs (Narodnyy komissariat vnutrennikh del, NKVD) – was the interior ministry and secret police of the Soviet Union from 1934 to 1946. The NKVD is known for carrying out political repression and the Great Purge under Joseph Stalin.

way, should you decide to stay human in times of war, someone will always mark you a traitor . . .

My grandparents – on both sides – didn't want to tell war stories. In times of war, they wanted to stay people of faith . . . people . . . humans . . . They wanted to see the human being in the other, the one that came to their doorstep with a need, even if the coming was marked with stuffing the sack with whatever met that need while keeping them at a gunpoint . . . Very rarely did they talk about their memories of war, and when they did, they'd stare blankly and mournfully, wringing their hands, speaking in disjointed, confusing phrases. For them, the war was humans destroying humans. That's why they had pity towards those who still had a spark of humanity left and whom they, as humans, could help.

The hardest thing to do in times of war is to stay human, to never change into a brutal beast that dehumanizes self and others. It's to stay a practising Christian, to stay human – not just a religious person that's "yoked" to this or that political ideology, which at times could lead to devilish wickedness. It's important to stay human, carrying that glimmer of the Kingdom of God, the image of God, Christ's likeness – to be seen even through a crack, even darkly in a mirror.

"As we went by ruins, I'd always think: how many years will it take to rebuild it all? War kills time, precious human time."[4] Mind yourself!

2:30 p.m. I have just boarded the plane. I really like Turkish Airlines and the music they play as passengers take their seats. My anxiety vanishes momentarily, only to return with a vengeance a few moments later.

3:00–5:00 p.m. Flight from Kyiv to Istanbul. After landing, I read the news that the Russian State Duma has passed an appeal to Putin "to protect civilians of the Donbas." How easy it is to twist history and truth! I recall that elderly retired paratrooper we visited as kids, who once claimed that he parachuted straight into hell a few times. Do those who are currently stoking the fires of war grasp the meaning of the real hell of war?

---

4. Aleksievich et al., *The Unwomanly Face of War: An Oral History of Women in World War II*, First Edition (Random House, 2017), 172.

I met up with Evan at Gate E4. We would be travelling together now. I exchanged a few messages with my daughter, Tanya, and made plans to call again once we made it to Chisinau. Then I called my parents. It was so nice to hear their voices, especially as realization had now set in that I'd never again hear the voice of Natalia's dad.

8:43 p.m. We landed in Chisinau. I found that the Ukrainian Christian clergy, Ukrainian Muslims, and the Chief Rabbi had called for prayer and voiced their support for peace.

10:00 p.m. Evan and I had dinner at Andy's Pizza. Our lodgings were room 5 on the second floor of the Divitia Gratiae University dormitory building. We discussed our plans for the next few days, but the conversation kept turning to the situation in Ukraine.

10:45 p.m. I just got off the phone with Tanya and Andrew (my daughter and son-in-law). I was happy to hear that they're doing fine. I pray that God will bless them as they work and study. After the call, I thought about how important it is to stay in touch with your loved ones, especially in such troubling times.

11:10 p.m. I just checked the latest news. NATO says there are indications that Russia is indeed planning a full-scale attack on Ukraine. At the same time, our authorities are reassuring Ukrainians, insisting that there will be no invasion and urging them to resist panic and worry. These contradictory messages remind me of my grandparents, on both my mother's and father's sides. I remember just how little they actually told us about the war, despite our persistent curiosity. Now, as we face the possibility of a new threat, I wonder why they were so quiet about their wartime experience. Perhaps their reluctance to share such memories was an attempt to protect us from the horrors of the past. Or maybe the wounds left by war were so deep that it was just too painful to recall and verbalize, especially to children. Perhaps now is the time to really listen to the few memories our older loved ones did share with us and learn some lessons for our volatile present. But will there be people in Russia willing to listen and come to the right conclusions?

11:50 p.m. I'm preparing for the next day's meetings, reviewing methodological resources. Come morning, Evan and I will begin our work with six different Eastern European and Central Asian institutions that offer higher theological education. This is part of the VSI. I think about how important it is to have honest discussions in order to continuously develop curricula for theological education, especially now that an impending full-scale invasion by Russia seems inevitable, even if we can't believe that this is really happening. I recognize the dilemma here: on the one hand, it's imperative to continue the process of developing theological education, but on the other hand, there's the looming threat and uncertainty about the future. How should curricula be adapted in light of potential crises? What role should theological education play in times of imminent war? How should students be prepared – not just theoretically but practically – for the challenges that a full-scale invasion may bring? I hope that our combined efforts will help prepare educational institutions to carry out their important mission should war prove unavoidable.

I'm going to bed heavy-hearted; yet I'm also hopeful that perhaps there will be no invasion. I pray for peace and for each of us to remain human.

First Lightning
Monday, 21 February 2022; location: Chisinau

> Out of the north he comes in golden splendour; God comes in awesome majesty.
>
> Job 37:22

7:30 a.m. Chisinau. Once again, I woke up with a heavy heart. The news is staggering: Putin recognized the independence of the self-proclaimed Luhansk People's Republic and Donetsk People's Republic. Russian Armed Forces enter ORDLO territories. Realities are shifting dramatically. I pray that the Lord will grant us all wisdom and strength. What will happen next?

8:00 a.m. Breakfast with Evan. We discuss the last-minute details of those strategic planning meetings with six different theological educational institutions. It's hard to stay focused on work when the world around you is ready to crumble. Evan is trying to be reassuring, but I can tell that he's worried, too.

9:00 a.m. Our meeting begins. We try to talk about strategic planning, but everyone's thoughts keep going back to the situation in Ukraine. Even I can't help but voice a rhetorical question: "How can we plan for the future if we don't know what tomorrow will bring?" The question lingers unanswered.

10:30 a.m. Coffee break. Water-cooler talk revolves around the situation in Ukraine. Our colleagues from the Divitia Gratiae University are expressing their support for us, but I sense that not everyone truly understands just how grim our reality is. Some still view all this as just political ploys.

1:30 p.m. Lunchtime. I read a statement by US President Joe Biden in support of Ukraine's sovereignty. It sounds hopeful; yet at the same time, it underscores the gravity of the situation. Once again, I wonder what Ukraine will be like when I return from Moldova. Will it still be the same country I left just days ago?

3:00 p.m. Our work continues. We discuss adapting curricula to crisis situations. This is no longer an issue simply to discuss but a dire need to be met.

4:55 p.m. The meetings are over. I hear on the news about shelling by the Russians. There have been more than thirty attacks involving Multiple Launch Rocket Systems (MLRS) strikes on Kherson's civil infrastructure. Innocent people are the first victims of Russian hostility. I'm overwhelmed by anger and helplessness, but what can I do?

6:30 p.m. I call home. Natalia is hanging in there, but I can hear the anxiety trembling in her voice. I wish I could be there with her right now, to hold her close and keep her safe.

7:30 p.m. Our work for the day is done. Evan and I are off to Andy's Pizza for our dinner. We talk about the lost humanity of the aggressor and how this leads to unpunished killings for the sake of the victory of "Russki mir." We finalize our meeting schedule for tomorrow. Evan posts his thoughts on the situation on Facebook. His words on "radical self-sacrifice" prompt me to reflect on the role of the church in this crucial hour.

> The mounting global tension provides a powerful backdrop as Taras N. Dyatlik and I are sitting in a cafe in Chisinau, planning for meetings with 6 schools from Russia, Ukraine, Moldova, and Kyrgyzstan over the course of the next 9 days. Prayers for peace are only a beginning. The impact of a war cannot be left in abstraction. Thousands of lives lost in direct combat, countless families who will lose loved ones, be displaced from homes, jobs, and lives, and the global economic and political impact are just the start of the list. One of the deepest scars of war is the inherent dehumanization that allows us to kill one another with the impunity required

to win. These are serious times indeed. Yet, we strive to find hope for a future that is better than today.⁵

9:30 p.m. We're back at the dormitory. A quick check of the news shows that the situation is deteriorating with every passing hour. It's hard to stay hopeful.

10:45 p.m. I'm reading through the Gospel of Mark: "After John was put in prison, Jesus went into Galilee, proclaiming the good news of God. 'The time has come,' he said. 'The kingdom of God has come near. Repent and believe the good news'" (Mark 1:14–15). I reflected on what Jesus *didn't* say in that situation – right after the last prophet of God was arrested – and also what he *did* say. Jesus spoke about the fact that although our kingdoms are ruined by sin, there is a new kingdom: the kingdom of God. There is a new people: the people of God. There is another king: the Lord of the universe. There is other news: the good news of the gospel. When John was arrested, Jesus went around calling more people into relationships within the kingdom of God – relationships based on love, trust, and care for one another. Being human is not for tomorrow or for some later time – it's for right now . . . and the rest is just between the lines . . .

11:10 p.m. I'm going to bed still dwelling on this thought: being human is not for tomorrow or for later; it's for right now – right here, in Chisinau.

Calm before the Storm
Tuesday, 22 February 2022; location: Chisinau

> The LORD said, "Go out and stand on the mountain in the presence of the LORD, for the LORD is about to pass by." Then a great and powerful wind tore the mountains apart and shattered the rocks before the LORD, but the LORD was not in the wind. After the wind there was an earthquake, but the LORD was not in the earthquake.
>
> 1 Kings 19:11

7:45 a.m. I woke up to the buzzing of notifications on my phone. The news of Russia's increased military presence at Ukraine's border is disturbing. I can feel anxiety's grip tightening. With such a start to the morning, how do I get through the day and stay focused on our work?

---
5. Evan Hunter, https://www.facebook.com/share/p/Q3S4B6rnjmstde8P/.

8:00 a.m. Breakfast time. Evan tries to keep the conversation going about our plans for today, but I can tell that he, too, is worried. We both recognize that today or tomorrow could be the turning point.

9:00 a.m. Another day of work as part of the VSI. We discovered that the team from the Tavriski Christian Institute would not be able to come to Chisinau on Thursday. There's been a lot of activity by the Armed Forces of Ukraine near Kharkiv due to the threat of invasion by the Russian Armed Forces from Crimea. For the first time, I wondered if the teams from Odesa Theological Seminary and the Ukrainian Evangelical Theological Seminary in Kyiv would be able to come here. War is drawing closer.

10:30 a.m. Coffee break. Our discussion revolves around the situation brought on by the build-up of Russian forces along Ukraine's border. Each one of us is trying to fathom the potential consequences of a possible war. Some of our colleagues – those not from Ukraine or Moldova – say that there will be no invasion because Russia only wants peace and has no intention of attacking. Their naïve stance is both impressive and annoying. Despite attempts to focus on work, our thoughts keep circling back to Ukraine and the possible scenarios that could play out. We are increasingly aware that this situation might have far-reaching consequences not just for Ukraine but for the entire region.

1:30 p.m. Lunchtime. News about partial mobilization in Ukraine comes in: the plan is to call up one hundred thousand reservists for up to ninety days of service. This decision triggers mixed feelings. On the one hand, this is a necessary step to defend our country; on the other hand, it makes the threat feel increasingly real. For the first time, I consider the fate of myself and my brothers, who might be mobilized as well. I can feel the war getting closer and more personal.

3:23 p.m. I received a text message:

> Attention Western region! Tomorrow in major cities you will hear sirens. Please, do not be alarmed, this is a test.

This message brought a mix of relief (as this was just a test) and concern (why now?). I tried to stay focused on work, but I kept thinking about my home.

5:00 p.m. Scrolling through Facebook, I notice increased tension displayed by people on my friends list. More and more are expressing their concern about the possibility of Russia invading Ukraine. At the same time, members of Russian evangelical churches and seminaries, almost without exception, are trying to reassure us that we're just hyping up ourselves and others and inciting "Russophobia." Oh Lord, how do we keep serenity and unity right now? Unity in terms of what? These questions keep nagging at me.

7:30 p.m. Dinner with Evan passed in almost complete silence. Both he and I were stunned by today's news and the ever-changing realities. This continuous tsunami of alarming news about rising tension and the threat of war has definitely left its mark on our emotions. I'm worried that this will impact tomorrow's meetings. What would have been incredulous yesterday or the day before has now become the new normal. We're trying to figure out how to adapt to these changes, but we are rarely able to keep up with the rate at which things keep changing.

9:45 p.m. I called Natalia, and then my kids and parents, to share what I've been feeling and ask how they've been doing. Natalia tried to sound calm and collected, but I could tell she's been really worried about me and my trip back to Ukraine. Her voice was shaky when she told me about packing a go-bag, but she tried to sound cheerful as she talked to me. I tackled my emails just as a distraction from my anxious thoughts.

11:50 p.m. I'm going to bed, but the thoughts in my head are buzzing like bees collecting honey. I try to fall asleep holding on to the thought that tomorrow will be a new day – and perhaps it will bring hope. But deep down, I recognize that we're on the verge of something terrible and irreversible.

On the Verge of the Storm
Wednesday, 23 February 2022; location: Chisinau

> Watch and pray so that you will not fall into temptation. The spirit is willing, but the flesh is weak.
> Matthew 26:41

7:30 a.m. I woke up feeling like I hadn't slept at all. My dreams were uneasy, filled with images of war and desolation. I've been trying to shake them off, but they cling to my thoughts. I pray the Lord will give me strength and clarity for today.

8:45 a.m. Breakfast with Evan. We talked about our plans for the day but kept circling back to the situation in Ukraine. Evan was trying to sound optimistic, but I could see the worry in his eyes.

9:15 a.m. Our meetings on project VSI began. I've been trying to stay focused on discussing strategies for the development of theological education. Still, everyone present understands that all our best-laid plans will be upended if a full-scale war breaks out.

10:30 a.m. Coffee break. We've been discussing the latest developments, deeply concerned that Russia has deployed forty-six battleships in the Black Sea and Azov Sea. I think about what this might mean – not just for the Tavriski Christian Institute but also for the Odesa Theological Seminary. Would they be able to continue operating under such circumstances? How can we support them?

3:00 p.m. We continue working, but it's getting harder and harder to stay focused. Every glance at my phone marks my apprehension of more alarming news. I'm trying to concentrate on our discussion, but my thoughts keep straying back to Ukraine, my family, and my colleagues there.

5:30 p.m. I got a message from Natalia. She says that shops are seeing long queues as people try to stock up on food and necessities and withdraw cash from ATMs. This reminds me of the beginning of the pandemic, but this time feels much scarier. My heart is clenched with helplessness – I'm here, they're there . . .

7:00 p.m. I posted on Facebook, sharing my thoughts about the ongoing situation and the potential long-lasting rift between Ukrainian and Russian evangelicals. As I was writing it, I felt a flood of emotions: anger, disappointment, pain.

> Friends! I don't often write about political topics, but those who know me, ask me directly, or read my blog are well aware of my stance. Even though the entire world is fallen, every single person is a sinner, and there are no blameless or infallible countries. I am reminded that Niemöller spent several decades (almost until his death) visiting different German Evangelical churches to expose and explain, biblically and theologically, the depth of sinfulness and devilry of Hitlerism and Nazism ideologies that had infiltrated German churches before and during WWII and wouldn't be readily expelled by many churches for years after the end of that war.
>
> How many years will it take to pluck out of Russian churches this ideology of Putinism, "red Christianity," and "Russki mir"? Friends and colleagues from Russia, I'm sorry to say, but even though many Germans were blissfully unaware of things or failed

to see them (be that because they lived in Germany or decided to disregard or turn a blind eye), it does not mean that those things never happened. Sadly, only a few evangelical believers and leaders from Russia have been able to express their stance on recent events and their views on the matter in private messages through messenger apps or email.

I understand that Russia is not Ukraine. I'm well aware of how speaking up can affect personal life and family (I've been through such things myself). However, I'm saddened that reticence is considered to be peacemaking. But peacemaking is impossible without truthfully calling things what they are – and that is known as confession. And without confession, there cannot be a change in thinking and world view (what is called "repentance" in the New Testament).

Sure, we are inspired by the many heroes of faith from WWI and WWII times. Yes, being faithful to Jesus has a high price. But being faithful to Jesus is not just being a "believer" – it's also being human, created in the image of God. And so, what is the price of reticence? What is the price of being and staying human? Where is that red line regarding faithfulness to Christ that we're willing to cross?

The rest is there, just read between the lines. This is nothing personal, just the lamentation of a soul at the funeral of the Russian-Ukrainian Evangelical movement. Once again, apologies for being brutally honest. I know I will be getting dozens of private messages from brothers and sisters in Christ, calling for the removal of this post for the sake of preserving unity and the good reputation of the so-called "Russian-Ukrainian evangelical Christian." But can one be called a real Christian after agreeing – whether publicly or silently – with the Kremlin's inhumane ideology and propaganda? How much does it pay to betray Christ? You could get for that sum a potter's field, at most. Why do you need Ukrainian land occupied by Russia? Forgive me, Jesus, for these words, and do not count them against me . . .

8:30 p.m. Evan and I returned from Andy's Pizza to the Divitia Gratiae University in complete silence. On our way, I thought about how Russian evangelical leaders have been reacting to current events. It pains me to see how many of them are either reticent or publicly accuse Ukrainian Christians of inciting

Russophobia, insisting there is clearly no intention of an attack. How is such blindness possible? Or is it a deliberate disregard for what's actually happening?

10:00 p.m. I just called home. Natalia is trying to stay strong and upbeat, but I could hear the worry in her quavering voice.

10:45 p.m. I re-read my Facebook post. I know it could draw a lot of criticism, but I cannot stay silent. Peacekeeping is impossible without telling it like it is. If we do not speak truth, what is the bedrock of righteous peace? Reticence cannot become the foundation for peace, certainly not in our relationship with God.

11:40 p.m. Before going to bed, I prayed for peace, for the safety of our family and loved ones, and for my friends and colleagues. I mull over the price of silence among Russian Christians. Deep down, I realize yet again that we're on the brink of something terrible.

Eye of the Storm
Thursday, 24 February 2022; location: Chisinau

> A furious squall came up, and the waves broke over the boat, so that it was nearly swamped.
>
> Mark 4:37

5:00 a.m. I was awakened by a WhatsApp call from Roman Soloviy: "Taras, the war has started." I can't believe it's happening. My heart is wrenched with anguish and fear . . . At 4:00 a.m., Vladimir Putin, the president of Russia, announced the beginning of a "special military operation" in Ukraine, claiming that its aim was the "demilitarization and denazification" of our country. The Russian Armed Forces began a full-scale invasion of Ukraine, with air strikes on military and civilian infrastructure across the entire country. Impacts are being reported in Kyiv, Kharkiv, Dnipro, Boryspil, Brovary, Kherson, Uman, Ivano-Frankivsk, Chuhuiv, Ozerne, Kulbakino, Kramatorsk, Chornobaivka, and dozens of other Ukrainian cities.

My hands are trembling as I dial Natalia's number. She picks up almost immediately. Her voice is even, but I can feel the tension. "We're fine. There were explosions near the airport," she says. I'm heartbroken and helpless – stuck here while they are there, under fire.

5:30 a.m. I woke Evan Hunter, who was staying in an adjacent room. We sent out messages to all the seminary teams to cancel their trip to Chisinau. Our planned programme is now suspended. Russia's missile strikes on multiple Ukrainian cities continue and intensify. The situation is changing rapidly. I can feel the changes every passing minute.

6:46 a.m. I messaged in our family group chat:

> War has started. They're bombing many places in Kyiv, Kharkiv, Lviv, Odesa, Kherson. My colleagues are messaging and sending videos. Airspace is closed. I'll have to figure out a way to get home. Let us all pray and support each other; don't panic or make hasty decisions or actions without asking for advice here. If anyone needs any help, message here or me directly. We are family, and that's what we're going to stay: a family. Andrii, you especially must stay in touch and keep us updated or message us if you need something. We're all praying really hard for you!

9:00 a.m. The president of Ukraine, Volodymyr Zelenskyy, held an urgent meeting of the National Security and Defence Council.

9:33 a.m. Another message for my family:

> Please pray for me as I'm looking into my options for leaving Moldova. Quite likely, I'll try to catch a car to Chernivtsi, and then whatever will take me to Kyiv – BlaBlaCar ride-share, express, or commuter train – and then home. I'm so sorry I'm not there with you right now. Please don't share any information about the location or movement of armed forces – that'll be considered treason. Andrii, how are you doing? Have you been assigned somewhere?

I have a hard time writing these words. I want to be with my family, but I must act sensibly right now . . .

Evan and I read the news online. Russia is attacking Ukraine from all directions: north, east, and south. Air strikes target military sites and airports all across the country. It's hard to believe this is actually happening in the twenty-first century. Andrii passed his physical exam and is getting ready to join the armed forces. The enlistment office instructed Pavlo to report for his exam by a military medical panel. It's a heart-wrenching thought: my brothers might end up on the front lines, in the hellfire of war.

1:17 p.m. Lunchtime was with Evan at Andy's Pizza. We planned his itinerary: by bus from Moldova to Romania, then by plane from Bucharest to the US, with a layover in Frankfurt. We try to stay calm, but our hearts are gripped by anguish. Another message for our family via Viber:

> Moldova closed its airspace. Evan Hunter's flight was cancelled, too. We're looking for ways to get Evan to Bucharest then on a flight to the US via Frankfurt. I've got to send people on their way, then I'll figure out something for myself. Thank you for your prayers!

4:55 p.m. We met for coffee with the university's leadership in Dean Dmytro Sevastian's office. Our joint prayer was for Evan's travels that evening – by bus from Chisinau to Bucharest – and my return to Ukraine tomorrow or the day after. I can see how important it is to support each other right now.

7:30 p.m. As I prepare to return to Ukraine, I know that challenges and uncertainty will mark my trip. I pray for God's protection over me so I can reach my family and loved ones and hold them close. I'm hoping to make it in two days, God willing.

9:45 p.m. I have so many thoughts about all that's been happening. It brings tears to my eyes to see how many Russian Christians we've worked alongside for years on mission and theological education remain silent or are supportive of this "special military operation." Some pastors are publicly rejoicing over "liberating Ukraine from Nazis." How could ministers fall for such dehumanizing propaganda?

11:30 p.m. I prayed for the safety of our cities tonight, asking that our families would sleep in their own beds, not bomb shelters or basements. I asked God to protect Ukraine from Russian missiles. Day one brought losses: 57 civilians killed and 169 wounded; and 137 soldiers killed and 317 wounded. Every loss is somebody's story, somebody's family, somebody's dream. I watch the news as the first pictures pour in: destroyed towns, frightened people, children seeking shelter in basements. And I can't help but ask: Where is God in all of this? Isn't this what we have been praying against since 2014? Isn't this the horror from which we tried to shield our children? The entire day, I felt like I was in a haze. My phone kept ringing – call after call. People were worried and scared. Oh Lord, may your mercy and grace abide with us.

11:40 p.m. I read a passage before going to bed: "And when the Lord saw her, he had compassion on her and said to her, 'Do not weep.'" (Luke 7:13 ESV) Jesus always had so much compassion for suffering people. He's probably crying now as he sees this tragedy unfold in Ukraine. My deepest respect goes out to those who are protecting our country. My prayers go out to all those who are wounded. May the Lord chastise the Russian invaders but also open their eyes to see the sinfulness of their actions . . . I posted the following on my Facebook page:

> Friends, I'll be returning to Ukraine tomorrow. The road before me is challenging and uncertain . . . I'd be grateful for your prayers for God's protection so I can make it to my family and hold them close . . . I don't know how long it'll take, but I'm hoping, God willing, to be there in two days . . . Moldova closed its airspace in an attempt to avoid what happened in Ukraine in 2014 . . .
>
> I've been awake since almost five this morning, just like many of you. There are so many issues that need planning and coordinating that I'm afraid there won't be much sleeping tonight . . .
>
> But it's hard not to cry just seeing how many Russian Christians we worked with for decades are staying silent . . . They do not believe us when we describe what's happening in Ukraine, but rather, they believe in the dehumanizing, devilish propaganda coming from the Kremlin. There are some who even rejoice in "liberating Ukraine from Nazis." Servants of the church . . . or are you servants of someone else? Liberating us . . . from what? From the peaceful lives we led before 2014?
>
> Pray, if you would, for the safety of our cities through the night, so our children, our wives, and our parents can sleep in their beds, not basements. Pray and do what you can so that Russian missiles won't rain on peaceful Ukrainian cities. Ukraine did not attack itself, my friends. Russian evangelicals, as you pray, also ask God's forgiveness for voting for Vladimir Putin, for writing him appreciation letters and greetings on his birthday, and for wishing him success in his endeavours . . .

I went to bed clinging to this thought: "When I am afraid, I put my trust in you" (Ps 56:3). We must entrust our lives to God's hands, for human hands are powerless here . . . Is there any hope that humanity will ever learn to live in peace?

In the Thick of the Storm
Friday, 25 February 2022; location: Chisinau, Chernivtsi, Ternopil, Rivne

> When you pass through the waters, I will be with you; and when you pass through the rivers, they will not sweep over you. When you walk through the fire, you will not be burned; the flames will not set you ablaze.
>
> Isaiah 43:2

7:00 a.m. I woke up from a restless sleep. My troubled dreams were haunted by explosions and air-raid sirens – probably influenced by the things I heard and saw on the news yesterday. The situation in Ukraine is worsening. I pray for protection over my family and loved ones.

7:30 a.m. Our group – joined by Dumitru Sevastian, Vadim Bulgak, and Viktor Ormanji – left Chisinau and headed for the Ukrainian border. Although I was plagued by thoughts and worries over what was happening in Ukraine, those few hours of travel became a precious memory of spiritual support and prayers offered by brothers from the Divitia Gratiae University.

9:15 a.m. I created a WhatsApp group called "We are from Ukraine" to keep our partners informed about the situation in Ukraine and our ministry to displaced people. It's an important step for subsequent aid and support planning.

11:40 a.m. As we travelled towards the Ukrainian border, the news kept rolling in about air strikes and shelling all across Ukraine. Russia keeps pressing on towards key cities and towns. My heart breaks for every life lost or destroyed. Many of our seminaries are already hosting thousands of refugees on their campuses. I keep mulling over other ways we could be of even more help.

1:19 p.m. We've arrived at the border. There's no going back now . . . Moldovan customs officers asked me if I was absolutely sure I wanted to return to Ukraine. I told them "yes." The same question was asked by Ukrainian officers, who warned me that once I entered Ukraine, I would not be able to leave again. I simply replied that I wanted to be where my wife, children, brothers, sisters, and loved ones were.

2:04 p.m. My friend and colleague Vasyl Malyk, president of Chernivtsi Bible Seminary, met me at the border. As I crossed the checkpoint, I couldn't hold back my tears for my land, my country, and my people. All international trips for Roman Soloviy, Helga Marchak (Dyatlik), and myself have been cancelled until airspace reopens and travel restrictions for men between the ages 18–60 are lifted. Now, I have to rethink my tasks and schedule. It looks like I'll be involved in more coordinating efforts, working with internally displaced persons (IDPs), partners, and hubs, just as I did back in 2014–2016. The only thing that's clear right now is that life and ministry will not be happening as usual.

2:20 p.m. I sent out an update on what's been happening in various seminaries. Ukrainian Evangelical Theological Seminary (located in the Pushcha-Vodytsya neighbourhood in Kyiv) is taking in refugees. Odesa Theological Seminary is getting ready for evacuation. I pray for the safety of all faculty and students.

> We're doing everything we can to take care of our students, faculty, and refugees. Our team has turned basements into bomb shelters. Right now, more than 100 people are staying on our premises, and we're expecting the arrival of more refugees. We are providing food and shelter to those in need. At the moment, everyone is safe. Thank you for your prayers!
>
> Ivan Rusyn, Rector of UETS

4:30 p.m. I continue to receive updates from rectors of different seminaries about what's happening on the ground. My heart breaks to hear their stories of shelling, evacuation, fear, and uncertainty.

> On the morning of 24 February 2022, Odesa woke up to the sound of explosions. It turned out to be an air raid on a number of military sites. Air defence also fired in response. Some of our employees saw Unmanned Aerial Vehicles (UAVs), but I'm not sure whose drones they were. This attack came right in the middle of our training session. We quickly arranged for the evacuation of all of our students from the campus. As arranged beforehand, a number of staff with small children moved to one of the western regions of Ukraine. Most of our faculty and staff, myself included, remained in Odesa.
>
> Today, 25 February, we had a meeting for all staff and faculty. In its course, we discussed the prospect of turning our campus into a refugee centre and logistics hub should refugees start coming our way. Everyone is ready and willing to help. Still, a lot depends on the combat action around Odesa. Local churches are gearing up to help people and continue holding services in the midst of war. I talked with the regional pastor of Odesa Baptist Church Union, and he confirmed that churches are ready to contribute

whenever such a centre is created. But at this moment, the largest waves of refugees are coming towards Moldova or the western regions of Ukraine.

We switched all classes to online mode and decided to take some time to reconfigure learning as most of our faculty relocated.

Oleksandr Geychenko, Rector of OTS

4:55 p.m. My sister Helga messaged me that she is in a bomb shelter – again – because of an air-raid alert. I pray for her safety and also for Kenyan students currently travelling from Kharkiv to Kyiv. Helga is facilitating their evacuation.

7:19 p.m. The roads from Kyiv to Lviv are jam-packed with tens of thousands of cars, vans, and buses carrying refugees fleeing the combat and shelling in Kyiv. Petrol stations in central, southern, and eastern Ukraine have pretty much run dry despite the government's efforts to keep them supplied and the imposition of various restrictions. Most of the petrol in reserves is earmarked for the Ukrainian army and military vehicles. Ukrainian Railways (also known as Ukrzaliznytsia) has introduced free train rides from Kyiv to several destinations, but for safety reasons, these announcements are not on its website.

7:53 p.m. Ivan Rusyn messaged me. He has been compelled to manage the seminary remotely because a destroyed bridge has prevented him from reaching the campus. He has left the bomb shelter in Bucha and is now in a relatively safe place.

7:55 p.m. I'm on my way from Ternopil to Rivne to join my family. I'm so thankful for Vitalii Varenytsia, the head of Ternopil Bible Seminary, for his hospitality – even if for just a few short hours – for food and an office space where I could continue my efforts to coordinate the evacuation of refugees.

Behind the wheel of an old car is firefighter Andrii, a good friend of my sister Liuba. Driving with him is his friend. The traffic is slow as the road is jam-packed with cars. Every five to ten minutes, ambulances fly by, sirens wailing as they transport the wounded from Kyiv. It's hard not to think about where these people are coming from and what's happened to them. This night is pivotal for Kyiv and for the country. If Kyiv falls, the country will most likely follow... My phone has been buzzing and ringing non-stop since Moldova. I coordinate the evacuation of a few other people, trying to help everyone who calls. There's so much fear and dismay in their voices.

The queue at the petrol station is incredibly long. The street lighting is spotty. People are anxious and upset. There's not enough fuel for everyone.

Payment cards have stopped working, so only cash is accepted. I see a woman holding a child – she is begging for just a splash of fuel as she doesn't have any money left. I share my hryvnia[6] cash stash I took to Chisinau just in case. Abandoned cars line the sides of the road – some have broken down, others have run out of fuel. People are walking, luggage in tow, trying to get to the nearest bus station or to a large intersection where they might catch a ride. We pass an elderly woman on the roadside, flagging down cars, and stop for her. It turns out that she had missed her bus at a petrol station. Her phone battery was completely dead. We try to help her get in touch with a dispatcher. We pass a military convoy moving in the opposite direction – towards Kyiv. There are tank transporters and armoured personnel carriers. The soldiers look tired, and it's obvious that this move took them by surprise.

The night falls, but the traffic doesn't ease up; in fact, it increases. Headlights everywhere create a surreal picture: it feels like the entire country is here, driving down this very road. There are long queues at each checkpoint because all documents and vehicles – including the boots – are thoroughly checked. People are growing increasingly frustrated, but they hold on. I understand that this is an important security measure, but there's just so much debasement and dehumanization in this process . . . We stop at yet another petrol station for a short break. Next to us is a family with three children. The youngest child is crying, confused, and distressed. His parents are trying to calm him down. I keep thinking about how many others must be on the road right now, how many lives are being upended over these past few days – our family among them . . .

9:17 p.m. Helga has asked for prayers for the Kenyan students. They've reached Kyiv and are now transferring to a train to Lviv, from where they will head to Poland.

9:45 p.m. I pray for Kseniia Trofymchuk as she prepares to leave. I pray for the safe evacuation of my sister Liuba, my brother Myshko, and their families as they make their way to the Polish border. I pray for the family of Roman Soloviy as he sends his children to a safe place. I pray for my brother Andrii, who is now protecting the Rivne airport. I also pray for the family of Kateryna Shutko, our financial administrator, because she, her mother, and her children have all decided to remain in Ukraine with her husband, Sasha.

---

6. Ukrainian currency.

9:55 p.m. While travelling from Ternopil to Rivne, I sent out an email to our partners:

> Please pray for truth to prevail. This is not "a situation"; this is not "a point of view." Those are the words that various Western partners use to ask me and avoid offending Russia at the same time. What's happening right now has happened before, on 1 September 1939 and 22 June 1941. We are here in Ukraine, not in "a situation," but in the middle of a brutal full-scale invasion happening to a country of 40 million people, and all this is in the twenty-first century. We didn't invite this war. Kremlin and Putin brought it to Ukraine. This is not "a perspective." There is a morality-based judgement of such acts of aggression. For example, it would not be proper during Holocaust to ask a Jewish rabbi at a Nazi concentration camp to give a Jewish point of view of that situation, then turn around and ask the point of view of a German pastor that supports Hitler's regime – all for the sake of "listening to all voices and determining the truth." This would be absurd and immoral because one is a victim of genocide, and the other is an accomplice to crimes against humanity. I hope you understand what I mean to say here . . . This is not a situation; this is not a point of view. These actions can be defined and judged based on the Bible: evil, aggression, and atrocities. Let us not be just Christians. Let us be people created in the image of God. Please pray for spiritual discernment regarding these things . . . Peace be unto you.

10:07 p.m. I sent out a WhatsApp message in the partners' group:

> Please pray for the family of Roman Soloviy, a Ukrainian evangelical theologian, as he moves them from Lviv to the Carpathian region. This will free up their apartment and office (they've been using it as a makeshift shelter) to accommodate other refugees pouring into Lviv from Kyiv, Central, Southern, and Eastern parts of Ukraine. Roman has to leave his elderly, frail parents for a few days just so he can get his family situated and then return. Please pray for his parents, wife, and children. Roman is the head of the Eastern European Institute of Theology, our regional educational centre . . .

10:30 p.m. Lord, I pray for my brother Andrii, standing guard at the Rivne airport. My heart breaks to see our big, loving family separated by this war that Russia has started.

10:42 p.m. A message from Helga in the partners' group:

> Kenyan students are on a train going from Kyiv to Kovel (it's closer to the border). Most of them are young people who don't speak Ukrainian; they are tired and don't have food. Thank you for your prayers. This means a lot to us!

11:14 p.m. I'm finally home and hugging my wife, Natalia. I'm so relieved that we're finally together, but at the same time, I realize that our challenges have only just begun.

11:30 p.m. Before going to bed, I drafted a message in English for our international partners. In it, I described what's been happening in Ukraine and asked for prayers and support. I felt that it was so important to keep our partners updated about the current state of affairs:

> Dear friends and colleagues, peace be unto you. Unfortunately, I was able to get to my emails only now, as I was busy with organizational and coordination matters since 5:00 a.m. Evan Hunter (Scholar Leaders) and I came to Moldova on Sunday evening. Our plan was to hold meetings with six seminaries from Eastern Europe and Central Asia as part of the Vital Sustainability project over the course of a few days until 2 March. But on 24 February 2022, I woke up in the wee hours because of a call from my friend in Lviv. It was a short message: "There's war, Taras . . ."
>
> The entire territory of Ukraine was heavily shelled for at least seven to eight hours by Russian missiles. After that came the so-called "special military operation" on the ground that involved Russian tanks, helicopters, fighter jets, and bombers. Russia attacked strategic Ukrainian cities. Russian forces took over the Chernobyl nuclear plant. Russian shelling and missile strikes targeted airports, defence depots, and civilian infrastructure all over Ukraine. Hundreds of civilians and Ukrainian soldiers were killed. Please pray for the following:
>
>> 1. Ukraine has announced general mobilization. This would mean that many students, alumni, and faculty

would be called up to serve in the army and engage in combat. Please pray for their families and mine. I have a son and five younger brothers. One of them is studying abroad, another is already in the Armed Forces of Ukraine, and yet another is going through a physical evaluation.

2. Please pray for the leaders of seminaries. Many of them are considering the evacuation of staff, faculty, and students to a safer place in Ukraine, but still, some don't have a way to do so.

3. Please pray for those seminaries that are hosting refugees in their dormitories. Together, we've decided to create a network of hubs called "People of the Bridge" to work with internally displaced persons and war-affected people.

4. Please pray for our wives. I talked with Natalia today about her possible evacuation from Ukraine. She immediately refused, saying: "I will be with you until the end, as I promised, in joy and in sorrow." Many wives refuse to leave as all men ages 18–60 cannot leave the country due to general mobilization.

I go to bed thinking that tomorrow will be yet another day of waging war. I pray for protection and strength for all those suffering because of this senseless Russian war . . .

Surges of Resistance: Breaking In
Saturday, 26 February 2022; location: Rivne

> Therefore we do not lose heart. Though outwardly we are wasting away, yet inwardly we are being renewed day by day.
>
> 2 Corinthians 4:16

12:47 a.m. I can't fall asleep. I keep thinking about yesterday's journey. As I travelled from Ternopil to Rivne, the road in our direction was almost empty. But the road in the opposite direction, away from Kyiv, was packed with tens of thousands of cars, vans, and buses, all filled with people. I had an eerie feeling, as if I were in a film that was about to end . . . But this isn't a film – it's the new reality we must deal with.

7:30 a.m. I wake up – at home, in Rivne. The joy of being with my family is intertwined with the painful realization of what is happening to my country because of Russia's invasion. Natalia is already up and making coffee. I see the worries lurking in the corners of her eyes, but she does her best to smile.

9:15 a.m. I'm so grateful for my friends' help on my journey home from Chisinau. Thank you, Vadim Bulgak, Viktor Ormanji, Vasyl Malyk, and Vitalii Varenytsia. I know all too well that in times of war, a journey is a challenge, not a joyful opportunity. Each one of them took a risk to help me.

10:30 a.m. Our small team gathered on Zoom to discuss plans for coordinating assistance for refugees and supporting our seminaries. I'm well aware of the importance of working quickly and efficiently right now.

12:10 p.m. The news rolled in about Russian advances towards Kharkiv and Mariupol. I can't shake the thoughts about thousands of refugees leaving their homes. My heart breaks for each and every one of them. We begin coordinating logistics for those trying to evacuate. Our team includes Roman Soloviy (director of the Eastern European Institute of Theology), Helga (my sister and Overseas Council team member), my son Nazar (a student), and other colleagues.

2:05 p.m. The future of Russian-Ukrainian Christianity – which currently feels like it's at its funeral (or, rather, the wake is over and the burial is underway) – will only be revived when every Russian Christian who supported and voted for Putin calls things by their proper names. Peacemaking is not reticence. Peacemaking is calling a spade a spade, calling a sin a sin – not a "mistake" – and recognizing fratricide as fratricide, rather than saying that "things are not so simple and straightforward."

3:04 p.m. I received a message from Roman Soloviy about what's been going on in Khust.

> Dear friends, this morning I took my family from Lviv to Khust, a city in the Transcarpathian region. Right now, we don't have a clear understanding of how the events will unfold or what our family will do. Regardless, I will be staying in Ukraine. I want to say a few words about the ministry of Ukrainian churches in these horrible times. From East to West, from Donbas to Transcarpathia, thousands of believers and hundreds of churches have joined efforts in saving lives. They arrange daily transportation runs, host people at temporary shelters, help cross the border into

neighbouring countries, and feed and clothe their neighbours – literally, anyone in need. Small congregations in Khust – moved by the spirit of brotherly love – daily take in dozens of refugees from various areas of Ukraine. Churches in Lviv welcome and provide for thousands of people. And even though these days we are watching, teary-eyed and desperate, the news of the suffering of our people, such examples of radical self-sacrifice give hope and strength to carry on our labour of love.

4:55 p.m. I stand in awe of the incredible self-organization of Ukrainian society. People have been taking the initiative to help one another without waiting for directions or instructions. I see this as God's grace and a gift for self-organization. I posted about this on Facebook, with great pride in our people:

> I am amazed by the people, by Ukrainians, by many Christians. I have experienced this powerful feeling three times in my life: in 2004, 2014, and 2015–2016. And now, I'm experiencing it again. So many people are not bossing others around, but rather looking to identify the need and their own strong suit, step up, roll up their sleeves, and get to work. Someone is good at coordinating; someone is capable in translation; someone is great at communicating; someone is able to serve with their possessions, like a car, and so on. As such, the miracle is revealed. People in hundreds and hundreds of thousands, millions even, are on the move – on the road – internally displaced persons, refugees, whatever the name. And so many people are helping them even as their own families are in need of protection. I see God's grace in this – this gift of self-organization of society, the glimmer of God's image still remaining in humans. For this, I will praise the Lord and hope to see more of this passion in our local churches after the war's end. This is my prayer . . .

5:37 p.m. I just wrapped up a conversation with my brother Mykhailo, who helps refugees on the Polish border. He won't be coming home tonight because of a car queue that stretches for almost twenty kilometres. Unfortunately, there is no official resource to assist refugees with many of the issues they face, including a lack of information. Mykhailo explained that two types of people come to the border by car. The first group consists of those who want to cross in their own car; the second consists of those who have caught a ride to the border and are just being dropped off. So, this second group doesn't have to go through a car queue – they can drive through the oncoming lane, park to unload, and then walk about three or four kilometres to the border crossing checkpoint. However, due to the lack of informational support, many people don't know this. For example, Natalia's relative – a young pregnant woman with little children – had to walk fifteen kilometres through a winding queue to get to the border crossing checkpoint. So Mykhailo walks along the queue, asking families direct questions and providing direct answers, all to help them cross the border more quickly and easily.

Our family business is temporarily on hold. It's a printing house that has received many state awards and published thousands of monographs, textbooks, historical scholarly works, and Christian books, operating underground during Soviet times until 24 February 2022. While Mykhailo was on the phone with me, he said, "I don't have anyone to go home to. I've sent Olha and the children off to France. At least here at the border, I can help hundreds of families who come to the border by ride-share avoid spending twelve to sixteen hours in a car queue and another four to five hours at the checkpoint." We don't know when our families will be reunited as the men are staying in the country to care for, protect, help, and support our people.

7:30 p.m. Dinner with Natalia. We tried to talk about anything other than the war, but it proved nearly impossible to do so.

8:47 p.m. Message from Roman Soloviy in the partners' group:

> Today, my friends in Khust, where I am at the moment, took in another family of refugees, this time from Uman, a town in the Cherkasy region. They lived very close to a military base and came under fire during the shelling on the first day of the war. Missiles hit the ammunition depot, and detonating shells went flying all over the neighbourhood, raining destruction. One of them blew a man into smithereens right in the centre of Uman. The pregnant wife, her husband, and their little son had to flee immediately. As they were travelling, the wife found out that her cousin had been killed in action. That brought on tears, despair, and pain. Only now do they feel safe, all because of the ministry done by my friends and a local church that will be taking care of them.

9:45 p.m. I heard the news about a baby being born in an underground metro station in Kyiv. What a stark contrast between death on the ground and new life underground. Above, there are explosions and death; below, like in an apocalypse film, a new life comes forth . . .

10:09 p.m. Helga sent a message:

> Kenyan students from Kharkiv are still waiting in a queue at the border on the Ukrainian side . . . please continue praying; there are some challenges . .

11:15 p.m. Before going to bed, I spent some time thinking about the future: What will happen to us? When and how will this war end? What will the postwar world be like? I didn't have answers to any of these questions, but I put my hope and trust in God. "Don't be afraid; just believe" (Mark 5:36). This verse has become a reverberating inner motif these days . . .

I've been trying to fall asleep, but I just can't, even though I've been awake for most of the past two days. Our go-bags are right by our bed. I think about our troops, about Andrii, and about how much sleep they must be losing. I think about those who spend their nights in metro stations, bomb shelters, and basements. I pray for my people's perseverance and fortitude, and for a quick end to this terror. I remember how, back in 2020, I saw my son-in-law Andrew Dalrymple off to the States after he had lived in Ukraine for two years. He told me: "Taras, you Ukrainians have got excellent survival skills, but when are you going to actually start living?" Yes, right now, those survival skills are very handy. Still, I'm compelled to do everything I can to make sure that those babies born underground would not merely survive but truly live and thrive.

Bursts of Unity
Sunday, 27 February 2022; location: Rivne

> There shall be one flock and one shepherd.
>
> John 10:16

8:10 a.m. I was awakened by the wailing of an air-raid siren. My heart was racing, but I tried to stay calm. I've been thinking constantly about those at the front lines, risking their lives to protect us. All at once, I'm overwhelmed by both profound gratitude and pain.

10:11 a.m. I sent the following message in the partners' group:

> Greetings, friends! This night went by more or less quietly. So much coordination is happening, and the information flow is

immense. Please pray for the team of the Eastern European Institute of Theology that's currently involved in this coordination ministry to the refugees by putting together people, seminaries, and organizations to assist with evacuation. Our team consists of Roman, Helga, Kseniia, Kateryna, Nazar, and me. I was able to sleep for about four hours and got back to working with our team. Thank you for your love and prayers.

10:16 a.m. Another message to the partners:

> Please pray right now for the team from the Divitia Gratiae University (seminary partner of the Overseas Council and Scholar Leaders). They are on the way from Chisinau to the border of Moldova to bring in several dozen more Ukrainian refugees, including a group from Kremenchuk Evangelical Seminary that is also undergoing evacuation. I get teary-eyed when I think that Moldova, being such a small country, has already taken in over 50,000 Ukrainian refugees fleeing war zones. Many thanks to our partners at the University! Love you all!

12:12 p.m. I received some good news from Helga. This brought a small measure of relief and prompted gratitude to the Lord for this small victory amid all the chaos.

> Thank you, Lord! Kenyan students just crossed the border to Poland and are moving on with the support of trustworthy people. The evacuation from Kharkiv and Kyiv was a miracle! The Lord is the Almighty One! They are also facilitating contact with other international students needing help, and we are trying to find ways to help them.

3:00 p.m. I continue to coordinate the assistance offered by volunteers. We're looking for drivers who can take people to the border crossing checkpoints. We're searching for places for refugees to stay. This February has been an especially rough month, not because of the weather but because of the Kremlin's hostility and invasion of Ukraine. I can't help but wonder how this war will change not just Ukraine but also Christianity in this region.

The Russian ideology of dehumanization – presented in the guise of "red Christianity" – must die. And it must first die within the Christians who cling to the idea that "it's not so clear-cut" or that "not everything was so terrible during Communist rule." A believer is called to be transformed into the image of Christ, reflecting his character. Leninist-Stalinist ideology is utterly incompatible with the principles and values of true Christianity. These two belief systems and world views are drastically different and cannot coexist within the same person or community. The doctrine of communism, as devised by Lenin and implemented by Stalin, is grounded in atheism, class struggle, party dictatorship, and the curtailment of freedoms. In contrast, Christianity teaches faith in God, love for neighbour, free will, and the dignity of each human being as created in the image of God. Therefore, a true Christian cannot adhere to Leninist-Stalinist ideals, just as a follower of such an ideology cannot be a genuine Christian. I hope that after 24 February 2022, Russian Evangelical Christians will stop the current practice of sending season's greetings to dictators and seeking or expecting acceptance and understanding from those being slaughtered by these dictators. It is not possible, in the same breath, to bless both dictators who protect "traditional values" (thus legitimizing their fratricidal tactics) and the people they are killing. A spring cannot pour forth, from the same opening, both fresh water and salt water.

5:30 p.m. I've been on phone calls with colleagues from various seminaries.

7:30 p.m. I heard that civilians who were trying to evacuate came under fire from Russian forces. Russian invaders shot a family with a small child as they were trying to leave Kyiv via a humanitarian corridor. Anger and pain wash over me. How can such actions ever be justified? I pray for justice and for the Lord to put an end to this madness.

9:45 p.m. I've been monitoring the status of border crossing checkpoints at the Polish border and trying to help evacuate international students. Thank you, Lord, for the financial and prayer support from our partners. There are so many people across Europe ready to meet refugees at the border that Ukraine and Poland cannot let them through quickly enough. All of my friends and acquaintances, both old and new, including some I've only met during these past four days of war – from Germany, the Netherlands, Poland, the Czech Republic, Moldova, and other countries – are incredible! This is true Christianity: to take in refugees and strangers, some of whom are my own family and their children.

11:30 p.m. Natalia and I prayed before going to bed. I'm so grateful to God for her and for us being together in these difficult times. Every day of this war is a challenge to our faith, to our being human, and to our ability to love. Yet it is also an opportunity to manifest the best in us. "Lord, your will be done, on earth as it is in heaven."

Never-Ending Storm
Monday, 28 February 2022; location: Rivne

> The Lord sits enthroned over the flood; the Lord is enthroned as King for ever.
>
> Psalm 29:10

12:09 a.m. A message from Roman Soloviy:

> Today, I sent my children over to Romania with a backpack, a suitcase, and some cash. My wife, Olenka, will be back tomorrow. She doesn't want to leave me here all by myself. I had to find a place to stay overnight in a village nearby. All of a sudden, I've been left all alone, without my family, and my travelling gear consists only of a backpack with my laptop; I don't even have a toothbrush. All of my stuff is in Lviv, maybe a few things in Khust. Day five of the war . . .

1:58 a.m. Since the beginning of the Russian invasion, 352 civilians have been killed, including 14 children. There are 1,684 wounded civilians, among them 116 children. These are the statistics from the Ministry of Health. The death toll would have been much higher if not for the many volunteers who promptly stepped up and helped people flee the combat zones. Now, the government is also getting involved – and that's a good thing. I appealed for prayer for all these volunteers – whether Orthodox, Protestant, Evangelical, Muslim, Jew, or Mormon – as they help refugees and internally displaced persons to overcome various challenges. As I see this extraordinary display of dedication, dignity, and passion over these four days of the war, I keep wondering: Why, oh why, aren't we just as dedicated to mission-minded theological education? Why aren't we as passionate about spreading the kingdom of God, not in the sense of a prospering society but as a community of hope, filled with relationships built on love, trust, and care for one another? Why can't we be a community of hope that seeks out the broken people in this world and invites them into a relationship with God and with one another through confession, acceptance, reconciliation, and cooperation for the sake of God's kingdom? Why, oh why?

2:00 a.m. I'm trying to catch some sleep, if only a few hours of it, when the air-raid siren goes off again. The coordination of evacuations goes on, an exhausting marathon that pushes us to the limits of our physical and emotional resources. Hundreds of requests begging for help whittle away at the heart...

We spent the entire day today coordinating evacuations. The process would start with a message in a chat: someone asking for help. We'd verify the information, weigh the risks, and then work out a route. It's a bit like piecing together a jigsaw puzzle: we try to account for everything, from the current locations of the Russian forces to the operational hours of checkpoints. The hardest part is bringing the person out of the immediate danger zone, where the greatest threat comes from shelling or attacks by Russian troops, who have been advancing rapidly across the country in recent days. We give step-by-step directions over the phone. If the person is in an occupied territory, we come up with a cover story to explain their reason for travelling in case they're stopped. Checkpoints are always a challenging place. We prepare people for possible interrogations and make sure all their documents are in order. We also anticipate likely questions and help people to be ready with acceptable answers. If the planned route goes through Russia, we involve a network of trusted volunteers who provide safe places to spend the night and also help with meals and train or bus tickets. It's like a relay race: a tag-team transfer of the travellers until they either reach safety or get to one of our hubs. We constantly monitor the situation, maintaining communication and remaining ready to change plans at a moment's notice. Our greatest asset is trust between all parties involved. At times, I'm amazed at just how much is pieced together and held together by trust during this time of war. Every successful evacuation is a small victory. Every single person rescued makes all our efforts worthwhile.

8:45 a.m. Once again, I'm awakened by the sound of air-raid sirens. This marks the fifth day of the war, yet it still feels like none of this is really happening. Natalia's face is tense as she checks the news.

9:00 a.m. My working day began with a Zoom meeting with our coordination team. We discussed new challenges: evacuations from hotspots, organizing humanitarian aid, and supporting refugees at our hubs. Every new day brings fresh challenges but also new ways to help. Our partners at the Overseas Council-United World Mission and Scholar Leaders, with some support from Langham, launched Project for Ukrainian Refugees in Europe (PURE). Through this project comes aid for our seminaries which had become hubs to support evacuation efforts, resources for IDPs and refugees, food supplies, etc.

11:20 a.m. I've been thinking about Russian mothers whose sons have been sent to Ukraine under the pretext of going through "military exercises." I wish I could get them to see the truth and bring their boys home. But it's becoming quite obvious to me that these soldiers have chosen to die in Ukraine as invaders. Regardless of whether this choice was made consciously or subconsciously, voluntarily or under pressure from the FSB,[7] it is still their own choice.

11:30 a.m. I pray for negotiations between Putin, Lukashenko, and Zelenskyy. I hope for a peaceful resolution, but I understand how difficult – even impossible – that would be.

11:40 a.m. I received news about an attack on an airport in Zaporizhzhia. I pray for the Zaporizhzhia Bible Seminary, its leaders, faculty, and students. This seminary is one of our hubs. I called the rector to offer our support.

1:30 p.m. Lunchtime. Natalia and I spend this time together eating and discussing the latest news.

1:41 p.m. Helga sends a message, followed by a request to share it:

> If anyone knows any international students from Africa who are currently stuck somewhere in Ukraine and can be reached, please ask them to get in touch with Dr. Albert Kitcher at his Office Room #6, 11 Volodymyrska St., Kyiv, Ukraine. Please pass along this information to students from Africa ASAP. Right now, time is a matter of life and death!

2:20 p.m. I received news about the evacuation of seventy people – faculty and students of the Ukrainian Evangelical Theological Seminary. Ivan's wife (Ivan Rusyn is the Rector of the Ukrainian Evangelical Theological Seminary in Kyiv) has brought five children from other families with her. I cry because I feel so helpless. I'm glad everyone is alive, but my heart breaks for those still in danger. Ivan messages me: he's crying tears of joy over the fact that nobody was killed. It's at times like this that we realize anew the preciousness of human life.

4:55 p.m. Helga is coordinating assistance for the Hutnyk family as they try to evacuate. Seven of their eight children are waiting at the border, in a line of over

---

7. The Federal Security Service of the Russian Federation (FSB) is the primary security agency of Russia and the main successor to the Soviet Union's KGB.

three hundred cars. We pray for their safety and successful border crossing. Right now, it's so important to support each other in both prayer and action.

7:10 p.m. I received a message from Valentyn Syniy, the rector of Tavriski Christian Institute. His words remind me of the high price that each one of us is paying in this war – not just physically but also emotionally and psychologically.

> We had to leave Kherson as it was shelled quite heavily. We are opening a temporary headquarters of the Tavriski Christian Institute in Ivano-Frankivsk. The plan is to rent some office space and begin working this week or the next. Then we'll have a better idea of how many people are still on board and able to work. We have seen that some of our faculty and staff have suffered psychological trauma from being under fire and need counselling. We want to be mindful of that and supportive. I tried to hold a meeting today, but it was quite unproductive . . . Please pray for the future of TCI.

7:30 p.m. The air-raid sirens are wailing again. We should go to a bomb shelter. Or, perhaps it's useless, and we shouldn't. I think about how this sound affects people's mental health, especially children. How will we ever recover from all of this? Natalia and I decide to stay in our apartment.

9:45 p.m. I wonder about the future of Christianity in Russia. I do think that there's a need for a new wave of evangelism, which includes the de-Putinization of the church and the Christian community in Russia. I posted my musings on Facebook:

> Revival of Christianity in Russia – including evangelical Christianity – will be possible with a new wave of evangelism that would also include de-Putinization of the Church and Christian community. There's so much to learn from Niemoller as he spent over 30 years in Germany after Hitler's demise – he would travel to various churches to preach and talk about denazification of the church and theology. And it's that denazification that made peacemaking dialogue and reconciliation with the German people possible.
>
> The "spiritual bonds"[8] of Russia – the very thing many Christians, Orthodox and Protestant alike, were very proud of – turned

---

8. "Spiritual bonds" or "spiritual ties" (Russian: "духовные скрепы") is an ideological concept in Russia that refers to "traditional values" for the population of the Russian Federation, which gained popularity during the late Putin era.

out to be demonic chains that bound conscience, theology, missiology, and ecclesiology. Reconciliation will need to happen, and peacemaking dialogues will need to open up. However, there absolutely must be an obligatory answer to the simple question that God so liked to ask each of his prophets: "What do you see?" The prophetic role of the church is wrapped up in answer to this question: do we look at the world through God's eyes or through the eyes of the demonic ideology of the Kremlin that has gained a presence in ecclesia-theological discourse?

Back in December of 2013, when I was at a conference in Novosibirsk (Russia), I often heard prayers coming from Russians in response to Ukraine's bid to become an EU candidate. Those prayers went along the lines of "God, please stop the Ukrainians as they're getting ready to sell out to Europe and gays for a piece of bread and renounce our real Russian spirituality." I couldn't (and didn't) say an Amen to prayers like that. I simply asked God for the wisdom to get through the conference and go home quickly. Any attempts to explain anything about Ukraine always ended with the response, "Not everything is so clear-cut."

Right now, things seem to be very clear. Yet, the question for the majority remains without an answer. "What do you see?" asks the Lord . . .

The prophets in Judges, Kings, and Chronicles had a clear differentiation of kings: wicked or righteous. If a prophet tried to justify the actions of murderous Ahab by saying that "things aren't so clear-cut," then he was a false prophet. Do God's people in Russia have enough of a prophetic voice to call a killer a killer without tacking on "not everything is so clear-cut"? Unfortunately, no, not enough . . .

Realizing something takes time. Healing both memory and world view takes time. Time is needed to be transformed and able to answer the question, "What do you see?" And that time begins from the moment of renouncing the Soviet world view, communist values, and Putinist ideas of gathering peoples into a single nation through fight and fire, through the bombing of peaceful cities and shooting of civilians. I will never stop reminding others of what came first: it was not Ukraine that attacked Ukraine back in 2014, it was Russia that attacked Ukraine through the creation of puppet states in an attempt to legalize its gathering conquest. And what do you see?

11:40 p.m. I went to bed with the same gnawing thought: reconciliation will only be possible when we can honestly and truthfully answer the Lord's question, "What do you see?" Tomorrow would be the first day of March. Lord, when will this war end? How many more days, weeks, months, or years? I fell asleep with a prayer in my heart, entrusting our future – whatever it might bring – into his hands.

Epilogue

These eleven days, as described in my diary, were only the beginning of a long and arduous journey for Ukraine and its people. The full-scale, unprovoked Russian invasion that began on 24 February 2022 continues to this day. It goes on and on, changing the lives of millions of people, destroying towns and villages, and separating families and communities. For me, as a theologian and a Christian, these months have been a time of deep reflection and reconsideration of many facets of my faith and ministry. The questions that arose in the first few days of the war have not disappeared; rather, they have compelled me to dig even deeper. How do we speak of God's love amid such suffering? How do we keep on being human when faced with such cruelty? How do we build bridges when others seem determined to blow them up?

Our theological seminaries and evangelical churches became places of aid and support for hundreds of thousands of refugees. Many of our students and faculty find themselves on the front lines: some serving with weapons, others ministering with prayers and words of comfort. We are learning how to be the church in times of war and how to bring the light of Christ to places engulfed by darkness. Coordinating evacuation, organizing humanitarian aid, and supporting victims both spiritually and emotionally is now an integral part of our ministry. We realize that theology cannot exist separately from reality; rather, it must offer answers to the pressing issues and challenges of the here and now.

The war has exposed many problems that exist within the Christian world, especially in the relationships between Ukrainian and Russian believers. We are confronted with the need to rethink what unity in Christ really means. Yet, amid these challenges, we have seen awe-inspiring examples of faith, love, and self-sacrifice. We have witnessed people of different faith traditions and beliefs coming together to help neighbours in need. We have seen how prayer has become not mere words shaking the air but a real force, comforting and empowering.

This diary is but a small piece of the great story of faith and the indomitable spirit of the Ukrainian people and the Ukrainian church. This story is still being written with blood and tears, in death and suffering, but also through incredible courage and hope.

We do not know when this war will end. But we do know that our faith, having gone through the fire of suffering, is growing stronger. We believe that the light of Christ shines even in the darkest hour. And we continue to pray and work towards the day when peace will come to our land and we will be able to rebuild our cities and restore our souls – steeled by trials but renewed by God's grace. May these pages serve not only as a testimony of the past but also as a call to the future – a future that is ruled by love and true unity in Christ. Mind yourself!

But who can measure the pain, suffering, and psychological damage inflicted on the Ukrainian people by those who orchestrated this unjust war? The lives of millions of Ukrainians were shattered. Everything we once knew has been wiped out. Nothing is left. Just a wilderness.
Oleksandr Geychenko (p. 53)

2

Theological Education among the Ruins

Oleksandr Geychenko

Rector, Odesa Theological Seminary, Ukraine

It is September 2024. The hot southern summer is giving way to the arrival of autumn. I am sitting at my desk in my office at Odesa Theological Seminary. Odesa is the largest Ukrainian city on the northern shores of the Black Sea. Known for its lively seaports and flourishing international trade, Odesa is sometimes called "a pearl by the sea," as the old song goes. A well-known cultural centre and resort area – once popular as a summer vacation destination – the city is celebrated for its character, wit, creativity, and international openness. Although the intensity of activity has decreased significantly, even now, two years and six months after the full-scale invasion, people still visit Odesa for the same reasons they did before the war.

The first Baptist Bible school in Ukraine was established in Odesa by a group of local ministers in 1989, during the final years of the USSR. Word spread like lightning, and students began coming from all across Ukraine and Moldova. In 1991, after the USSR collapsed, the school evolved into a seminary – Odesa Theological Seminary (OTS). OTS played an active role in developing an accrediting agency and was involved in numerous theological initiatives through its faculty. I enrolled at OTS in 1996 and completed my BTh programme in 2001. I then joined OTS as the librarian and later became its academic dean. While working at OTS, I was also involved in various publishing and scholarly projects, through which I got to know many excellent Ukrainian theologians and dedicated educators. After completing my PhD at St. Andrews, I returned to OTS as its rector, and it was in this role that I faced the full-scale invasion.

The events of 24 February 2022 served as a clear dividing line between how things were before and what came after. As I recall the events before and after this date, I realize that the war has completely changed everything I knew about theological education. It has changed the normal academic routine, the composition of our student bodies, and the way Ukrainian theological educators view the content of theological education and its relationship to public issues. It has changed the community of educators across Eastern Europe and Central Asia, exposing realities we would never have imagined before. It has certainly changed us as Ukrainian theological educators and theologians. Ultimately, I must reluctantly admit, it has changed me and all of us permanently. We cannot yet imagine the final shape of these transformations since this brutal and bloody war is still going on. We are still on the move.

On the Eve

The months leading up to the full-scale invasion were a strange period, filled with a mix of worry and hope. The Russian Armed Forces (RAF) were performing drills at our borders and amassing troops and heavy weaponry. The intelligence reports and statements from Ukrainian and foreign officials were often contradictory, and the news changed in tone like a weathercock. However, the emails from our partners asking what was happening and what my plans were, along with growing concerns expressed by fellow educators during private conversations over coffee or lunch, were indicators that something inescapable was approaching.

Looking back, I can see more clearly what was happening and when. But at that time, when I was caught in the midst of the events, it was hard to see beyond the horizon. My emotions and hopes were very similar to those of the Jews described by Elie Wiesel – the Jewish Holocaust survivor and Nobel Prize winner – in his novel *The Night*. The Jews in Wiesel's novel heard the news about the German army entering Hungary, but they thought that these events would pass, leaving them unaffected. Intuitively, I sensed that danger was approaching as the atmosphere was becoming thicker and more electrified. At the same time, I hoped that some level of sanity and decisiveness would prevail among global political leaders to prevent a tragedy. Well, we all know what happened . . .

Since the tension was growing, we at OTS decided to draw up a plan in case of invasion. We made copies of our statutory documents and sent them to our partners abroad, packed important documents, as well as valuable equipment, and secured extra funds. We also negotiated with a local church in western Ukraine to secure rooms for our families in case of any emergency or evacuation. We had two meetings with all employees to give instructions on how to prepare for evacuation and to discuss our action plan in detail. I still remember the strange feeling in my heart and the surprised looks I received from employees – is this all a bad dream they wondered?

The final event that made me realize the gravity of the situation was a meeting of the Council of the All-Ukrainian Union of Churches of Evangelical Christian-Baptists, which took place in Kyiv eight days before the invasion began. I was there as the chair of the Union's Educational Committee. I had travelled to Kyiv with a group of Baptist youth leaders who were in Odesa exploring facilities for a future youth congress. On our way to Kyiv, we discussed the situation. Although all of us were concerned, we were still hoping that nothing would happen. The council meeting was like a bucket of cold water poured over my head. The leadership of the Union warned that invasion seemed imminent and urged all regional Baptist associations of churches situated in the eastern and southern parts of Ukraine to create evacuation plans. The churches in the western parts of the country were advised to prepare for a wave of refugees. On my way back to Odesa, I felt certain that Ukraine was at the threshold of something horrible. Nevertheless, deep in my heart, I still hoped we would never have to implement our evacuation plan.

When I try to understand why the possibility of the invasion seemed so inconceivable to many, myself included, the only explanation I can come up with is that it was a defence mechanism. My mind frantically clung to even the smallest signs of hope because it could not imagine that the world I knew and used to live in was collapsing before my eyes.

When Things Fell Apart

I remember the night before 24 February and the morning of that day as clearly as if it all happened yesterday. I was at home alone because my family had gone to Lviv for a holiday the week before. We had a brief conversation over the phone. My wife said she planned to purchase return tickets to Odesa the next day. I told her not to hurry but to wait for a few more days if possible. Before going to bed, I decided to start reading Paul Tillich's *The Courage to Be*. It seemed like the right book for the moment since it might help me to accept the reality I couldn't prevent. I fell asleep reflecting on what I had read.

Most Ukrainians were awakened by the sounds of missile strikes on the morning of 24 February. I was awakened by a call from my colleague and friend, Roman Soloviy, who said, "It has begun, Oleksandr." I opened an app on my smartphone, and the news burst in. The RAF (Russian Armed Forces) had invaded Ukraine from three directions – south, north, and east. I immediately sent a message in the seminary's chat, informing employees that we must implement our emergency plan.

Events unfolded quickly. The Russian army was advancing fast. The southern regions were captured within the first few days. The RAF came very close to Kyiv. The news was disturbing and sometimes contradictory. No one was certain what exactly was happening and where. There were rumours that Russian forces were near Mykolaiv, a city that was a two-hour drive southeast from Odesa. Due to its geographical and strategic location between the annexed Crimean Peninsula and Transnistria – an unrecognized Russian-controlled enclave on the territory of Moldova – Odesa was one of the RAF's key targets. The chances were high that the RAF would attempt to cut off the city from the rest of the country and launch an amphibious assault.

Most people didn't want to stay in the city, waiting for events to unfold. By the end of the first day of the invasion, Odesa was almost deserted. The streets emptied, although stores and businesses were still open. Gas stations limited the volume of fuel one person could purchase. Drivers queued up, hoping to get some fuel before setting off. Tickets for trains and buses were sold out in the blink of an eye. Thousands of people fled to the western parts of the country or to the Moldovan border. It was just a matter of days before supermarket shelves emptied and could not be restocked because suppliers were afraid to bring goods to Odesa. The city was preparing for an assault from the Black Sea. The streets were barricaded with multiple checkpoints and strongholds, aimed at stopping the Russian units. Elderly people recalled the German blockade of the city during World War II.

Most of the OTS faculty and their families evacuated on the first day of the full-scale invasion. I think our experience was fairly typical of most Ukrainian theological schools. But behind this typicality, one can easily miss the unique stories and tragedies of different individuals.

The OTS dean's wife and three daughters went to the west of Ukraine with other faculty members. The dean himself remained in Odesa with his elderly and fragile father, who had limited mobility. The dean's family safely reached their home town in the Volyn region. When the situation in the Kyiv and Zhytomyr regions became threatening, they went to Poland and, later, to Germany. The dean and his father were evacuated in an overcrowded train to a relatively safe place in western Ukraine. Unfortunately, his father did not survive the period of displacement and passed away far from his home. This family was separated under tragic circumstances, not knowing what hardships they would face and whether or when they would meet again.

I remained in Odesa because I had important matters to complete before I could leave. When I finally joined my family, the four of us – my wife, our two grown-up daughters, and I – lived in a single room for almost six months. Three other families lived with us under the same roof. Sometimes, it was hard, but we couldn't complain because others were living in far more difficult conditions under occupation or in towns and villages destroyed by shelling and bombing. Each of us had only a small suitcase of clothes and documents with us; everything else we owned had been left behind in Odesa. This was a time when we learned to value relationships, be content with a simple life and basic necessities, and realize that our loved ones are more important than anything else.

The full-scale invasion took us by surprise at OTS during a training session. We had students on campus at the time; and on 24 February, we sent them home. Although most students left, one of our female students could not return to her home town in the east because the front line was very close to it and all trains in that direction had been cancelled. So, we convinced her to evacuate to one of the western regions. She was concerned about her elderly mother, who was still in their home town. When the fighting escalated, the apartment block where her mother lived was partially destroyed and set on fire by the invaders. Although their apartment was damaged, thank God her mother survived and was evacuated to the place where her daughter was. With no place to live and no job, they became refugees.

Multiply this scenario by 4.9 million, and you will get an approximate projection of the situation in Ukraine. Each of these 4.9 million people has a name, a face, and a unique story. Families hurriedly packed their belongings and went to other parts of the country or abroad. Many people fitted their lives into a suitcase, not knowing where their journey would end. But who can measure the pain, suffering, and psychological damage inflicted on the Ukrainian people by those who orchestrated this unjust war? The lives of millions of Ukrainians were shattered. Everything we once knew has been wiped out. Nothing is left. Just a wilderness.

I don't think it would be an exaggeration to describe the first days after the invasion with words like "chaos," "shock," and "uncertainty." Most of us were in deep shock for a few days. Everything felt surreal. The full-scale war became the focus of our thoughts and conversations. Whatever topic someone started inevitably led to sharing thoughts and feelings about current events. The newsfeed on our smartphones consumed all our attention. We scrolled through, hoping to find good news from the front lines to share with one another. All this created deep anxiety, stress, and exhaustion. The newsfeed was full of so much blood, pain, and death. A normal human being cannot process so much painful information without paying a price, and most of us did. I remember that at some point in March 2022, I suddenly realized that I couldn't feel anything at all. At first, this discovery frightened me, but upon reflection, I realized this was my body's reaction to stress – it had shut down my emotions to protect my health.

All of us were traumatized in one way or another, but we didn't realize it at the time because we were still living through it. I remember my older daughter telling me, after returning from the annual meeting of the Conference of European Churches in Tallinn in June 2023, "Dad, it was only there that I realized how traumatized I am." This kind of realization only comes when a person is surrounded by circumstances and people who don't bear the marks of war.

In addition to this traumatic experience, we encountered a phenomenon that most of us had never experienced before: the phenomenon of a delayed life. This was caused by the expectation that the war would end soon, a feeling that was reinforced by official government spokespeople. They even coined a phrase that was later turned into a meme: "two–three weeks." Since no one knew what was happening or how long this war would last, waiting seemed like the only reasonable choice for many: Well, let's wait for two–three weeks and see what happens. Why plan something if, after two–three weeks, or a month, you could return home to your normal life? Why make friends in another part of the country if you expect to be back home soon? This waiting for a return to normalcy was paralyzing and demotivating. I soon realized that the only way to break free from this condition was to accept the uncertainty and the fact that the war could last for years, not months. When I shared this thought with my family, my daughters burst into tears. It was clear they wanted their old life back; instead, they had to face the harsh reality of a prolonged war and its consequences. And even if the war ended sooner than expected, we had to accept that things would never be the same as before. This realization was painful, but it was also healing.

For me as the principal of OTS, one of the most difficult aspects of this war-impacted life was that my horizon for making decisions was limited to one or two days. Under such conditions I could only focus on the immediate. Before the full-scale war, I used to think in terms of years. We planned well ahead of time to ensure that our schedule would not be overcrowded when the time came. But after the invasion, no mid-term or long-term planning was possible. To remain sane, I had to focus on the things I could control. For me, this involved writing emails to partners, meeting with employees over Zoom, visiting the local church, and trying to help others in more precarious situations. This was not the time for passive waiting. Things were developing rapidly, and this demanded quick decisions and full involvement.

Transforming Theological Education

Theological education in Ukraine has been evolving since our country gained independence. But the most significant transformations in both its content and form were a result of the full-scale war. The educational process was postponed until the end of March, and some theological schools stopped work until the end of the spring semester because of other pressing issues that required full attention.

Instead of running educational programmes, these schools transformed into hubs that connected those in need with those with the means to help them. We also helped people directly by evacuating them and providing food, medicine, or shelter. There are numerous stories of heroism, as well as simple compassion, that we can recall and retell. Some campuses were turned into temporary shelters for people fleeing from the east to the west of the country. Faculty members delivered food, medicine, and clothes to people in devastated towns and villages. The names of many of these people will never be known to the public, but it is thanks to them and many others that our country survived and was able to turn the tide in a more favourable direction.

Active involvement in social aid projects helped many Christian educators to break free from the grip of endless newsfeeds and the phenomenon of the delayed life. Very quickly, they realized that this was no time for despair, self-pity, or retreating to the safety of private life. The situation demanded action, and this action not only brought healing but also reshaped our perspective on theological education.

When courses and training programmes resumed, these sessions were initially conducted over Zoom or similar platforms. The lecturers didn't just focus on teaching and discussing the course content with students; instead, these sessions also became a time for group therapy. Students and faculty shared their experiences, prayed for one another, and exchanged valuable information and ideas related to their ministry. Faculty referred to common experiences of students to anchor their teaching and help students to integrate the course content into their ministry or use it as an interpretive lens through which to process their experiences.

Our interactions with many people helped us realize that any educational programme that trains individuals to work with people should include courses that address the issue of traumatic experiences. Theological institutions began offering training programmes to eradicate illiteracy in this area. More comprehensive courses were developed to provide students with diagnostic and therapeutic skills. Old Testament lecturers delved into the biblical texts dealing with sorrow and despair and developed new lecture cycles that focused on how to deal with such experiences. Psalms of lament provided valuable insights into this important aspect of human life.

The war prompted fresh discussions on issues such as patriotism, national identity, and public theology. The existential threat caused many Christians to rethink their attitudes towards their country and people. Many realized that although Christianity does create some tension between national identity and Christian identity, it is impossible to think of an ethnically neutral Christianity. Scholars, pastors, and denominational leaders discussed these issues at conferences and produced valuable resources that could be used to develop courses in public theology.

The shrinking of human resources led to a greater need for short-term training for those already in leadership roles within churches and Christian organizations. Since the horizon for decision-making narrowed significantly, many people could only commit to shorter training courses, usually from six months to a year. This development complicated the regular activities of theological institutions because their full-length programmes became less attractive than their shorter courses. In addition, safety concerns and the inability of many institutions to provide bomb shelters caused a switch to more distributed forms of instruction, such as online learning or conducting classes in smaller groups in various locations rather than in one central location. These institutions have developed flexible approaches that accommodate students' needs and learning preferences. Most programmes now use some form of hybrid instruction. In these ways, Ukrainian theological institutions have proven flexible and resilient, adapting well to the situation. However, the war has significantly depleted their human resources, and this will significantly impact the development – and even the survival – of these institutions.

The Night

Since February 2022, it has become clear that Russia is waging a total war against the Ukrainian population. This war has caused massive human and material losses in Ukraine. It is an undeniable fact that the RAF have fought not only against Ukrainian soldiers but also against the Ukrainian people. According to the most conservative estimates, there have been 35,160 casualties – 11,520 killed (including 633 children) and 23,640 wounded (including 1,551 children).[1] Multiple reports point to Russian attacks on hospitals, schools, apartment blocks, and theatres. There is not a single undamaged building in Mariupol, a city with more than 450,000 citizens. Most casualties were caused by artillery strikes, MLRS strikes, and air strikes with non-precision bombs on civilian areas.

Dozens of cities have been destroyed by the RAF leading to depopulation. Kyiv School of Economics (KSE) estimates the documented losses of residential and non-residential real estate at $135.9 billion.[2] This includes industrial enterprises ($13 billion), energy infrastructure ($6.8 billion), and housing ($52.5 billion). The likelihood of complete restoration is low.

Since October 2022, Russia has changed its tactics, launching attacks on critical infrastructure with massive cruise missile and drone strikes aimed at destroying power plants, fuel refineries and storage centres, electricity distribution hubs, and dams. These attacks are intended to undermine Ukraine's ability to provide heating, electricity, and water to its civilians. As a result, Ukraine's energy grids have become unstable and vulnerable, threatening the lives of millions. When the outside temperature drops, electricity consumption rises, resulting in scheduled or emergency sectoral power outages for private and business clients. These outages disrupt normal life and compel Ukrainians to adapt their daily routines to this new reality.

After Kyiv, Chernihiv, Sumy, and Kharkiv were liberated, survivors testified to the RAF's war crimes against civilians. In de-occupied territories, war crime prosecutors have identified twenty-six locations where detained individuals were held and tortured by Russian soldiers and security services.

The brutality of the war, especially the war crimes against civilians and prisoners of war, has also caused extreme moral pain. It seems as if all the powers of hell have been unleashed to destroy the lives of Ukrainians. The intense media coverage of the war created a sense of presence and participation in these events. Together with my fellow citizens, I felt a deep sense of solidarity with

---

1. United Nations in Ukraine, "Protection of Civilians in Armed Conflict — July 2024," 9 August 2024, https://ukraine.un.org/en/276097-protection-civilians-armed-conflict-%E2%80%94-july-2024.

2. Kyiv School of Economics, "As of November 2022, the Total Amount of Losses Caused to the Infrastructure of Ukraine Increased to Almost $136 Billion," *Kyiv School of Economics*, 15 December 2022, https://kse.ua/about-the-school/news/as-of-november-2022-the-total-amount-of-losses-caused-to-the-infrastructure-of-ukraine-increased-to-almost-136-billion/.

the victims. I could not help thinking about those who suffered and feeling for them in their pain. We were witnessing the atrocities of war and the senseless and irrational cruelty of the invaders, and I felt as if it was happening to me. I felt as if I had died with the pregnant lady and her unborn baby who were severely wounded during the bombing of the maternity hospital in Mariupol. I was hit by a mortar, along with those people who had lined up for bread in Chernihiv. The Russian soldiers shot me, together with those who were fleeing for their lives from Irpin, Hostomel, Bucha, Kharkiv, and Sumy. Many souls were burned to ashes. The pain has been real, almost tangible.

But the most challenging aspect for me was the realization that I could do nothing about any of this. I felt completely powerless. I also felt indignation, anger, and hatred. These complex emotions did not fit into the traditional shape of a Christian's life. These emotions were not directed at some abstract powers of evil but at evil personified and embodied in those military invaders, Russian politicians, government officials, propagandists, and priests who planned, carried out, supported, or justified the genocidal war against Ukraine.

This war prompted many Ukrainian Christians, myself included, to reconsider our traditional beliefs and practices. Since I could not find in my devotional vocabulary words and concepts that could help me to properly frame and express my new feelings, I turned to the Bible. There I discovered the language of imprecation in psalms that appealed to God for retribution and the restoration of justice. These texts resonated with me and helped me to give voice to my feelings of anger and pain. They spoke *to* me and *for* me. From the Old Testament prophets and poets, I learned how to cry with those who were crying and suffer with those who were in pain. I also learned how to pray for our enemies and how to transform my pain into prayer and my tears into trust that God will bring forth justice in due time.

Another deeply puzzling, regretful, and discouraging aspect was the level of support for this war among the Russian people, including celebrities, politicians, media pundits, and simple labourers. Even a significant group of Russian ministers, evangelical celebrities, and average Christians either support this war or silently avoid condemning the perpetrators and refuse to stand with the victims. Although most "experts" claim that this is Putin's war, I believe they are mistaken. On a personal note, on 24 February, after I commented on my Facebook page that we were now living in another reality because of a new, open, and brutal phase of the war, my cousin from Moscow called me a Nazi because I disagreed with the "Russian world" narrative she was promoting. I believe this incident is a representative one.

By August 2022, six months into the war, hope had returned for many of us. The liberation of the northern regions of Ukraine – the cities of Izium, Kupiansk, and Kherson – served as signs that we had withstood the first wave of the invasion. The prospect of a just peace and the restoration of Ukraine's territorial integrity appeared on the horizon. However, I now see that these hopes were too bold and premature. After two and a half years of war, I still see no end in sight.

My primary concern now is how to remain sane under these frenzied circumstances and how to distribute my emotional and physical strength evenly over a long and undefined period. The challenge is how to keep going despite the constant emotional swings caused by the war. Imagine living in a state of constant stress due to regular shelling and nightly missile attacks on your city or region. Add to this the emotional impact of disturbing news from the eastern or southern front about friends or acquaintances killed in action, along with complaints about ammunition shortages. Even more disconcerting is information about the western border being blocked due to the economic demands from farmers who are fighting for a better life for themselves at the expense of the Ukrainian people. The final straw that may break the camel's back is the news of the recess of the lower house of Congress at a time when my country and its people are in critical need of military aid. Another cause for concern is the desire of some Western politicians to assume the role of peacemakers at the expense of surrendering Ukrainian territories and people to Russia. Who can endure this, and by what strength?

Being the Body of Christ

Against the background of the events described above, Ukrainian Christians have experienced tremendous unity and solidarity. During the first months of the invasion, churches, educators, and Christians of different traditions joined forces to help those in need and supported the Ukrainian army that was protecting our people. Wherever possible, local churches held daily prayer meetings. Many Christians volunteered to transport people from war zones to safer places, distributed food and water to those in need, dug trenches, and guarded their neighbourhoods as part of their responsibilities as members of territorial defence units. Churches opened their basements to those who had nowhere to hide and served as refugee hubs, sheltering people for a night or two as they made their way to the west of the country or abroad.

But it was not only the solidarity of Ukrainian Christians that struck me. These years of full-scale war taught me personally what it means to be the body of Jesus Christ. While I had always known this truth at an intellectual level, these tragic days allowed me to experience this as a daily reality. Even now, two and a half years after the invasion, I am amazed and encouraged by the depth of compassion, involvement, solidarity, and help from brothers and sisters in Christ, whether I knew them personally or hardly knew them at all. Their prayers, emails with expressions of concern and encouragement, involvement in advocacy and financial support of our needs were, and continue to be, a practical enactment of being the body of Christ here and now. This practical expression of the unity of Christ's body and the involvement of my brothers and sisters in the lives of the needy and disadvantaged has encouraged me personally and helped me to survive this war.

I recall one particular Lord's Supper celebrated by Ukrainian churches in 2022, the first since the full-scale invasion began. It took place on the first Sunday of March. At the church I visited that day, we had people from all across Ukraine – Zaporizhzhia, the Donetsk and Luhansk regions, Kharkiv, Kyiv, Chernihiv, Odesa, and Mykolaiv. We all gathered to worship our crucified Saviour. Apart from the usual reflections on Christ's sacrifice for our sins, participation in the life of the Trinity through Jesus Christ, and the anticipation of his second coming, the high point of the Lord's Table was identification with the pain of our fellow believers. As we were breaking bread, I recalled the broken bodies of my fellow citizens. I thought about those who had lost their dear ones in Mariupol, Kharkiv, Bucha, Hostomel, Irpin, Chernihiv, Sumy, and Izum. I prayerfully reflected on all those who were fleeing to safety along Ukrainian roads, those missing their dear ones who had fled to foreign lands. At that moment, I knew God was, and still is, present in the midst of our people's sufferings. He shares the pain and sorrow of all who have been impacted by this cruel and inhumane war. I took the bread, and I knew that I was part of the body of Christ scattered across my war torn country. "If one part suffers, every part suffers with it; if one part is honoured, every part rejoices with it. Now you are the body of Christ, and each one of you is a part of it" (1 Cor 12:26–27).

I also thought about those who were my brothers and sisters in Christ by name but failed to express their solidarity with the victims of war, either publicly or privately. I felt deep sorrow for those who actively supported the Russian invasion of Ukraine or passively agreed with it. I cried for those who were led astray by Russian geopolitical narratives and mass-media propaganda. Their attitude intensified my pain. I thought that for some of them imperial unity based on the "Russian World" ideology was more valuable and real than identifying with suffering Ukrainian fellow believers. I prayed that they would regain the spiritual sight to see things clearly, the courage to stand with the victims of war, and the ability to make moral decisions regardless of the consequences.

It struck me that when the war ends, any conversation about reconciliation and restoration of relations will have to begin in the presence – tangible or imagined – of the witnesses to the war's atrocities. The presence of these witnesses is necessary because they embody and represent the tragic fate of my people. Those who wish to talk about reconciliation will first have to look into the eyes of these witnesses, listen to the stories of survivors, and realize how the active support of the Russian imperial regime – or even mere civil passivity – turned this war into the monster that claimed thousands of lives.

On Leadership

This war has become a crash test for leaders. Some have not passed this test. I have realized that leadership is not about a position, a title, or education but about core convictions that drive a leader's actions, commitment, love for people, willingness to lend a shoulder and bear another's burden, and resilience in the exhausting conditions of war. Difficult circumstances often become an environment that reveals a person's deepest convictions, much like the process of developing a photographic film in a darkroom. Some leaders turned out to be mere celebrities, lacking the proper DNA of leadership. But there were enough people with strong convictions and commitment, which explains why we are still alive and fighting. These leaders persist in serving the people despite a shortage of human and financial resources, overloaded schedules, restless nights, unexpected demands, and the heavy burden of losing people – both military personnel and civilians. They remain true to their calling and pay the price for doing so.

Unfortunately, I have also come to some negative conclusions based on my observations during these last two and a half years. I was deeply disappointed by international organizations that should have addressed challenges such as the Russian invasion but, instead, demonstrated impotence in the face of it. I was also disappointed by most conservative Christian political forces, who proved to be consummate pragmatists, willing to play by the rules of mad dictators if it served their own political agendas. Unfortunately, as in the parable of the good Samaritan, these people passed by because their own interests and goals were more important to them than the poor man who was bleeding to death on the side of the road. We, lying alongside the Ukrainian people on the side of the road, observed how a UN employee and a representative of a well-known political party disappeared at the turn of the road, rushing off to their own important affairs. May our gracious God grant us opportunities to meet along this path those who can set aside their own affairs and take responsibility for those condemned to slaughter – people who will keep taking responsibility and acting on their convictions even when the cause is no longer trending on social media.

When I am feeling down – and this often happens because of painful news or endless hard questions about the near and distant future – I ask myself: Should I continue doing what I am doing, or should I try to find a way into another reality, where I can think about ordinary things and not about things on which my existence and the existence of those who depend on me hangs? I admit that I am neither a hero nor a titan. I am just an ordinary person who wants to love, to be loved, and to enjoy life and the simple pleasures it offers.

Every time such thoughts cross my mind, I remember Dmytro, my younger colleague, the OTS senior librarian and New Testament Greek lecturer, who has been mobilized into the army and is now defending my country by serving as a chaplain. At home, Dmytro has a young wife and a little son, born after his mobilization. Dmytro is neither a titan nor a hero, but he continues to defend our country. During my low moments, I also recall those people who, despite very difficult economic conditions, keep donating to the various needs of Ukraine's armed forces and continue working in a country that is fighting for its very existence. I think of the military, most of whom were farmers, teachers, engineers, or business people before the war. They are also ordinary people who, in a moment of acute danger, took responsibility for their country and for other people. Such people are the backbone of our country. They embody moral leadership against all odds.

At those moments when I am at my lowest point emotionally, I try to remind myself: You have not chosen this time, it is the time that chose you. You are where you must be. You do what you must do because that's what you've been preparing for. Sometimes, God's power comes down on me, and I carry on refreshed and energized. Other times, nothing happens, and I just keep moving forward, driven by sheer will and a sense of duty. God only knows how long I, and we all, will be able to carry this burden.

What Is Next?

Unfortunately, the future of theological education is quite uncertain right now. I cannot predict how things will develop if the war continues for another year or so. However, I am certain that theological education will only survive if

Ukraine's territorial integrity is preserved. The war has already changed theological education in Ukraine and will continue to transform it.

I know for certain that seminaries and colleges are not just the buildings that house them but are made up of their faculty, staff and students. Nevertheless, the place is also important in shaping the identity of both faculty and students. It serves as the point of gravity that attracts others, preserving the ethos of the community and transmitting it to newcomers. We need the faculty and staff of Ukrainian theological schools. They carry a unique DNA.

If you look at the Flightradar24 map, you will notice that the airspace over Ukraine is completely empty. No flights dare to fly over my country for obvious reasons. I'm sure there's no comparable map for theological education. Before the full-scale war, Ukraine would host world-class luminaries such as Richard Hays, Don Carson, John Panteleimon Manousakis, and Emanuel Tov. Today, almost nobody – except a few faithful friends and committed partners – dares to come to Ukraine due to safety and logistical concerns. Many view Ukraine as a dangerous zone and a theological wilderness. Yet just like in the wilderness, there is theological life in Ukraine. Although it may be understated and adapted to the specifics of the current climate and landscape, it is there. It continues because of our partners who still believe in Ukrainian theological education and because of those Ukrainian theological educators who remain in the country and do their best to keep things going. Just as the wilderness awaits the rain to begin blooming and producing fruit, so does theological education in Ukraine. Lord, bless this wilderness with the rain of your blessings as we move forward!

"I know that somewhere close to me is a bleeding, vulnerable God who became homeless so each of us could begin our journey to the home that no one can take away, destroy, or leave without light. Frankly, this is the only thing that gives me hope: the light of his birth in our midst." Nadiyka Gerbish (p. 76)

3

Homeless God

Nadiyka Gerbish
Ukrainian writer

At the end of the day, the crux of the matter is this: our longing for home and the ongoing journey homeward.

***

I think each one of us can recall exactly where we were on the morning of 24 February 2022 when the news of the war broke.

My husband and I were still dozing in bed. In the next room, Bohdana, our daughter, was sound asleep, with our dog curled up at her feet, as usual. Then my phone rang. My mother's voice sounded sharp and short, like staccato.

My husband rushed to the vet to make sure our dog's vaccinations and papers were up to date, in case we had to cross the border. My daughter and I made sure we had a sufficient supply of water. We packed a small suitcase: documents, handwritten family letters, warm clothes, and a small stack of our most cherished books.

At the time, we lived in downtown Ternopil, in an old house built in 1891 during the time of the Austro-Hungarian Empire. Although damaged by bombs during World War II, the house, along with the people sheltered in its cellars, survived. Before that, it was the home of Blessed Father Mykola Konrad and his family. Father Konrad was born in 1876 in Strusiv, a small village in the Ternopil region. He was an author and scholar who received his education and PhD in Rome. He served as academic counsellor at the Obnova Society of Ukrainian Greek Catholic Students. He was a teacher at a "gymnasium" (high school) and also a university lecturer – and among his students was the future patriarch Josyf Slipyj. Father Konrad was also a public figure, dean of the Faculty of Philosophy, and a publicist. Furthermore, he was a refugee, a prisoner of conscience, and a martyr. On 26 June 1941, NKVD[1] agents shot Father Konrad as he was returning after administering the sacrament of confession to a sick woman. He was later beatified by Pope John Paul II. Father Konrad's wife, Antonina, and their four children survived and later emigrated to the US. Antonina kept a black dress made from her husband's shot-up cassock.

As I packed our little suitcase that dreadful morning, I tucked into the important papers folder the handwritten letters from my grandfather – who was also a priest – and his well-worn service book that I had inherited. The cellar, which had once protected residents from Nazi bombs, was cold and dank. We spent the night on the floor in a hallway, listening to the warning wails of air-raid sirens. I took down our large wall mirror, just in case.

The next day, my daughter, our dog, and I set out for a small mountain house in Poland, where a family friend had invited us to stay and wait out this brutal attack. My husband stayed at home in Ukraine, where he was joined by a friend's family from Kyiv. At that time, we still hoped for an imminent no-fly zone over our skies and a decisive stop to our deranged neighbour's actions. After all, it was the twenty-first century, marked by belief in progress, negotiations, justice, and the miracle formula "never again." Somehow, we felt confident that such unambiguous situations would be resolved without delay according to prearranged protocols and with predesignated resources.

The evacuation train was packed. Elderly people, women with children, pets, suitcases, and only a few young men – those holding infants. One of them, noticing my daughter and me, offered us his seat. He had a newborn baby, and since my daughter had a runny nose, it would have been, at the very least, impolite – according to the rules of peaceful times when we were still worried about COVID-19 – to plop down with a pack of Kleenex next to an infant. We managed to find a different spot – one seat for the three of us. At our stop in Lviv, the last one before the border crossing, all men were asked to get off the train, and the weary mothers were left cradling their babies. The train was delayed for many hours. The light was dim, and the air was stuffy. Children grew fussy. Adults' voices were hushed. I looked at the woman whose husband had offered us a seat earlier. She looked pale and overwhelmed. I moved closer and offered to give her a little break. She handed over her baby and rushed off to the vestibule. I held her baby boy while my daughter tried to keep him entertained as best she could. The days of apprehension and petty concerns were over. On that train, we all had to take off our masks.

---

1. That is, the Russian secret police agency at the time.

The following days, weeks, and months blurred together, and we were swept up by endless torrents of time. We were frantic, pulled in all directions, scrambling to subdue the evil with our bare hands. We flooded the Western media with calls for NATO to close the sky over Ukraine. We helped evacuate those who couldn't take up arms and fight off the enemy – and tried our best to equip those who could. We wrote to just about anyone and everyone, prayed hard, and still clung to hope that this senseless, wicked war was about to end and that justice and peace would reign. By April, our naïve thinking had been bruised and battered, and a more realistic, albeit horrifying, realization settled in: this war might go on for years. And no one knew for sure how it would end.

That April, snow fell in the mountains where we stayed. The night sky was deep and intense, and the Seven Sisters stars were strikingly bright. I bought some art supplies for my daughter and marvelled as I watched her create peaceful, colourful worlds on fine art paper. I stacked her drawings on a shelf in the kitchen, although I knew all too well that when the time came for us to go, we'd have to leave them behind.

Maya, the owner of the cosy wooden chalet that became our temporary home, visited us occasionally on weekends. One Saturday, she arrived with an origami set for Bohdana and some news for me. At that time, Ukrainian armed forces were in dire need of bulletproof vests, and we had been scouring the land to find some. Maya shared that she had found a manufacturer of armour plates and had gone to a shooting range to test them. The plates turned out to be defective – bullets would ricochet off them. She smiled as she mentioned this, and we both thought how fitting it would be to have a shot rebound to the one who had fired it, delivering swift justice. Still, we knew all too well that ricochet was not the same as boomerang and that swift justice was never a certainty.

As we sat in a snowed-in wood-and-stone house, my kiddo quietly transformed pieces of paper into colourful birds, while we, peaceful ladies with minds far from military matters, sipped hot tea and talked about armour ratings and options for timely deliveries across the border. Maya left as the night quietly settled among the spruces outside our window. I stood by the window and watched her go. Suddenly, a movement in the dusky woods caught my eye – three roe deer heading down from the mountain towards our yard. Our dog sensed their coming and barked, spooking them. But the feeling of wonder remained, along with an aching sadness, for this delicate, gentle majesty felt unfathomably immense. I gazed at it, and it took my breath away, yet I could not fully accept this gift. It was a bittersweet moment indeed: the raging war, my faraway husband, unprotected soldiers, defective armour, and heartbreaking news. And our wide-open, wounded, unwanted sky that no one seemed to care enough to cover. It felt as if the world itself was too cruel to protect the entrusted beauty from its crippling ways.

The next morning, I woke up with a sharp pain. The ambulance took a while to arrive. As I suffered a miscarriage so far from home, I cried for the first time since the beginning of the full-scale invasion. There was nobody by my side in the hospital room – nobody but broken-hearted Jesus.

We returned home after a few weeks.

A parcel was waiting for us at the post office. In the first few days of the invasion, my old friend Paul, a Dutch publisher, had asked what he could send over for me personally. My answer might have sounded strange. I remembered a wish from before the war that now took on a whole new layer of meaning. I asked for an old candlestick that had survived World War II, as a reminder to me that wars are finite. I had forgotten about this request, but Paul hadn't. The parcel contained a pair of charcoal grey candlesticks – old and weathered but also tall and elegant – and a photo book titled *The Crown of Creation: Masterpieces and Their Stories* from the Museum of Humanity in the Netherlands. The masterpieces are people; the stories are their testimonies of pain and perseverance.

Phan Thi Kim Phuc wrote the foreword to this edition. She is the woman in the iconic photograph taken in 1972 by Nick Ut to expose the horrors of the Vietnam War to the world. The picture shows Kim Phuc as a nine-year-old girl – naked, barefoot, and burned – with other children and soldiers, running away from the flames that destroyed her village, Trang Bang, after it was hit by a napalm bomb. Nick Ut took that photo and later saved that girl's life. Today, Kim Phuc is a grandmother. She lives with her husband in Canada and runs a non-profit that supports victims of war. In 2022, she travelled the world carrying a Ukrainian flag that bore the words "Do not give up hope" in bold black ink.

That's exactly what Ivanka Dymyd says, time and time again. She's my dear friend, whose son, Artem Dymyd, was killed in the war.

I'm trying my best to hold on to hope – to sow hope, to give it away just like friendly neighbours give away zucchini from their bounty in July, to make hope preserves for winter, to exercise hope, to regain hope, to dig deep for the hidden springs of hope, and to recharge hope like one would a power bank. I keep telling myself that wars are finite but love is eternal. I repeat this as many times as it takes for me to calm down and reach out (or rather grope) for an antidote to day-to-day despondency. Sometimes, I succeed in finding it. But the truth is, this newfound hope doesn't last long. It's like manna that needs to be gathered daily. Except on the day of rest – then yesterday's hope will last, provided you gathered a little extra.

On the other hand, I must admit that when we returned home, we were able once again to take a deep breath. We decided to put down roots: we built a small house outside town, drilled a water well, and began exploring alternative energy sources. We sent our daughter to a different school – one with a better basement. It turned out that the community there was better, too. And in wartime, a safe environment is just as important as a safe space. We've been told, repeatedly, that investing in real estate in a country at war is, to put it mildly, not the most prudent decision. We would agree . . . but pursued it anyway. I doubt we could find anywhere else that offers the sense of inner peace we've found here.

It is sometimes said that people living close to the front line have an easier time coping with war on an emotional level. Their fears are limited by their day-to-day reality. The farther you are from immediate threat, the greater the fear and the wilder the imagination. I often notice that my friends – well-protected and well-settled in another country – suffer much more than I, who stayed at home. Obviously, life is still complicated in more ways than one. And yet, we're doing a bit better with hope here *at home*.

Flipping through the pages of the photo book from the Netherlands, I keep thinking that the light in the beautiful eyes of people whose faces and bodies have been scarred by illness, war, and tragedies illuminates for us the reasons for hope. Their lives have not been easy, but they go on. Their lives are still marked by love, meaning, and joy. On the other hand, the daily news from Ukraine and around the world relentlessly reminds us that this is not always the case. Not everyone has had, or still has, a chance to make it through. Not every family that hoped and prayed for a miracle received one. Not everyone has seen justice, and not everyone will receive it. As a Christian raised in a caring church, I want to tell them the good news that God loves them. Yet far too often, I don't know how to do so. Right now, every word of hope spoken to them feels weak and, at times, almost hypocritical.

As we look upon the place of God's greatest vulnerability – the cross of Christ – we, as believers, have the firm confidence that this is not the end but, rather, a momentary yet great affliction that will be followed by the revelation of great glory. In this, there is another assurance for us: our present troubles are not the final chapter of our story. After all, we are still prisoners of time. Even though we do believe in the final victory of light and eternal joy, right now, we are still here in our own Calvary moment, caught in the tension of our affliction. Some of us are crucified with Christ. Some are standing with John and Mary.

Sometimes I think that the only way we can stay true to the image of Christ crucified is by caring for our neighbour, especially one who is in unbearable, hopeless pain. In a time of great expectation, while Christ's hands are nailed to the cross, we can extend the touching warmth of his love to others. Words are not always necessary – but sometimes, they still are. As much as we sit quietly with those close to us, we must also speak up – loudly and persistently – to those far away.

In May 2022, there were rising fears that Russian propaganda, coupled with Western "war fatigue" – also awkwardly named "Ukraine fatigue" – would displace Ukraine from the news cycle and make the world forget the bloodshed that Ukrainians were enduring and their fight for freedom. So, when Catherine Burke, the UK head of Little, Brown Book Group – a reputable imprint of the global publishing giant Hachette – asked me how they could support Ukraine, I responded, "By publishing Ukrainian authors." The news is a one-day wonder. In contrast, a book publication contract typically lasts at least five years. In addition, books end up in libraries and remain there even longer. People who buy and read books do not usually shy away from making difficult and critical decisions. Those who frequent bookstores also don't pass on the opportunity to cast a ballot. I offered a curated list of Ukrainian authors whom I personally found influential, but, instead, the publisher asked me to share my own writings. That's how we ended up with *A Ukrainian Christmas* – the abridged English translation of *The Great Christmas Book*, which historian Yaroslav Hrytsak and I had co-authored a few years earlier. It came out at the end of 2022, with our new, wartime-prompted foreword, which concluded with the following words:

> Christmas is a time that reminds us that justice and love prevail, even when it seems that both are slowly dying. It ensures the indestructibility of hope in times of the greatest hopelessness. For as long as we celebrate Christmas, we can neither be defeated nor destroyed. This is the message that Ukraine is trying to convey to the world, and this is what our book is about.[2]

---

2. Nadiyka Gerbish and Yaroslav Hrytsak, *A Ukrainian Christmas* (London: Sphere, 2022), 15.

This edition also has a dedication prompted by the war: "In memory of Artem Dymyd (1995–2022) and other children of Rachel murdered by the modern-day Herod."[3]

Ivanka, Artem's mother, is the woman who speaks so much about hope, as I've mentioned already. At her son's funeral, she sang one last lullaby for him, followed by the Paschal troparion "Christ is risen from the dead."[4] With Christ's resurrection, she insists, our hope – however senseless it may seem right now – will not be put to shame.

This book, along with other things that sprang from it, became one of the little bridges that brought tangible support from the Western world to Ukraine and its people. For one thing, it triggered donations to support Ukraine. It also became a platform for our outspokenness. To our surprise – and, I suppose, the publisher's as well – the book became a bestseller and received numerous accolades. Leading publications wrote glowing, in-depth reviews, and readers offered heartfelt comments. The audio version was recorded by the award-winning actress Juliet Stevenson, who was hosting a Ukrainian family at the time. Translation rights were purchased by publishing houses in Germany, Estonia, and the Netherlands. Following this publication, other books have been published in various languages. As I had ardently dreamed of in the spring of 2022, the works of Ukrainian writers are now on the shelves of bookstores and libraries, read in schools, and studied at universities. Their words get people talking about Ukraine, and people are starting to listen when we speak. However, sometimes (well, almost always), we have to work extra hard to communicate more about a country that, until recently, was a blank space on the map for most of the world – just to make sure that we're not only heard but also understood.

In December 2022, a few days before Christmas, I was interviewed on *Saturday Live* on BBC Radio 4. The show was hosted by the brilliant Nikki Bede and the Reverend Richard Coles. There were three other guests on the programme that afternoon. It was the "season to be merry," at least for most of the global audience of this radio station. The conversation was lively and terrifically funny, and I was laughing, too – despite the air-raid sirens wailing

---

3. Gerbish and Hrytsak, *A Ukrainian Christmas*.

4. The Paschal Troparion is a short stanza often used as a refrain between verses of a psalm, but also used separately:
    Christ is risen from the dead,
    by death trampling death,
    and to those in the tombs
    granting life!

outside my window and the awareness that my MacBook's battery was running low and the scheduled blackout due to Russian missiles targeting our critical infrastructure was about to begin.

The funniest questions went to the other guests. I was asked questions about the war – questions that evoked sadness. However, my answers must have sounded too gloomy because, at one point, the host tried to change the subject by asking me about family Christmas heirlooms, such as the Christmas decorations I'd inherited from grandmothers. I realized that this was supposed to be a joyful question, intended to draw me away from today's pain and carry me back to touching memories of pre-war times or maybe even childhood times. The irony of the situation felt like a thorn in my side. As I listened to the other guests share hilarious Christmas stories, I really wanted to share one of my own. But, instead, this question stirred up bitterness and anger, cutting deep because it tapped into generational, inherited pain.

I did my best to explain – somewhat awkwardly – that the invasion taking place in our country right now is not the first time Ukraine and its people have suffered war since the tradition of decorating Christmas trees was established in our culture. World War I swept through Ukraine, followed by World War II, and then the Soviet terror – which ensured that any and all glass and crystal items in homes were shattered into smithereens. I explained that even if some of my peers had thought to keep as heirlooms the ugly glass squash made by Soviet decorations factories for the so-called New Year tree – bought by their grandmother out of sheer desperation – they would hardly have taken these with them when they left their homes to flee from yet another invasion coming from the northeast.

When I wrote earlier about the heirlooms I inherited from my great-grandfather, I did so deliberately, for two reasons: first, these heirlooms really mean a lot to me, and second, having touched on the topic of our deep need for home, I felt it important to emphasize this point by drawing a contrast. For many centuries, people around the world have regarded home as an important heritage. But in the fabric of our history, even a single handwritten letter that has been preserved and passed down is viewed as a great luxury. We are longing for home and traumatized by our profound, and often unmet, need for it. And that is why it hurts so intensely, so unbearably, when someone tries to take it away.

Aside from the old candlesticks (which, by the way, are also part of what makes a house a home) given to me by my friend in the Netherlands, a few others have come into my possession since the war began. One candlestick was given to me by another friend, a Ukrainian soldier who fashioned it out of the fragments of a mine. Another came from a friend with whom I worked together on a book – she now works as a professional in humanitarian landmine clearance. A couple more were gifts from a friend who became a refugee in Switzerland, along with her daughter, after her husband was deployed to the front line. In lieu of therapy, she visits antique shops there, searching for things that embody the continuity of comfort at home. And, also in lieu of therapy, she brings me some of the things she finds.

Her name is Natalia, and we've been friends for quite some time. C. S. Lewis once wrote that "friendship is born at the moment when one man says to another: 'What! You too? I thought that no one but myself . . .'"[5] For Natalia and me, that moment of "inner intersection" hinged on Christmas. A few years ago, while we were both temporarily residing abroad, we made our only trip to Ukraine that year – in August, no less. In the corner of the living room stood a Christmas tree, lit up, while kutia, uzvar, a candle, a shoppka,[6] cinnamon sticks, and marigolds in a vase graced the table. After celebrating Christmas in August, we went out to see the Perseids meteor shower and sang carols. In fact, the retelling of this story is featured at the back of the first Ukrainian edition of *The Great Christmas Book*. And the very house where we used to celebrate Christmas together in August was the one Natalia had to leave when she was forced to flee.

Writing about Christmas and home, G. K. Chesterton notes, "Christmas is built on the beautiful and intentional paradox; that the birth of a homeless should be celebrated in every home."[7] But does this also mean that the homeless of today – those who have lost their homes and those who have not yet found their homes – are even closer to the heart of Christmas than those who have the privilege of celebrating it at home?

***

As I write this, I'm failing to meet the deadline. I can't seem to string together those last few paragraphs. It's not because I'm being lazy or even shying away from a painful subject. It's just that I've been running out of words for a long time. Although, perhaps, it would be more honest to say that the illusion that pain and hope can be captured, conveyed, and healed through words has long since crumbled. I long for this piece to bring hope, to carry at least faint

---

5. C. S. Lewis, *The Four Loves* (London: Geoffrey Bles, 1960), 92.

6. A shoppka is the Ukrainian version of a nativity scene, an exhibition, especially during the Christmas season, of art objects depicting the birth of Jesus.

7. G. K. Chesterton, *Brave New Family: G. K. Chesterton on Men and Women, Children, Sex, Divorce, Marriage and the Family* (San Francisco: Ignatius Press, 1990), 257.

overtones of optimism (and a sense of Christmas, no matter the time of year), but I also want it to be honest.

As I write, I think about the fact that a crisis is often a time of rapid growth, marked by pain that is often just as profound. The crisis itself, and the growth we experience through it, are inseparable from sorrow and pain. Yet as we grow through it, we, in turn, begin to grow something within us that is not of us. And this creation is best done not from a place of trauma and pain but from a place of healing and wholeness. As Victoria Borodina – who was forced to become an internally displaced person after leaving her native Donetsk in 2014 – once told me, we need sadness in order to go deeper and joy for the strength to keep moving forward. I want so much for us to have that strength to keep going and to have that joy. And healing to create new things and rebuild what needs to be restored. And for us to be whole. And to have hope. And home.

And yet, I cannot piece it all together and put it into words. I know that somewhere close to me is a bleeding, vulnerable God, who became homeless so that each of us could begin our journey to the home that no one can take away, destroy, or leave without light. Frankly, this is the only thing that gives me hope: the light of his birth in our midst.

"The Other always transcends the notions we might have, and the infinitude of the Other cannot be fully grasped, measured or confined within our boundaries. This infinitude cannot be mastered or seized. Yet, something else must come before that something that's so casually called 'hospitality'." Kseniia Trofymchuk (p. 83)

4

Finding Yourself When You're Tossed in a Sea of Lost Faces

Kseniia Trofymchuk

*Manager of Educational Programmes and Projects,
Eastern European Institute of Theology, Lviv, Ukraine*

Homelessness as a Symbol of the Global World or Return to the Unprocessed Past Trauma

> We are no longer limited by tradition, language or distance. What once was fixed is fluid and there's no one path.
>
> We work more jobs, learn more skills and share more ideas than ever before.
>
> And, we don't have to stop our lives to start new ones. When we understand this: Our world is infinite. Everything is possible. Everything is open.[1]

I came across these words in the book *The Gift of the Other* – the author had seen them in an advertisement from New Zealand. This book refers to a new experience of human existence in the twenty-first century, characterized by cultural, economic, and political "interdependence," "openness," and "borderlessness." Even though the world in the twenty-first century is still far from perfecting hospitality, this tendency to view oneself as a resident of a "global village" – despite the differences and diversity among "human civilizations" – is gaining ground.

---

1. Andrew Shepherd, *The Gift of the Other: Levinas, Derrida, and a Theology of Hospitality* (Cambridge: James Clarke & Co, 2014), 1–2.

In such a world, relocation is viewed as an opportunity or a necessary expansion of individual world views and professional skills. It seems that the notions of "home," "grounding," and "own ground" are losing meaning in this cross-cultural network. "Homelessness" is becoming a symbol of globality.

However, "homelessness" as a positive experience of "life without borders" is not a phenomenon or invention of the twenty-first century; rather, it's at least a hundred years old. This topic took on a particularly ambiguous and tragic tone in the Ukrainian milieu during the Soviet era. In 1942, Ukrainian writer Viktor Domontovych referred to this experience in his novel *On Shaky Ground*: "A modern person has gotten into a habit of not having a place to call your own."² Domontovych wrote his novel amid social shifts due to World War I, technological advances, and urbanization that undermined stability and universal values, particularly Christian ones. The storyline centres around an old unfinished cathedral that's slated for demolition in order to build something new and useful in its place. However, this unfinished cathedral stands not only as an image of a modern Ukrainian project but also as an image of the identity of a person, vulnerable to the fear of losing touch with the past, a place of belonging, and the authority of God. Of course, Domontovych reflects on this existential experience of "groundlessness" as both an opportunity to find one's own cultural and artistic bearings and a trauma due to losing the underlying foundations of identity.

Ukrainian intellectuals who experienced forced migration to Europe due to Soviet repressions in the 1930s and, later, to the Americas because of World War II also reflected on this issue of groundlessness. Among them were George Y. Shevelov – a Ukrainian linguist, literary critic, and writer – literary critic Yurii Lavrinenko, and, most notably, Yurii Kosach with his *Aeneus and the Lives of Others*, a work dealing with the trauma of losing his homeland – at the time, Ukraine did not exist as an independent state – and searching for a new homeland and a new identity in a foreign land. Different waves of emigrants dealt with this experience in various ways: some longed to understand their Ukrainian identity in dialogue with other cultures, while others, believing that their relocation was temporary, were reluctant to put down roots in new cultural landscapes. Despite these differences, Ukrainian emigrants in the twenty-first century are united by the same experience: being forcibly uprooted from their home ground.

---

2. Translators Note: to leverage the nuanced meaning used by the author here, this quote is translated from the original text. A full translation is available: Viktor Domontovych, *On Shaky Ground*, trans. Oksana Rosenblum (Budapest: Central European University Press, 2024), 11.

Such "uprooting from home ground" is what we experienced during Russia's occupation of Ukrainian land in the twenty-first century. The Russian-Ukrainian war that began in 2014 thrust us into a new existential experience: fear of losing home ground, fear of losing that sacred something that tells us who we were, are, and long to be, and the fear of being helpless and unable to change anything. This occupation means you cannot be who you want to be wherever you are and cannot be wherever you want to be. Your borders – and your "borderlessness" as well – are defined for you without your input.

Russia's full-scale invasion of Ukraine in 2022 caused massive waves of displacement. Within the first few months, more than six million Ukrainians became refugees and more than three million became internally displaced persons. As of the summer of 2024, the total number of refugees still hovers around seven million. However, experts predict an increase of about a million within the next two years due to continuous power supply disruptions, missile strikes across Ukrainian territory, and the realization that this war is unlikely to end any time soon. Many people were forced to leave behind their families, loved ones, jobs, childhood homes, and all the near and dear things that formed their personality and identity and made them who they are today.

For me the Russian invasion has been a challenge as I seek to process this experience of being uprooted and struggle to find myself among and along with thousands, even millions, of lost faces. For over ten years, I've been working in various organizations that, amid the rubble of an anti-religious Soviet world view, sought to bring meaningful change to the Ukrainian education system and especially to develop theological education. I was getting ready to move to Lviv for my new job and the next step in my calling after receiving my graduate degree in Kyiv barely three months before the full-scale invasion.

I was forced to leave Ukraine in the early days of the full-scale war, but it took me some time to realize that I was, in fact, a refugee. This realization started to sink in because of a chance encounter in Belgium a few months after Russia's invasion.

Face to Face with a Refugee

> I see myself from the point of view of another, I expose myself to another,

I reveal myself...[3]

Never did I imagine that I would face such an experience. I remember exactly how it happened. On 20 August 2022, I was standing on the platform at the Brussels railway station, waiting for my train to Leuven, where I was doing a research internship. A very young woman came up to me and, somewhat ashamed, asked for some money to buy food. On hearing her story of being a refugee from Gaza, I dug into my almost empty pockets and gave her all the cash I could find. I didn't expect our conversation to continue, but she blurted out:

"Where are you from?"

I choked up.

"I'm from Ukraine..."

My answer must have caught her off guard. Flustered, she stared at me with her dark eyes for a moment, then averted her gaze and rushed off to her train. That moment knocked the wind out of me. My eyes welled up with tears. That evening, I missed my train.

On the one hand, this encounter became a moment of truly recognizing myself the way Domontovych describes it – when you feel with every cell in your body that it's not just the ground slipping away from under your feet but that you're being uprooted from it, like a tree. On the other hand, it was also that feeling of defenceless nudity in the face of the Other, as described by the French philosopher Emmanuel Lévinas. When you come into this world, you're surrounded by love and care. You go to school, then to university, and, little by little, ambitions, plans, and dreams emerge. Life feels fulfilling and meaningful. You look forward to the future... and then war turns your world upside down. You find yourself on a platform next to another refugee, and you realize that your life will never be the same again. You meet the gaze of the other refugee – and the compassion you see there cuts deeply into your dignity. You are defenceless before the Other and feel vulnerable, exposed, and weak. You wish you could have avoided this encounter, but you're caught off guard by it because it was not a response to your invitation but a "traumatic intrusion" that exposes your wound. A dark-haired, dark-eyed young woman, about my age – it was not hard for me to see myself in her face.

That was the first time I met a refugee while being a refugee myself. It was not that I had never seen a refugee before; on the contrary, I'd seen many

---

3. Еманюель Левінас, *Між нами: Дослідження. Думки-про-іншого* (Київ: Дух і Літера; Задруга, 1999), 99. [Emmanuel Levinas, *Between Us: A Study. Thoughts-about-the-Other* (Kyiv: Dukh I Litera; Zadruga, 1999), 99.]

refugees, especially over the past two years. During that encounter, however, I saw the Other – the Stranger – in myself. I did not exist as a refugee before the full-scale invasion. All too often, we think of the Other as someone who comes to us from the outside, seeking hospitality and welcome. Yet sometimes, we must deal not with fundamentally different otherness but with the Other in regard to ourselves. I can still feel that gaze, ripping open my wound. Time after time, this confronts me with the experience of being a stranger to myself. Still, this encounter, this wound, is probably necessary to be able to recognize the face of the Other. Not just a physical face but the boundless vastness that cannot be distilled down to definitions such as "refugee," "internally displaced person," or "immigrant." The Other always transcends the notions we might have, and the infinitude of the Other cannot be fully grasped, measured, or confined within our boundaries. This infinitude cannot be mastered or seized. Yet, something else must come before that something that's so casually called "hospitality." Perhaps true hospitality begins with welcoming the Other within yourself: "Therefore, I look at myself as if I had become the Other, having first opened myself to him: 'I see myself from the point of view of the Other, I expose myself to the Other, I reveal myself.'"[4]

That day at the railway station, I did not just meet a refugee from Gaza – I met myself as someone totally Other. It wasn't me, but she who met me with her gaze. It was a touch. Sometimes, you think you're touching someone but, in fact, it's you who is being touched because a touch is always reciprocal. (Think about Jesus's encounter with the woman who had been suffering from bleeding for twelve years.) And so, in this painful yet poignant touching of eyes, you realize that you are the Other who needs to be welcomed and accepted.

How It All Began

For many Ukrainians, 24 February 2022 became the reference date marking absolutely different – not only in terms of history but also in the level of horror – the existential experience of being uprooted. Granted, looking at the experience of the previous generations, it becomes obvious that this day is part of a certain logical pattern, and the experience of those born in sovereign Ukraine is not all that different from generations before them, each being able to pinpoint its own reference date with its own tragedies, oftentimes just as horrific.

---

4. Левінас, *Між нами*, 99. [Levinas, *Between Us*, 99.]

However, thousands and millions of Ukrainians, including my family and me, were caught off guard by 24 February 2022 – not because we didn't realize that war was a possibility but because understanding possibilities does not always prepare you to accept reality. I was woken up at 6:00 a.m. by a frantic phone call from my cousin in Kyiv, crying, "We're being bombed here! We're heading to you!" At the time, I was visiting my parents, who live in a small town not far from the capital. Since it was a bit farther from the northern border, things were calmer there.

This was a time when my family had just experienced two tragedies – two funerals, one after the other. I remember standing at the Baikove Cemetery on 16 February, just a week before the full-scale invasion, feeling the cool winter air thick with unease and fear of what was to come. Of course, this feeling wasn't unfounded. Apart from this family tragedy, there was the constant buzzing about the alarming threat of war, accompanied by advice on how to pack a go-bag, how to evacuate safely, where to find shelter in case of shelling, and so on.

My relatives didn't leave their home immediately. They, too, needed time to come to terms with this new reality and make some hard decisions. My cousin was seven months pregnant and had a six-year-old daughter. My parents insisted, "You're going with them! They must be taken across the border." Although I had imagined various scenarios, none included leaving the country. Nevertheless, without any argument, I packed my bag according to the media's recommendations: two pairs of pants, two shirts, a sweater, and, most importantly, my personal papers.

The hardest part was leaving my family behind. The recent funeral had been for my mother's younger brother – so, my grandma had lost her son. Family tragedy was followed by extensive missile attacks. In the early days of the full-scale invasion, Russian forces took over towns and villages in the northern parts of the Kyiv and Zhytomyr regions. We already knew what Russian occupation looked like, having heard about it since 2014 when the RAF first crossed the border and took over Crimea and parts of the Donetsk and Luhansk regions. We had read about Ukrainian prisoners being held in jails such as Izoliatsiia, torture, crackdowns on locals who supported Ukraine, and repressions targeting religious minorities. It was all too easy to extrapolate and imagine possible scenarios. I remember bawling in front of my six-year-old niece when I said goodbye to my parents. At that moment, I felt like a little girl, too, unable to protect myself or others. This was the helplessness of a child facing her own imagination that kept painting horrors more terrifying than reality. My parents hugged me tightly and hurried me and my hastily packed go-bag into the car.

It took us a couple of days to reach the border. There was no special treatment for pregnant women with little children because most of the fleeing people were women, children, and the elderly. I have never seen such long queues – a couple of days' worth – at border checkpoints. We waited for almost fifteen hours, making hardly any progress. My cousin wasn't feeling well, so we had to leave the queue and find a place to spend the night. We stayed at a small dormitory, already filled to the brim with refugees from the north and east of Ukraine, each with their own heartbreaking stories. Many had come from the Kharkiv, Sumy, and Chernihiv regions. People had left behind everything – apartments, houses, valuable belongings, and trinkets dear to their hearts. In my case, I had packed old family photos that weren't saved digitally because I couldn't bear the thought of them being reduced to ashes. Some people just managed to grab their personal papers. Some had to leave behind not just their belongings but also their fragile and elderly parents who refused to evacuate. These stories sent shivers down my spine. There were many such stories, and they kept pouring in, along with new people. Some stopped for a short break; others stayed at the dorm for longer, stuck between nowhere to go and no place to return to.

We finally crossed the border on 28 February. Three refugees – tiny droplets that vanished in the wave of hundreds of thousands of Ukrainians fleeing the country during those first few days of the full-scale invasion. In the days that followed, these hundreds of thousands swelled into millions . . .

Miracle of Hospitality

> Borders are the place for hospitality . . .[5]
>
> Welcome [accueil] . . . always expresses the first gesture in the direction of the other: the first movement as good movement.[6]

Ukrainians and Europeans quickly rallied to help displaced persons and refugees. For me, this experience was a real miracle of hospitality. People opened up their homes; and churches, universities, and office buildings were transformed into shelters. After crossing the border into Europe, we were met by volun-

---

5. Jacques Derrida, *Hospitality*, vol. 2, ed. Pascale-Anne Brault and Peggy Kamuf, trans. Peggy Kamuf (Chicago: University of Chicago Press, 2024), 74.

6. Derrida, *Hospitality*, 5.

teers, security guards, and medical personnel – and we gladly accepted their help. Strangers brought bags of groceries and warm clothes for the refugees. Volunteers handed out warm tea in paper cups. I was holding the leash with one hand (yes, we also had a dog with us), and with the other, I clutched the warm tea, which had a certain soul-soothing power. The kindness of people to those fleeing the war was enough to feed way more than five thousand souls.

I remember how a volunteer – I can't recall his name – drove us from Moldova to Romania. On the way, we stopped at a small but tidy grocery stall – similar to what is often found in small Ukrainian towns, though not usually in winter. A modestly dressed woman (probably the shopkeeper) hurried out of the stall and reached out to my sister. She was holding fifty euros in her hand and speaking passionately. Although we did not understand Romanian, it seemed clear that she was talking about the war since the driver had already told us that he was transporting refugees. My sister's eyes welled up with tears because certain actions touch the soul far more deeply than any words. Those fifty euros could not save us from the war, but a gesture of sincere care in the midst of barbaric violence saves the human being in you. It gives hope for light even as darkness seeks to extinguish it.

That encounter reminded me of the New Testament story of the widow who gave her last two mites to the temple treasury. The story is just two lines and may seem insignificant, but Christ took note of this woman's action and highlighted her sincerity. And I wanted to write at least two lines here about the kindness of that woman who gave her fifty euros to strangers. There is a certain Levinasian "face of the unconditional" in this story. There were no questions about who we were, whether we were Christians, whether we needed money, or even whether we were hungry – she helped without asking and without expecting anything in return. Levinas believed that the Other is not primarily someone to be understood but someone to whose ethical call we are meant to respond. This was not an act of charity for the sake of self-fulfilment but what Levinas calls responsibility in the face of the Other, in which I bow down to wash their feet or share their pain.[7] In a world full of distrust, in which hospitality is often reduced to a pragmatic and commercial tit-for-tat, it is rare to come across a selfless action like this. We have lost the courage to be hospitable and to love without any reason or conditions, but it is precisely such actions that help to save the face of the Other and give us a chance to accept what is so difficult to accept. This woman understood that our situation

---

7. See Emmanuel Levinas, "Ethics and the Face," in *Totality and Infinity. An Essay on Exteriority* (Pittsburgh: Duquesne University Press, 2007).

could not be helped, but she wanted to offer her two cents to share in the pain of these strangers. She didn't have to do this... But thanks to her openness, this miracle happened – and it will forever be etched into my personal story, just like the widow's story recorded on the pages of the New Testament.

Since my cousin was pregnant and could not travel more than ten hours a day, we had to plan for stops along our route. In Romania, a young family – husband, wife, and two sweet teenagers – took us in for the night, despite us being complete strangers. Those teens gave us small gifts to remember them by, and I still keep them as a reminder of the human kindness that helped us on our journey. I will forever remember the hot tea from volunteers at the border, the fifty euros from the shopkeeper, the open doors of Ruksandra's home, Julian's car that took us from Cluj-Napoca to Budapest, train tickets from Tamás, and the warm sweater from Elsie... The list of unconditional acts and gestures goes on and on. I remember that journey of five countries over five days – a journey characterized by unity and hospitality from people I had never met before and will probably never see again. Yet this help they provided saved the lives of not just the three of us but also those of millions of our fellow citizens. To be honest, at that time, we could never have imagined that those five days were just the beginning of a journey that continues even today.

From Hospitality as an Event to Hospitality as Ethics

> For I was hungry and you gave me something to eat, I was thirsty and you gave me something to drink, I was a stranger and you invited me in.
>
> Matt 25:35

These past two and a half years have been a real challenge, both for those who needed welcome and for those who welcomed them.

My sister and I travelled to several European countries before she and her (now two) children were able to settle down in one of them. My journey continued, with stops for a few months in the Czech Republic, Belgium, and the US. During my wanderings through different countries, a passage from the Gospel of Matthew often came to mind: "For I was hungry and you gave me something to eat, I was thirsty and you gave me something to drink, I was a stranger and you invited me in."

Once, on a car ride to Leuven, a stranger asked me, "What's your name?"

"Kseniia."

"Isn't that Greek in origin?"

"Yes, as a matter of fact, it is of Greek origin."

"If I'm not mistaken, it means 'stranger' . . ."

My parents had always told me that my name was a prophetic one because my mother had dreamed that she would give birth to a girl named Kseniia. I have always been proud of my name – up until the point of becoming a refugee. This reminds me of the way names are treated in the Bible, how a name becomes an integral part of a person's identity. My name does indeed come from the Greek word ξένος (*xenos*), which means "stranger" or "guest," and so ξενία (*xenia*) means "hospitality towards a stranger." A name is the first gift given to someone as they are brought into this world. Why wouldn't such a gift be welcomed? But perhaps it takes a journey or two – from Israel to Moab and back again – to transform your harrowing experience into a practice of sincere hospitality.

During our travels, everywhere we went, everyone was trying to help refugees from Ukraine. Countries in the free world provided financial and social support, legal work permits, free education for children, and integration classes for newcomers. Foreign volunteer organizations provided integration assistance, and churches were actively involved in helping refugees with everything from free language courses to housing and job searches.

The openness of churches depended largely on their previous experience ministering to refugees. Leaders who have had personal experience of this or been missionaries in other countries are generally more flexible in working with people who need assistance in integrating into a new culture. Such churches usually have language learning groups and hold services that actively involve people of different nationalities and with different physical needs. Openness to one form of otherness tends to promote understanding of another, and then another. For example, I am engaged in theological research, my sister has a university degree and is the mother of two children – a six-year-old and an infant – and has a dog. These are four completely different realities that require different approaches and different forms of openness. Someone may have a child with Down Syndrome or autism. Someone else may have a serious illness or disability. Some women have husbands who stayed back in Ukraine to fight, leaving them to cope with their children and the financial challenges of living in a new country with a completely unfamiliar language and culture.

It's a little different with churches that are focused on their own internal audience. In such communities, a refugee will always feel like an outsider. Although leaders in such churches may be ready to provide immediate help based on a list of needs (which is good and vital), they are not always ready to offer lasting relationships and support, which is especially important for those whose normal lives and relationships world have been undermined by war. I realize that this is a bold claim, but as a refugee myself, I know that a person cannot be reduced to a single list of prayers or needs, nor to a template of "refugee" needs such as housing, employment, language, healthcare, and mental health support. We could spend a few days analyzing statistics to identify the basic needs of refugees, a few more days assessing which needs are most urgent in a particular country, and then more time trying to determine which countries and institutions could best respond to a particular issue. But a refugee is not a list of needs. A refugee is an incomprehensible Other. This person has unconditional preciousness beyond my responsibility for him or her.

I remember hearing on the news that, during the first year of the war, most refugees who returned to Ukraine did so because of the lack of personal connections and friendships. European societies, unlike Ukrainian ones, are extremely individualistic and tend to instrumentalize relationships pragmatically. Therefore, many Ukrainians abroad are terribly lonely due to the lack of social connections. Usually, whenever someone plans to move to another country, they try to find out more about its customs and social norms beforehand. However, in cases of forced or unexpected migration, the realities of new life often clash with preconceived expectations, and this comes as a shock for the unprepared.

I was fortunate to be taken in by my relatives across the border, and I also managed to secure an internship at a university, where I came across some familiar faces. But later, I had to choose between my favourite job and my emotional attachments – and in choosing one, the other is often lost.

Among the refugees, some had lost not only their social connections but everything. They, too, stood at the borders, with the small bundles they had managed to save from the flames of war, waiting for some miracle. However, those with no money to spare had the most challenging time – unable to afford the difficult and expensive living arrangements abroad, they were often compelled to return and start over in their own country in the midst of war. Here, it seems appropriate to mention the talented literary critic Yurii Kosach, who, before becoming an immigrant, attended lectures at the Sorbonne. After immigrating, however, he was not accepted by the community and, with no social support, was forced to clean offices to make a living. Just like back then, not all refugees can find a position in their own field; therefore, they often accept menial, low-paying jobs. This is how war first turns human life upside down and then casts the face of the Other beneath the feet of the Other.

A stranger is a visitor from another country, someone who has lost their own ground, someone who needs welcome and protection. There's a very good reason why, when we talk about hospitality, we lean on the metaphor of a house that not only welcomes someone in but also protects them. Forced migration is an existential problem, and its solution may lie in hospitality, as proposed by Levinas, unlimited in time: "Don't urge me to leave you or to turn back from you. Where you go I will go" (Ruth 1:16). This hospitality expects nothing in return because a refugee has little, if anything, to offer as the war has taken away most or everything they own. Some have been left with only the ashes of memories of the past. I do believe that those ministry leaders in Ukraine who opened their churches and converted them into shelters for refugees who had lost everything know what it means to welcome them, to be present day in and day out, rearranging their own space and schedule to meet the needs of others. It's not that a stranger doesn't need the basics – water, bread, a box of noodles, or some clothing – but a person is always more than a checklist of needs.

Of course, such hospitality brings with it a number of issues for church leaders, volunteers, and ordinary people who are trying to support refugees or displaced persons.

- *The issue of fatigue.* This is a challenge for both those who are helping and those in need of help because there is no respite; and given the constant uncertainty, it is impossible to truly rest.
- *The issue of time.* We have entered the third year of the war (for many Ukrainians, this is the eleventh year of the war). The illusion of solving individual problems in order to return to a comfortable position is unsustainable for both those in need and those who help.
- *The issue of community.* In a world with six million refugees from Ukraine, no one is under any illusion that they can single-handedly tackle the flood of needs of the people pouring in.
- *The issue of personhood.* We cannot reduce a refugee to a list of problems to be solved or a sociological category.
- *The issue of diversity.* Refugees belong to various Christian denominations, or may even be atheists. They are old and young, highly educated and not so much. They are unique, differing in culture, faith, and lived experience.
- *The issue of inclusion.* We are ontologically equal, but physically, we are different, with varying needs, abilities, and disabilities. In just three years of war, the number of Ukrainian soldiers with amputations has reached more than twenty thousand, and this number is increasing daily.

- *The issue of education.* Helping and receiving help is not just about implementing a charity programme with donors and beneficiaries; it is a real transformation of individuals.

Ukraine has never had to deal with migration in the same way as Europe. Our society within Ukraine's borders is quite homogeneous. But in the difficult circumstances of the current war, we – in the relative safety of the home front – are learning to welcome immigrants and open the doors of our homes and churches to those fleeing parts of the country where life has become increasingly threatening or impossible.

The war continues. Every single day, it torments and scars both those who stayed in the country and those who were forced to leave.[8] That miracle of hospitality that many of us have experienced at the border must now turn into the miracle of presence that can come as we reimagine our ethics of hospitality. The Croatian theologian Miroslav Volf wrote that we are often driven by ostensible hospitality, which leads to the exclusion of a person from a coexisting community.[9] This may come through pushing for assimilation, objectifying a person for the sake of our own desires, or valuing a person based on economic relations – if the other person has no means to repay our hospitality, we may keep them at arm's length or turn our faces away from them so that we do not feel their call for real hospitality. Such practices, even when referred to as "hospitality," have little to do with true hospitality.

Sometimes, we want to live in a world without the Other. Nobody likes it when somebody disrupts their peace and quiet. The Other is always a challenge, always a matter of angst and unease.

> Nevertheless, the most important experience of welcoming the Other / the Alien is gaining the ability to respond to a number of challenges: the capacity to change through overcoming limitations, the desire for freedom and discovery, the possibility to embrace what is difficult to accept, the ability to cope with unsettling otherness, etc.[10]

---

8. Approximately four million Ukrainians lost their homes – either fully or partially – due to Russia's invasion.

9. Miroslav Volf, *Exclusion and Embrace, Revised and Updated: A Theological Exploration of Identity, Otherness, and Reconciliation* (Nashville: Abingdon Press, 2019), 69–70.

10. Тарас Лютий, «Інший, Чужий у структурі людського Я», *Наукові записки НаУКМА. Філософія та релігієзнавство* (2018): 27. [Taras Lyuty, "The Other, the Alien in the Structure of Human Self," *Research Notes of NaUKMA, Philosophy and Religious Studies* (2018): 27.]

But at the risk of angst comes love, as well. Isn't this what Christianity is about? "Keep on loving one another as brothers and sisters. Do not forget to show hospitality to strangers, for by so doing some people have shown hospitality to angels without knowing it" (Heb 13:1–2). The entire Bible speaks of the Other; and without that Other, we cannot grasp the miracles therein.

Finding Yourself in Giving to the Other

> My ethical relation of love for the other stems from the fact that the self cannot survive by itself alone, cannot find meaning within its own being-in-the-world, within the ontology of sameness.[11]

The war forced me, like many Ukrainians, to make a difficult choice. In the autumn of 2022, a family invited me to the US to stay with them for a few years. At that time, I had already returned to Ukraine after several months of an internship abroad and travelling around Europe. In October, when Russia launched a series of massive missile attacks on the Ukrainian energy infrastructure, I decided to leave. I can't call my decision logical or even emotional because everything within me wanted to stay in Ukraine or at least be somewhere closer to the Ukrainian border, but the decision had to be made, and I couldn't put it off any longer. Terrible emotional fatigue, fear of an uncertain future, and concern for the fate of my family prompted me to leave.

On 27 October 2022, I crossed the Atlantic Ocean – and I felt shattered. Anyone who knows me well understands that I made a choice that was too much for my heart to bear. At first, you tell yourself that you're going for a year – for a new experience (which had actually been my dream before the war) and to wait and see how the situation in Ukraine unfolds. After all, a war like this cannot last forever. The first year passes with a feeling of motivated ungroundedness. The second year brings perplexity. And as the third year begins, you slowly realize that there is probably no way back – not because you don't want to go back but because you no longer know where to go.

Some people talk about their experience as refugees as a dislocation from existence into nothingness. For me, this experience became a place in between: you are hovering over the abyss of nothingness, with one foot still on your home ground, and the other on a new one, albeit to it you have not yet had

---

11. Emmanuel Levinas, "Ethics of the Infinite: An Interview with Emmanuel Levinas, in *Dialogues with Contemporary Continental Thinkers*, ed. Richard Kearney (Manchester: Manchester University Press, 1984), 60.

time or, perhaps, the desire, to be tied. This sense of not being grounded here, in a foreign land, makes you feel like you are losing touch with life back home. Refugee life is a painful hovering between worlds – hardly something that could be called normal. But it is precisely this painful experience that gives you the ability to notice and accept the Other. After all, who else, if not a refugee, understands what it means to be a stranger and without ground in today's global world? Who else but a refugee understands the value of acceptance and the power of hospitality to change lives that have been shattered by war or other calamities? Who, if not such a person, having been through this experience, is called to acts of hospitality?

According to Jacques Derrida, another French philosopher, hospitality comes to us in order to happen again.[12] Because once you have experienced a miracle, you can never be indifferent. Witnessing real hospitality invariably makes you responsible to repeat it. This is how we discover that we are welcomed so that we can become hospitable because "the self cannot survive by itself alone, cannot find meaning within its own being-in-the-world."[13] We welcome because we have been welcomed. As the apostle John said, "We love because he first loved us" (1 John 4:19). It is in the giving of ourselves to the Other in love – which reveals itself as my responsibility to the Other – that we rediscover what it means to be human.

Hospitality is the ability not only to give something to another person but, in giving, to accept the Other as a gift. True hospitality is always preceded by an understanding of the Other as an infinity that opens up to us, beyond the visible, something that cannot be seen with the human eye. True hospitality is like that touch: we cannot touch someone without being touched as well.

The story of Abraham and Sarah in Mamre is brought to life anew: you encounter the Other as an absolute transcendence before whom you fall down and wash their feet. Then follows the story of Christ's supper with the apostles, where you no longer distance yourself from the Other but share your experiences with them: "Take and eat; this is my body" (Matt 26:26). Hospitality is the "eating" of the Other – that is, when their story becomes yours. You are "filled" with their fragility, brokenness, and tears. You are the one who welcomes them not only into your home but also into yourself. You have to "open up" yourself to receive the suffering and life of the Other, to receive their wounds, not only to give something but also to receive. It is in recognition of one's own vulner-

---

12. Jacques Derrida, *Hospitality*, vol. 2, ed. Pascale-Anne Brault and Peggy Kamuf, trans. Peggy Kamuf (Chicago: University of Chicago Press, 2024), 78–79.
13. Levinas, "Ethics of the Infinite," 60.

ability to the Other and one's need for the Other that the host opens up to the possibility of being received as well. In this way, continuous and mutual giving and receiving unfold. "This is my body" marks the culmination of not only humanity but also community.

I am talking about my experience not because it is universal or special, and not because I think I can teach anyone anything. My experience is but one among many; I have gone through and am still dealing with personal challenges and wounds that the Russian aggression has inflicted on me. But this is not just a story about painful uprooting. It's also about how the Other comes from outside and brings me more than I can hold just when it seems like everything has been lost. It is about what it means to receive and be received. It is a path of encounters that hurt yet bestow the ability to embrace both yourself and the Other.

So, whenever I feel lost in a world that doesn't seem to see me and that I find hard to call my own, I open my little treasury with all the unconditional gifts I have collected during my wanderings. I look at them to remind myself that the miracle of hospitality is possible and real. The process of contemplating these unassuming bits and pieces becomes a prayer, a request, and a hope that the Other will be accepted and, in turn, discover their own gift of hospitality. I implore both myself and everyone else to be part of this miracle of humanity: to receive and give, to welcome and be welcomed.

"I am grateful to God that despite complicated and confusing events, I continue to trust him. I truly believe that God is with me, that God does not leave me, that God is working out his salvation story even now, at a time when all I see around me is gloom and darkness." Pavlo Horbunov (p. 113)

5

Reclaiming Home

Pavlo Horbunov

*Lecturer, Ukrainian Evangelical Theological Seminary;
Military Chaplain, Territorial Defence Forces of the Armed Forces of Ukraine*

About Me

Greetings! My name is Pavlo. I'm a little over forty, married, with a daughter and a son. I've been a believer since I was fourteen. I have a Master of Theology and teach at a seminary. Before the war, I taught various theology classes – both at the seminary and at church – ran seminars on biblical studies, and lived and loved life. The only thing I knew about war came from watching *Saving Private Ryan*.

Regarding Chaos and Uncertainty

I enlisted voluntarily to fight in the full-scale war. On 24 February, when Russia invaded Ukraine, I was away on a trip, teaching at a branch of our seminary. A full-scale war in the twenty-first century seemed unbelievable to me for quite some time. Sure, there was a lot of buzz about amassing troops at the border and the possibility of military action by Putin, but I considered all this nothing more than attempts to pressure Ukraine politically. Once again, a set of Minsk agreements, once again, schemes regarding the Russian language, EU integration, the Black Sea fleet, natural gas, or whatnot.[1] So, I was shocked to learn that the RAF had crossed the border and begun taking over Ukrainian territories,

---

1. The Minsk Agreements of 2014–2015 are a set of political agreements on the terms and mechanisms of a peaceful settlement of Russia's hybrid war against Ukraine, reached on the basis of a multilateral compromise during two rounds of negotiations in Minsk (Belarus) in September 2014 and February 2015.

bombing cities and military stations alike, dropping air assault forces right at Kyiv's doorstep. In the middle of my lecture, I received a phone call from my wife. Because of the time zone difference, it was night in Kyiv. She said that explosions were heard in the area of Boryspil airport. Residents of the capital were waking up and panicking. Many were attempting to leave the city. There were traffic jams and long queues at petrol stations. It was like a scene from an apocalyptic film, and it was hard to believe this was actually happening.

Immediately, I decided to go back home, and that very day, I changed my plane ticket. Leaders of the seminary branch were so helpful, changing their schedule, arranging tickets, and raising funds to get me across Europe and back to Kyiv. Ukraine's airspace was already closed, so their contingency plan for me to travel through Budapest came in handy.

When I arrived in Ukraine, I didn't know what to do at first. My family had relocated to Poland, and I was very happy about that. I had no plans to join them because I was convinced that I should remain in the country and do something to help. However, all around me was chaos and confusion. Even reaching my friends on the phone was almost impossible. The seminary where I worked did not have a clear plan of action and did not need my help at that time. I remember so well the third day of the war – I was far from home, visiting friends, praying, and trying to decide what to do next. Through the window, I saw a man in a camouflage uniform passing by. It's hard to explain, but I felt that this was a sign for me: I had to go to the military enlistment office. I had never served in the army before, but I felt it was my duty to defend what I hold most dear by taking up arms.

New Realities

I enlisted, and I am still serving in the Territorial Defence Forces of the Armed Forces of Ukraine. During the first two months of the war, our military unit was guarding critical infrastructure facilities and learning basic military skills as part of our duties. It was an interesting experience but certainly not an easy one. The living conditions in the barracks left much to be desired, and the frequent night patrols and poor quality of food soon began to adversely impact our health. The war continued, and we did not know what the future held for us. The soldiers with military experience tried to explain to the rest of us that combat operations would be more than just a little difficult. Some of us listened, while others dreamed of destroying a tank and receiving a medal. I tried not to overthink things and to take it one day at a time. It was the only possible decision to maintain my mental and emotional health. I love freedom, so the barracks regulations became a challenge for me. People crowding around denied me personal space, and the officers made it clear that an ordinary soldier was a nobody there. The army mentality itself was new to me and many others, and I would soon come to hate this with my whole heart.

I had to make considerable efforts to stay true to my Christian identity and to find time for prayer and reading the Bible. My commanding officer respected my faith and gave me leave on Sundays so that I could attend church services. He even referred to me as the unofficial chaplain of our unit. At that time, the law regulating military chaplain posts in battalions had not yet been introduced, so any chaplaincy had to be offered on a personal level. I was constantly asked questions like "What will you do when you come under fire?" or "How about 'Thou shalt not kill' and 'turn the other cheek'?" I saw once again (and repeatedly later on) how many myths about Christians and Christianity circulate in our society. I was able to dispel some of these misconceptions for a few soldiers.

I will forever remember Easter of 2022. We were shuffled aboard a train and went off to gain our first combat experience. What I am writing here may seem simple and calm. In reality, everything was complicated and challenging. Many of us were unprepared. Everyone was afraid, but while some were able to conquer their fear, others could not. I wrote a letter to my family in case of my death, and I still have it. I hope it will never be read for its intended purpose but that I will be able to show it to my children when I reach a ripe old age. The unknown, the danger, and the constant uncertainty weighed down on me. The war didn't teach me anything I didn't know before, but I was *experiencing* it all now. As a result, I was changing, and so was my outlook on life. I began to value family, freedom, and the bare necessities of life above all else. Previously, all of this had been overshadowed by hollow imaginings of happiness, such as owning things or being popular. The war quickly and ruthlessly dealt with these illusions.

Painful Loss

During the first months of the war, I received news that my friend Andrii Shostak had been killed in action. Andrii was one of those near and dear people you find only a few times in a lifetime. He, too, had enlisted in the Armed Forces of Ukraine, fought to defend the Kyiv region, and worked to evacuate civilians. Unfortunately, he was captured during a combat mission. There was no news of him for a few weeks. It was only after the liberation of the Kyiv, Zhytomyr, and Chernihiv regions, as the RAF withdrew from those territories, that volunteers found his tortured body in one of the villages. This news hit us hard. Andrii is survived by his wife, Svitlana, and three children. It's one thing to hear of the death of people you don't know, but it's totally different to experience the reality of loss when it involves someone you care about. I was quite close with Andrii, spending time together and debating theological matters. Whenever he visited me, we had a tradition of going for a walk in the woods. First, we would go to the shop and buy Pepsi – which had to be in a glass bottle – and an ice cream – which had to be "Eskimos" by Rud. As we walked, we would talk, share our lives, and just relax. It was a special time, very meaningful, and now I realize that it will never happen again – not in this world. I was able to visit Andrii's grave some time later, but I have to admit that I still haven't been able to say goodbye and let go. Perhaps after the war, when I am not in a hurry, I will be able to go to his grave with two bottles of Pepsi and two "Eskimos" ice creams and reminisce about how we walked in the woods and talked. Then, perhaps, I will pray, find peace, and let my friend go – and wait until we meet again in the new, resurrected world.

The Apostle John Was Right

I keep pondering the causes of this war. In the twenty-first century, with all our technological advancements and having experienced the horrors of wars, the whole world knows all too well that aggression is an evil that brings pain and suffering. So how is it even possible that Russia invaded Ukraine, once again bringing death to so many, destroying cities, and shattering the lives of so many families? How could the Russian people ever consent to this? Why, in the third year of the war, are Christian evangelical churches still silent, not calling this a war and not decrying their governments' actions? Beyond Russia's particular political system, its economic processes, the mentality of its citizens, and the personal ambitions of the wannabe emperor Putin, I believe (and I feel strongly about this) that the spiritual and universal cause of most wars throughout human history is deception. Unfortunately, the situation in Ukraine is no exception.

The book of Revelation describes the four horsemen of the Apocalypse. The first rider is said to be on a white horse, the second on a red horse, the third on a black horse, and the fourth on a pale horse (Rev 6:2–8). I happen to teach this book at the seminary, and I know that most scholars agree that the horsemen represent, in that order, the antichrist, war, famine, and death.

It's as if John is speaking prophetically to the church: "Look at what's going on in the world. There's an antichrist who's posing as a messiah, faking his shining white because his nature is utterly different. This antichrist is sending out arrows from his bow: war, symbolized by the rider on a red horse, and famine, represented by the rider on a black horse. The red rider is given the power to take peace from the earth. The black rider brings forth a shortage of essentials. The fourth rider is death, an inevitable consequence of war and famine."

Allow me to point out that chapters 6 and 7 of Revelation, which describe the breaking of the seals, probably refer to the big picture of the situation of the world in the last days. According to the Bible, these "last days" refer to the time period from Jesus's resurrection to his second coming – the big picture, indeed. Some Christian communities in Asia Minor needed a reminder that there are adversarial forces at work in the world and that they must not be careless or spiritually asleep. Some Christians around the world, including in Ukraine, also need this reminder. I get very emotional when I think about how many people are living in an illusion – whether it's the idea of optimistic humanism, the prosperity gospel, the comfortable gospel, or simply the principle of "not my concern" – and fail to recognize the existence of war, hunger, and death. Instead, they are sheltered in a rose-tinted bubble, deaf and blind to human suffering and the shattering concept of evil.

But I digress. I'd like to focus on a specific and important detail in John's account because it explains the origins of all the woes. According to Revelation, the universal sorrows that plague our world – war, famine, and death – owe their existence to deception. Deception is the main attribute of the rider on the white horse. He impersonates and pretends to be someone other than who he really is. Deception is his essence and his weapon. The apostle Paul, in his epistle to the Corinthians, says, "For Satan himself masquerades as an angel of light" (2 Cor 11:14). In John's Gospel, Jesus calls him "the father of lies" (John 8:44). The story of the fall is rooted in the deception of the serpent. Job's tale begins with a similar lie uttered by Satan: "Does Job fear God for nothing?" (Job 1:9). Revelation also mentions "the accuser of our brothers and sisters" (Rev 12:10). Deception and lies are at the core of the devil's every move.

I can draw some clear parallels between Revelation 6–7 and the war in Ukraine. Not that Revelation is only relevant to the twenty-first century, but its ever-relevant message helps the reader see that deception lies at the beginning of wars throughout history. Russia's war against Ukraine also began with long-standing, reality-twisting lies. Long before the full-scale invasion, the Kremlin routinely and consistently lied about Ukraine. Mass media and the propaganda mill successfully convinced not only Russia's own population but also many people around the world that Ukraine – as a sovereign country – simply does not exist. Moreover, there were snowballing lies: that Ukraine is no more than a peripheral province of Russia; that the Ukrainian language is not a real language but a mangled version of the venerable Russian language; that the majority of people in Ukraine are Nazis, celebrating Hitler and reviving fascist Germany; that Russian-speaking people are oppressed; that Crimea was unlawfully passed to Ukraine; that, since 2014, the Ukrainian armed forces have been shelling civilians in the so-called Donetsk People's Republic and Luhansk People's Republic; that NATO is using Ukraine in its master plan to take over Russia; trickery and manipulations regarding history, language, and natural gas supply. The Kremlin's rendition of reality warps the very foundations of truth by twisting, distorting, and turning it on its head. Never did I think such deception was possible, let alone that it could be so successful. I was proved very wrong. The Russians now believe that they are protecting peace, not starting a bloody war. And if it doesn't appear that way, then they blame the government and army, rather than the kind-hearted, highly cultured common people of Russia.

The lies continue throughout the war – lies about what happened in Bucha and Mariupol, lies about the bombing of a children's hospital in Kyiv, lies that are copious, masterfully crafted, and continuously spun. The Kremlin has been hugely successful in sophisticated information warfare. Russia distorts reality, muddles concepts, and skews information. It is a terrible weapon – one that, like nuclear radiation, quietly poisons everything around it.

This leads to two conclusions. First, we must always tell the truth. The truth is inherently sacred. It deserves to be told for the very reason that it is the truth. There is no sense in saying that everyone has their own truth. No! Everyone may have their own interests, but there is only one truth. Second, we must learn to discern lies so as not to be deceived. This demands hard work and sustained effort. It's a process and a struggle but also a responsibility. At this point, no one could claim that they've been beguiled and are, therefore, innocent. Being beguiled – led by deception – still requires a willingness to follow. It is true that no one is infallible. We all make mistakes, but once we realize our mistakes, we must change our ways. Persisting in deception is a decision driven by spiritual blindness, cowardice, and complacency. I'm originally from Russia, but I've lived most of my life in Ukraine. I must admit that until the Revolution of Dignity in 2014, I didn't see much difference between Russia and Ukraine. But those events forced me to see the light. There is a great divide between Ukraine and Russia – in every respect.

First Combat Experience

I remember our battalion's first combat experience. We were transferred to the Luhansk region in May 2022. We were supposed to settle into our positions and block the movement of Russian troops. As it turned out, there wasn't much to settle into – just flat land, interrupted by narrow strips of site-protective forests. No trenches, no dugouts, and, worst of all, no overwatch from our artillery. Well, there was some artillery but not enough to provide suppressive fire. It was so outnumbered that it could only return fire at about 2:10 – and not in our favour.

It was a challenging time, mainly due to miscommunication and confusion. The objectives of the Territorial Defence Battalion of the Armed Forces of Ukraine – to which I belonged – did not include direct participation in combat operations. At most, our job was to hold the third line of defence, guard strategically important facilities, man checkpoints, and so on, and our level of training and equipment reflected this. I remember, back at the training ground, we asked for an opportunity to practise shooting with a grenade launcher and were told, "You're Territorial Defence; you're not allowed." And yet, here we were, being deployed to the first line of defence, with no armoured vehicles and no proper weapons. I remember getting to the debussing point on yellow school buses. Looking back, I smile. We used to joke with each other that the Russians on the other side must surely be stunned by an unknown type of troops travelling to the contact line in brightly coloured public transport and terrified by such boldness. In reality, it was utter madness and lack of competence.

I ended up in a platoon guarding a command post. It was a good thing we managed to dig the first round of trenches before the shelling began. I had seen this being done in films, but now I was part of the film. Admittedly, it was far more fun watching such scenes in the cinema than living through it. With mortar shelling, you hear the "blomp" of a round being launched and then the explosion when it hits. There's just enough time in between to hit the ground or duck into a trench. Once, a missile hit and created a crater large enough to fit one of our infamous yellow buses. By God's grace, it narrowly missed our command post. Otherwise, this story would have had a far grimmer ending. The truly scary part is that you can't hear an incoming missile. One moment, we're standing around and talking; the next, we're astounded by a tall pillar of soil rising about ten metres high. Then a thought pops up, "Good God, I hope the guys aren't hurt." Only then does the reality sink in, and we take cover from the lumps of soil that were kicked up by the explosion and now start raining down on us.

It's Hard Being a Part of Something Big

During that first combat experience, we found ourselves in a position with enemy troops on three sides and only one way to fall back. The risk of being surrounded loomed, and this was rather unsettling. I was far away from home, unsure when – or if – I would see my family again. The situation on the battlefield was unclear. What were we supposed to do? How should we fight? No one seemed to know. Did we even need to be here right now? No one could give a proper answer. I vividly remember seeing a spider sitting serenely in its web, woven among the branches of a tree. I don't know what came over me, but at that moment, I envied that spider. "I wish I were a spider, sitting pretty in its web, free of worries, far away from this war," I thought. But after a moment, I realized that the spider could rest comfortably in its web precisely because, ironically, it wasn't attached to events happening around it. The spider wasn't part of the Ukrainians' great struggle for life and freedom, and so it could rest on the sidelines. This thought cheered me up a little. Yes, it was a tough spot for me, but this also meant I was part of something big, something much bigger than myself. It was a fleeting comfort, I admit, and I still envied that spider.

During our stay in the Luhansk region, I became keenly aware of just how little one really needs for day-to-day living. At first, we lived in a dusty shed with no windows. Then, it was a trench, and later, just a pit made of two concrete hoops with a metal hatch, on which we threw a bundle of hay. Sleeping there was more comfortable, but I still preferred sleeping in the trench – at least there were no frogs in it, unlike in the concrete "room." We had no shower, no proper food, and no bed. Once, in a conversation with an old friend, I talked about how I dreamed of a simple cup of hot tea or coffee – no sweets, no cupcakes, just a good cup of piping hot tea. It turned out that he had a portable gas stove and a stash of 3-in-1 coffee packets. The cup of coffee he made that day became a slice of heaven for me, delivering such an intense sense of pleasure that I still remember it to this day. I realized then how little I really needed for a comfortable life.

Prayer Has Never Been More Important

When I went off to war, I took with me a book that was small in size but grand in meaning and significance: *Great Prayers of the Old Testament* by Walter Brueggemann. I had read this book before, during peaceful times, but re-reading it in the trenches, I discovered a number of new insights. The prayers of Abraham and Moses described in it came alive for me on a deeper level. Their prayers became my prayers during that time. It is difficult for me to fully explain the profoundness of my experiences, and I cannot always define it clearly even for myself, but the way the prayers of Abraham and Moses influenced – in the appropriate sense of this word – the decisions and actions of God, especially in his intention to destroy Sodom and Israel, became my own words. Abraham spoke up, saying, "Will you sweep away the righteous with the wicked?" (Gen 18:23). Moses spoke up, saying, "Otherwise, the country from which you brought us will say, 'Because the LORD was not able to take them into the land he had promised them, and because he hated them, he brought them out to put them to death in the wilderness'" (Deut 9:28). Similarly, I spoke up: "Lord, if I perish, it's one thing, but think of the people who pray for me, what will they say?" I still believe that because of the prayers of my family, my friends, and my church, the Lord protected me time and time again so that their faith would not be shaken. It is so good to have family, friends, and a church that pray for us.

My First Leave and Surgery

After some time in the Luhansk and Donetsk regions, we were transferred to the Sumy region to defend the border. This was still a combat zone but not as active as the Donetsk, Luhansk, Zaporizhzhia, or Kherson sectors. Here, our tasks included setting up defence lines and standing guard. Before arriving in the Sumy region, I had leave, as well as time off for knee surgery. It turned out that my meniscus had been damaged by the weight of a tile carrier, assault rifle, combat kit, backpack, and other gear. It was a strange experience being back home again after being away for so many months. Everything seemed surreal. Since my family was still in Poland and would not return to Kyiv until later, we couldn't even see each other. I have never felt so lonely. My knee surgery took place after my leave; as strange as it may sound, this was one of the best times of my life. For one thing, my family finally came to Kyiv. In addition, I was given thirty days for rehab after surgery instead of just ten days of leave. The fact that the surgeon was tinkering with my knee no longer seemed to matter.

False Hopes

My deployment in the Sumy region continued. My routine included position patrols, drills at training grounds, the challenges of daily living, health troubles, and unannounced inspections. The inspections were the biggest challenge. Figuring out the exact expectations of your superiors is next to impossible, so any interaction with senior commanders felt like a whole different type of warfare. And I'm going to hold my tongue about the battle with the army's paperwork – logs, records, and forms of various kinds.

Meanwhile, I kept pondering what was going through the minds of the Russians, especially Russian believers. Ever since the annexation of Crimea and the hostilities in the Donetsk and Luhansk regions, my Christian friends in Russia had been repeating the TV message that the "little green men" in Crimea were not actual Russian troops and that, in the Donetsk and Luhansk regions, they were just local resistance fighters. They insisted that Russia truly cared about Ukraine and only wanted to help in any way possible. I could not but wonder: How can anyone be so blind? As subsequent events demonstrated, I should not have been so perplexed.

When the full-scale war began with Russia's open attack on Ukraine, I thought that now, finally, Russian believers would see the true nature of their leaders and their country, reconsider their support, and stand with Ukraine. And yet, the majority of Christians in Russia continued to justify this war, calling it a "special military operation" that would only target military sites and not affect civilians. Russian Christians continued to deny the indisputable events that took place in places such as Bucha, Irpen, and Mariupol – rape, torture, and murders of civilians, along with the rest of the war crimes committed by the RAF. Time and time again, I would hear bizarre calls to love and claims that hatred is a sin. It was then that I realized that attempts to explain and reason with such people would be utterly futile because this was not a case of being blind or deaf but a case of demonic madness. Now I began to see the biblical references to spiritually closed eyes and ears in a whole new light. I felt the devastation that Jesus must have experienced when he had to deal with such madness: "It is only by Beelzebul, the prince of demons, that this fellow drives out demons" (Matt 12:24). Utter folly, beyond correction. When the apostle Paul encountered Christians who taught that one should sin more in order to receive more grace, his response was quite simple: "Their condemnation is just!" (Rom 3:8). Paul understood that such minds could not be set straight because such thinking was simply madness. That's why, when I was asked in an interview whether the Christians of Russia would be reformed, whether they would admit their wrongdoing and repent, I replied, heartbrokenly, that most likely they would not.

Peace and Justice

During the first months of the full-scale war, while we were still completing our training, I was able to attend worship services on Sundays. My commanding officer had great respect for Christian churches and always granted me leave on Sundays. One Sunday, Fedir Raichynets, my seminary colleague, was preaching. We hadn't seen each other since the beginning of the full-scale invasion, and I was so glad to see a familiar, friendly face. I remember well his sermon on justice and peace and often thought about it as I grappled with a number of war-related questions: How does God view war? How are we to deal with an enemy? Can an enemy be forgiven while still on a rampage, killing and destroying? Should a Christian take up arms? Although his sermon didn't provide all the answers, it offered a biblical foundation for me to explore these questions further. Fedir's main point was that true peace is impossible without justice; if justice is ignored, there can only be an illusion of peace. For this reason, God considers justice a matter of great importance and weaves it into his creation. An enemy must first acknowledge wrongdoing and stop killing. Only then can the issue of forgiveness be addressed. Jesus restores justice on the cross, he does not simply forgive humanity because he feels like it. Therefore, when soldiers take up arms to defend their family, their friends, the weak, and the defenceless, they are not murderers but a servant of God who brings peace. Peace is only possible if evil is defeated and justice is restored – that was my key takeaway from that sermon. Later, when I began serving as chaplain in the battalion, I often recalled that sermon, which helped me to remind the soldiers of this truth: "You are not murderers; you are peacemakers who defend peace and justice." Some believers from other churches would thank me and say that they now had a better understanding of God's principles regarding war, love, forgiveness, and peace. I myself am grateful to Fedir for what he preached that day because his sermon brought me clarity as well.

New Challenges for Our Battalion

We were stationed in the Sumy region for about eight months. During that time, most of the Kharkiv region was liberated. Everyone was waiting eagerly for the war to end. The Russian army appeared weak, and many thought that it was holding on purely because it was so large. The arrival of military aid from our allies, the news that the first Leopard tanks were arriving, and the Ukrainian army's preparations for a counteroffensive brought optimism and a sense of impending triumph, even though the tragic news from Bakhmut lay heavily on everyone's mind. If only we had known what really lay ahead for us . . .

Around March, our battalion received orders to deploy to the Kupiansk sector. There were rumours of a breakthrough and, therefore, an urgent need for reinforcements. Since we already knew what to expect, we were fully prepared mentally. War, however, can be overwhelming. In the Kupiansk sector, I was riding in an armoured vehicle for the first time when I heard the sound of enemy drones (I still hate the buzz of a quadcopter). Only a year had passed since our last engagement in active combat, but everyone already felt and understood that the war had changed – things were certainly different from before. Unfortunately, it was near Kupiansk that we suffered our first significant losses. Situations where we had recently spoken to a fellow soldier and then, shortly after, received news of his death became all too real for us.

Once again, I was admitted to hospital to have my knees treated. I was not wounded, and I am grateful to God that the war did not claim my health. However, injuries related to my military service resurfaced. I spent two months in Kyiv with my family and underwent outpatient treatment. Frankly, it was a real miracle that I was permitted to receive such a treatment protocol. I don't know how this was possible, but I was grateful to God for this blessing.

Chaplaincy

After returning to my battalion in late summer 2023, I was offered the post of chaplain. The battalion command officers knew that I was a believer, so when our current chaplain was discharged for family-related reasons, they asked if I would take on this responsibility. I said I would think about it – and the commander responded that it was an order, not a suggestion. In September 2023, I began to perform chaplain duties. Soon thereafter, I received a mandate from the Ukrainian Evangelical Church, of which I am a member, to perform chaplaincy ministry. After a probationary period, I assumed the position of military chaplain of the Territorial Defence Forces of the Armed Forces of Ukraine. I was granted non-combatant status and was no longer issued weapons and ammunition.

I Am a Captive of My Theological Beliefs

My friends ask me if I regret enlisting in the army. I tell them I had no choice. This response surprises them a bit, so I have to explain: yes, I volunteered because – given what I taught my students, what I read in the Bible, and what I learned from history about courage, duty, the value of freedom and the fight against evil – I could not have made any other decision. I am a captive to my convictions, if you will. There is no glamour or sentiment here, only raw reality; but it is still full of hope. The path of a soldier during a war is a very difficult one. I did not crack or give up because God is with me and because friends support me. But if I were offered the opportunity to return to civilian life today, I would not hesitate even for a moment.

This war taught me a lesson in humility – one that was painful yet valuable. Perhaps nothing humbles you as much as the awareness of the fragility of the flesh amid exploding shells and flying bullets, knowing that a small piece of shrapnel can halt the entire stream of your consciousness, full of thoughts, ideas, goals, and notions that rival the volume of countless books, both read and unread. Perhaps nothing humbles you more than the realization of your own insignificance in the vast theatre of war, where the death of a single soldier often goes unnoticed. While at war, I am acutely aware of my weakness and insignificance against the mighty roar of a tank engine or giant blasts of energy released by an exploding missile or air bomb. Writing about it is easier than living it, and such experiences leave an indelible mark.

So why did I voluntarily join the army? Because I know that all that is important and precious must be fought for and paid for. If Ukraine, as a sovereign country with its own culture and identity, is important to me, if people and friends living here mean something to me, then I will certainly fight for it. I also know that evil must be opposed simply because it is the right thing to do. There is no other way. Evil exists, and it is objectively real. It may not always manifest as something purely evil, so it is not always easy to recognize. But when an armed person comes to kill simply because he desires more power, there is no need to attend lectures on philosophy and psychoanalysis to properly judge his actions: this is evil, and it must be stopped. There's nothing more to say here. Evil will always exist in this world. Even after another victory over evil, it will not disappear; eventually, it will rear its ugly head again somewhere. The hydra's head will grow back again and again. But if you do not fight evil, it will swallow up everything and everyone, and its destructive power will be immense. Yet, even in such a situation, God will find a way for evil to consume itself. However, this profound truth should not be used as an excuse for irresponsibility or a lack of accountability.

Another important factor shaping my beliefs was my study of the book of Revelation. For a long time, as a teacher, I tried to avoid this book. I thought it was confusing, strange, and simply extraneous to the New Testament. Truth be told, throughout my years as a Christian, I had seen so many strange ideas and claims connected to this book that I even thought it would be better if it had never been written. Without a doubt, I was ready to throw away a pearl hidden behind a thick layer of numerous self-serving, short-sighted interpretations. But one day, I told myself that it was time to go deeper into this book, that I should not continue giving students a broad summary of it in my New Testament Overview class and avoid difficult, complicated questions on the pretext that such questions were unimportant or uninteresting. For almost five years, I have been delving into the book of Revelation for my own personal study. I had to spend a great deal of money to purchase substantive and thorough commentaries, and it took considerable emotional and intellectual efforts, as well as time, to find satisfactory, albeit uncomfortable, answers. But it was worth it! I discovered a whole world within the New Testament – a world full of deep, relevant insights. These insights are present in one way or another in other books of the Old and New Testaments, but the perspective and emphasis they are given in the Revelation simply blew me away. My study of the book of Revelation has led me to one fundamental statement that has forced me to rethink my entire theology and ethics. This fundamental statement is that God cares about his creation. It is as simple as that. But believe me, it's a lot to think about. God is in a covenant relationship with his creation, including human beings. God is weaving a story of redemption for all of his creation, including humans. I believe with all my heart that when Christians see someone destroying God's creation, it is their duty to stand up for creation. I gained a few adversaries by giving seminars on the Apocalypse, but at one point – well into the war – I received a video message from one of the attendees of my seminars, someone I knew. The message said: "Thank you, brother Pavlo, your seminars on the book of Revelation have changed my stance on the events that are happening in this world. I went from the attitude of 'it is not my business' to the attitude of 'it is my responsibility.'" I couldn't have asked for a better response to my lectures on the Apocalypse of John!

Back to Chaplaincy

Chaplaincy is a creative endeavour. In fact, it is an innovation for the Ukrainian army. When adopting NATO standards, the armed forces introduced new positions, but it will take time for these to be fully integrated into the overall structure. At first, everyone asked this question: "What is a chaplain, and why do we need one at all?" Some suggested that a chaplain was just a new version of a Soviet zampolit – a political officer who makes sure that troops toe the party line. I had to explain to everyone that these roles are fundamentally different. The Ukrainian law "On the Military Chaplaincy Service" clearly states the chaplain's duty: to provide pastoral care to the personnel. The problem is that no one knows exactly how to do this, especially during wartime in an army that is just beginning to purge its Soviet past. We had to get creative in our approach to our duties. Constant relocations, scattered units, myths about the

Christian church, pagan elements in the Orthodox tradition that have nothing to do with biblical truth, and many other factors presented challenges to this ministry. Nevertheless, its benefits are undeniable. The church is present among the troops, and, in one way or another, the troops hear the truth of the gospel. The very existence of chaplaincy in the military brings about change – and definitely for the better. Whenever I remind myself of this, I am encouraged.

Unfortunately, some events indirectly tarnished the ministry of military chaplains. After the unsuccessful counteroffensive of our troops in the summer of 2023 and the growing firepower of the Russian army, Ukraine faced a difficult situation. The enemy was pushing along the entire front line, and military aid from the allies was running out. Arguments between Democrats and Republicans in the US over the allocation of further aid to Ukraine led to delays in arms shipments. We were running out of both shells and military equipment. Behind the façade of alleged support for Ukraine, there was political plotting, which seemed like a game for some. The most unfortunate aspect of this situation was that the Republicans – people who are usually viewed as having strong ties to evangelical Christianity – were blocking aid to Ukraine. Here we were, losing Avdiivka to the Russians bit by bit, people dying, the situation on the battlefield becoming dire, and over there, across the ocean, Congress was still undecided about whether or not to help us. I remember hearing the news that the Ukrainian issue had been blocked at one meeting and that they hadn't reached agreement even at a second meeting. But then came the news that since Democrats and Republicans were on their Christmas recess, the discussion of aid to Ukraine would be postponed until the next session. I didn't know how to react. A mix of sadness and anger welled up inside me. Yet I was expected to organize religious events for the military to celebrate Christmas, now that the date for it, based on the Western church calendar, had been approved by the members of the Verkhovna Rada of Ukraine.[2] How was I supposed to talk about Christmas to soldiers when this Christmas of 2023 had caused a delay in their receiving aid? Christmas is supposed to be a message of hope when there is no other source of hope. When it seems like darkness has engulfed the whole world, Christmas comes with a light that no darkness can overcome. Christmas is hope against all odds. But in 2023, Christmas added to the already dire state of the people of Ukraine. Fortunately, Democrats and Republicans were later able to reach an agreement, but for me, that Christmas was marked by a lingering sense of pain and sadness.

---

2. Verkhovna Rada – Ukrainian parlament.

Questions Better Left Unasked

As I chat with my friends, I'm often asked to share a Christian testimony – something remarkable that happened during the war. I understand this kind of interest, and I am convinced that it's not mere curiosity but a genuine desire to hear how God acts in times of war as he works out the story of salvation. Unfortunately, I don't have any traditional testimonies like "God miraculously saved us from danger. Praise the Lord!" Many different things happened. For example, one night, a plane dropped a bomb on a nearby building instead of directly on us, so we escaped with just shock and cuts from flying glass shards. There was also a time when an enemy mortar shell missed us while we were moving out into position at night simply because we stopped just in time. On one occasion, our platoon was relocated to protect another area, and we later found out that an enemy reconnaissance team had entered that very spot where we had recently been positioned. Unfortunately, on many occasions, there were casualties. Some of my fellow soldiers were killed and others were wounded while holding their positions near Kupyansk – but I was safe because I was being treated in a Kyiv hospital at the time. Therefore, I find it difficult to share a traditional Christian testimony in church because, in my case, it is story after story of "by the grace of God, it missed me . . . but not others." I don't know how to testify about that. I am well aware that I don't understand everything that's happening. Before the war, it was easier to understand. Now, I feel with all my heart that my interpretation of events is inadequate. I don't understand why things happen, I don't see the whole picture. I'm neither an expert nor a prophet. I would like to hear the voice of God explaining what is happening and setting everything straight, but there is no voice – or rather, there is no voice thundering from heaven. But there is a voice deep inside: "Where were you when I laid the earth's foundation? Tell me, if you understand" (Job 38:4). In ordinary, peaceful times, these words may sound like a reprimand, but in times of darkness, pain, emptiness, and misunderstanding, they offer tremendous comfort.

Over the course of the war, I've accumulated dozens of "whys." I still have these questions today. Why is there war in our country? Why did our battalion get into such trouble? Why did they die and not someone else? Over the years of teaching and interacting with wise people, I have concluded that there are no answers to such questions in this world – those answers simply do not exist. And those "answers" that are floating around only distort reality because they are neither true nor unambiguous. Once, when the disciples saw a blind man, they asked the Lord: "Rabbi, who sinned, this man or his parents, that he was born blind?" (John 9:2). Jesus's answer is crucial. He shifted the focus of the question, not asking "Why?" but "What now should be done about it?" The question of "why" is devastating, and millions have been crushed by it, never finding an answer. But the question "What now should be done about it?" has changed the lives of millions, helping them to find a way forward when, at first glance, there seemed to be not just a dead end but a bottomless abyss. I tried to share this wisdom of the gospel with the soldiers. Some listened, others did not.

Speaking of Christian testimony, I recall a minister from Cherkasy asking me about my testimony. I replied, "I didn't start hitting the bottle, I didn't lose my faith – does that count?" The answer was "Yes." This is important to me. I cannot offer a traditional testimony, but I can tell you why I am grateful to God.

God Is Our Sustainer

The journey of a soldier is difficult. Many times, I have found myself on the brink, but I feel that God sustains me, and that gives me the strength to go on. Psalm 139 has become my prayer and my comfort song. Everything in it seems to be written for me. I am grateful to God that I am alive. The dangers have been many, but, by God's grace, I live and breathe today. I am grateful to God that I am on solid ground spiritually and emotionally. I find great comfort in prayer. I am grateful that my family is relatively safe and well. I am grateful to God for my friends who support me in this war, in both word and deed, and I will always remember their help. I am grateful to God that despite complicated and confusing events, I continue to trust him. I truly believe that God is with me, that God does not leave me, that God is working out his salvation story even now, at a time when all I see around me is gloom and darkness. I truly believe this and consider this sense of assurance God's greatest gift to me. That's my testimony, but I don't know if I should share it in a church service. I wonder ... will it be understood?

I've titled these reflections *Reclaiming Home* because this whole war is, in a sense, about getting back or reclaiming our home. As Ukrainians, we are fighting for a home that we have partly lost. We have lost territories, and we have lost many people – some died defending others, some left and are unlikely to return. Ukraine is our home. Yes, it will not be the same as it was before 2022. It is different now, but it needs to be reclaimed, protected, strengthened, and made better. However, this is a very long journey. In a way, every soldier has also lost a home – his or her own home. Perhaps it has not been destroyed, perhaps it is intact and in good order, but for two and a half years, we have not been able to return to it. Home has become distant and, for many of us, even strange. For two and a half years, we have been on the move, living in barns, abandoned houses, dugouts, trenches, tents, sleeping bags, cars, farms, garages, administrative buildings, cultural centres, clubs, or libraries. We have lived in all kinds of places. But I know that we all want to go *home*. For some, it will be harder to return; for others, it may never be possible to do so. And yet, we are all fighting for our home. For now, we are wanderers without a roof over our heads. No sooner do we get used to one place than it's time to move to another. The song "I Have No Home" by the band Odyn v Kanoe resonates strongly with me. My most fervent desire is to return – in every sense of the word – to my home. This is my daily prayer.

I don't know how long or how far we have to go before the war ends. I don't know what efforts and sacrifices it will take, what price we will have to pay. It is hard for us; we shed blood and suffer losses every day. But the struggle is worth it. We are fighting against evil and fighting for our home. The stakes are high. Christians should remember that victories don't happen on their own; they require effort. Sometimes, titanic efforts are needed, and then we realize our weakness and turn to God. As we walk down this road, we must keep trusting God. Yes, it's difficult, and I'm not ready to advise others on how to do it. I've barely found – and try not to lose – my foundation of faith. Thanks to my faith, I manage to remain steadfast, even when it doesn't seem possible to do so. But I have become convinced that Christians who have no lived experience of war should delve more deeply and earnestly into the concepts of biblical justice, peace, love for neighbour and enemy, and the preciousness of God's creation. Many Christians would also do well to realize that it is not necessary to give an expert opinion on every issue. If there is nothing to say, it is better to say nothing at all. Often, even if you do have something to say, it may still be better not to say it. I must emphasize the gravity of deception. It is a terrible sin that corrupts God's creation. Deception distorts reality, like creating an alternate world. The destructive effects of this are inevitable. We must not allow this to happen.

How Now Shall We Live?

Does Ukraine have a future? I am certain that it does. However, we should not expect a rosy, happy ending because we will still face many challenges and have much work to do after the war. The pain of loss will not fade overnight. The challenge of forgiving the enemy also looms somewhere on the horizon. It's too early to talk or even think about forgiveness, but as I look towards the future, I am horrified to realize that we, as Christians, cannot avoid this topic. Nevertheless, everything happens in its own time, so let's not get too far ahead of ourselves. At the moment, we have a more pressing problem that requires our utmost attention. If we, the people of Ukraine, want to have a future, we need to change. I'm not talking so much about sinfulness (although it all comes down to that in a global sense) but about what we have done on the social, economic, and political levels that allowed this war to happen. Without offering too many insights or sounding too cryptic, I am deeply convinced that if we had taken our culture more seriously, reduced corruption, and strengthened our economy and army, there would have been no war in 2014 or 2022. We became soft and feeble – intellectually, morally, economically – and the enemy took advantage of this. What we must learn from the war is that we can no longer afford to be weak. We must be stronger in every respect than our crazy and godless neighbour. And this requires change. We have no moral right to continue living the way we did before this great war. Changes must take place across the board. I am sure that they are already happening, but the road ahead is still long, and backsliding is inevitable. However, this is not a reason to give up. On the contrary, it is a reason to find and hold on to hope, to work hard to protect and improve our home, remembering that even in this present darkness, God still reigns. This is what John saw when he looked through the open door in heaven (Rev 4:1–8).

"His shoulder marks had no stars that signified a higher rank; he was just an ordinary soldier. However, there was now one star – the most important one – shining for him. And now ahead of him was not just the unknown but also the glimmer of the light for a luminary yet to exist. He smiled, for everything had been done right. And that was the sixth day." Denis Gorenkov (p. 137)

6

It's Still Too Dark Here, but I'm No Longer Afraid

Denis Gorenkov

*Junior Lieutenant, Chaplaincy Service of the Armed Forces of Ukraine;
Lecturer, Centre for Training of Military Chaplains, Military Institute,
Taras Shevchenko National University of Kyiv*

In the Beginning

> And the earth was without form, and void; and darkness was upon the face of the deep. And the Spirit of God moved upon the face of the waters.
>
> Genesis 1:2 (KJV)

He stopped drinking. That's how it all began. Before that, the earth was formless and life was empty. The darkness brooded upon the void, and the void lured him closer and closer. The Spirit of God was also there, hovering ever so close – he just didn't know it yet.

The earth gave rise to the roads that were going each and every way. He worked up their dust and mud like a lifeless grey dough. Whichever direction he chose, his car would arrive at war. This war would take on many shapes and faces. At first, just like many others, he would take photo after photo: a rusty shell of a burned-out car; an image of a tower block, cleaved by a monstrous cutlass; a Russian army ration pack and stripy undershirt, discarded in Ukrainian bushes. Only later does it become clear that there aren't really many different shapes and forms of war but, rather, a singular panoramic view – the distinctive sight of the dusty earth into which the war has returned everything. Torn, ravaged, formless earth.

The family had left. He took them all the way to the Polish border himself. They walked along a road for a while, luggage in hand and a carrier holding two cats in tow. Hundreds of stranded cars lined the road. People were making campfires, weeping, abandoning their possessions on the side of the road – and slogging forward. Going back was certain death. These were the days when spring had sprung. Precocious and precious. Promptly pounded by tank convoys and slashed by the blades of KA-52 attack helicopters. His road back was stippled by wet snow. He felt like he was drowning in it, sinking deeper and deeper into the dark void, tiny air bubbles escaping his body and travelling back towards border guards, frightened children, and two cats crammed into a carrier. He was drifting ever further into a life that was as empty as a cracked cup.

Dusk was falling. The darkness began to thicken and swell – first in the hidden corners of life. Yet light still trickled through from above; and the blankets and pillows left in the car held on to the faint scent of children. But darkness built up – at dusk and at dawn. Night would turn into day, yet light would not come.

Over the past year, he had spent his nights in some of the most unexpected places. Houses, abandoned by owners who had fled the war. These dwellings now housed other people, displaced by war but unwilling to leave the country. In the wee hours, he'd enter a room that would be his bedroom for the night, crash on the bed, and fall asleep. Waking up in the morning, he'd stare for a minute at unfamiliar furniture, plastered with pictures – probably by teens – at mirrors blackened by soot, at vanity desks cluttered with make-up bottles and jars.

In those moments, he'd try to figure out where he was, try to imagine the people who had lived there. It was a strange yet fleeting feeling, quickly replaced by the usual dark sense of futility and irrelevance that now followed him everywhere, no matter where he'd fallen asleep or woken up.

The void gaped wide when, amid the darkness that now surrounded him day and night, he began drinking. The drinks were shared with journalists, soldiers, humanitarian aid workers, priests, or random acquaintances from seedy drinking dens. Sometimes, he'd wake up in the middle of the night and drink until the world dissolved into a fog. Late next evening, he'd dig through text messages and calls on his phone, trying to piece together who he had talked to and about what. And then he'd go outside – and his gut instinct would always lead him to a place in this abyss that would pour him a drink. And another, and then another.

He stopped drinking abruptly. It was in the month of May, the second May since the beginning of the war. The earth was still formless, and life still empty. The darkness still swirled above the void, but above the face of the deep waters he'd been sinking in, the Spirit of God had moved. He stopped drinking, picked up his papers as a humanitarian aid delivery driver, and crossed the border. This was the end of the first year of the war and the morning of day one.

First Day: And There Was Light

And God said, Let there be light: and there was light.
Genesis 1:3 (KJV)

There was light inside the church, but the doors were closed. On Easter, he ended up in the main street of an old city in the Netherlands. There were several churches, their stone fingers reaching for the sky, pointing to heaven, yet the tourists were unfazed. People were eyeing cheeses and wooden clogs in the display windows, popping open doors of coffee shops, sipping on beer, and taking pictures against the backdrop of waterways. The Lord's stone fingers kept reaching upwards to the sky; but on the ground, bronzed fingers of Arab youth deftly rolled marijuana joints.

He felt that no one here thought about God. The churches were well maintained; their stone fingers were kept neatly polished. That's the proper way. And that's the way Dutch people are – doing what's proper during the day and doing what feels good in the evening. Obviously, at some point, God had become both useless and irrelevant. At least, that's how he felt in this lovely country where everyone was polite and nice, even the dogs. But he himself wasn't nice. He carried deep inside a darkness that hovered over an ever-deepening void.

Easter was coming – a Jewish feast, an export of the apostles and their local representatives, carried to the ends of the earth, including the Netherlands.

Back in his home town, early on Easter morning, people would come out to the main street – Lenin Avenue – to sit on benches and green lawns, spreading out newspapers to hold hard-boiled eggs, cucumbers, tomatoes, bottles of booze, and shot glasses. And, of course, there was salt stashed in small matchboxes. Men would wear white shirts, women would don dresses, and old ladies would come bedecked in their best kerchiefs. Almost all of them would have been to Orthodox churches earlier that morning and would come back carrying wicker baskets filled with the usual fare: bottles of booze, hard-boiled eggs painted various colours, and special Easter sweetbread called *paska*. Children would frolic among the spreads; adults would sit, peaceful and quiet, even a little solemn. Easter was almost like May Day, except with the addition of this Jesus Christ guy that the authorities hadn't approved of yet, but he has risen nonetheless.

Christ's resurrection was a mystery. It's early morning. Birds warble and trill. Women come to the tomb and find it empty. Then the angel appears and speaks: "Why seek ye the living among the dead?" (Luke 24:5 KJV). And after that, those confusing words of the apostle Paul about Jesus being the firstborn to be raised from death into eternal life and how others – whosoever is willing – will follow him (1 Cor 15:20–23).

His father would say these were convoluted fairy tales for adults. In their house, no Easter bread was ever made, and no one would go to an Orthodox church. On Easter morning, his parents would just stay at home and have breakfast in their tiny kitchen, and his mother would boil dirty clothes in large pots on a gas stove, trying to get the stains out.

His father was a member of the Communist Party and the proud owner of books on scientific atheism that explained everything about Christ's resurrection in terms of myths and church politics. His father also subscribed to and regularly read a magazine called *Literary Learning*. Then, all of a sudden – perhaps to commemorate the approaching 1000th anniversary of the Christianization of Rus – the magazine began to publish some excerpts from the New Testament. These titbits included the words of the Teacher about the birds of the air that neither sow nor reap, his resurrection from the dead, and his promise to the thief on a cross next to him that he would be with the Teacher in paradise.

It was an Easter morning, laced with birdsong, when he got on his bike and rode to an old temple that thrust its stone finger upwards into a gloomy Easter sky. He was a bit late. The service had already started, and a bike rack at the side was filled with a dozen or so bicycles. But the doors were closed – and that threw him off a bit. Inside the temple, there was light, and there was singing, but he couldn't get in. Confused, he went around the temple a few times, trying to open each door that he came across – but none of them opened. Inside the temple, the service went on, bright light streaming through the windows while he remained outside, unable to enter. Suddenly, one of the doors opened to let a couple out. He rushed to the door and tried to enter, but two men in uniform shirts stopped him. He tried to explain to them, in his broken English, that he was a Christian, that it was Easter, and that all he wanted was to enter. In just as broken English, they told him that he could – but tomorrow, not today. And then, the doors were closed.

Did the orderly Dutch Lord not allow latecomers into the temple? Had he just been cast out of Eden by two angels dressed in uniform shirts? It was almost inconceivable that he was not permitted to enter the church!

He had been baptized some time ago – twice, in fact – in both an Orthodox church and a Baptist one. A graduate of a Christian seminary, he knew the Bible well and had preached in various countries. On his social media accounts, many young people reached out with words of gratitude and questions about life and marriage. The war created a great demand for humanitarian projects. Being the head of one of these, he could enter the offices of any Christian leader of his country. In churches and houses of worship, wherever their humanitarian aid would arrive, he was a welcome guest, always invited to speak or preach. So, he felt as though he had unhindered access to God. The apostle Paul's local representatives became his business partners and sent him reports on their completed work. Churches and houses of worship threw open their gates for his trucks filled with humanitarian aid.

The country was plunged into war. He was drinking. The darkness could barely conceal the void it had once hidden. Yet he kept thinking that God was near and on his side. It took quitting drinking and being late to an Easter service in a Dutch temple for him to realize that the doors had been locked for a while now and that there was no fellowship between the darkness within him and the light.

He was sitting on a stone bench by the temple, and he was crying. These tears, it seemed, turned his heart of stone into a living one. It was broken, groaning, and wailing in pain, but it was trembling and ablaze. He was only a few steps away from the singing, the light, and the church people. Getting in was impossible, but, suddenly, he saw the church clearly – all the Christians in big cities and tiny villages, in peaceful countries and in his own, ravaged by war. Everywhere there was light, but inside him was darkness. He had drifted too far from the shore and the campfire where the Teacher had prepared fish for his disciples. That's how it happens when you're a child – you swim out on a float and doze off, only to wake up and realize that the wind and waves have carried you far from the strip of life-saving land.

So, on that Easter morning, right there by the locked doors of a temple, he understood just how far he had drifted away. And right then, for the first time in many months, he felt his heart beating again and believed that the darkness dwelling within it could become light once more. He asked God, who had kept him out of a Dutch church, to give him back the light. He believed that despite the shut doors, he was part of the church again, that he was heard and cared for. Life began to change course – sailing farther away from the void, moving closer to the shore. He wept, and the darkness within him dissolved into a grey fog. Then deep inside it, the sun came forth. And there was light. And so it was Easter. The first day.

Second Day: The Ukrainian Sky

And God called the firmament Heaven.

Genesis 1:8 (KJV)

A taxi driver – a Tajik – drove through Warsaw as if he were high and still cruising the streets of his home town, Khujand. This driver really liked talking to his passengers.

"Where are you from?"

"Ukraine."

"Where are you going now?"

"Coming back home."

"Why would you do that? Isn't there a war there?"

He didn't know how to reply. He just knew that he had to go back. He had cargo to deliver – medical supplies gathered by a volunteer group that worked day and night to ensure that vulnerable elderly people and wounded soldiers would have all the medicine they needed. So he picked it up and headed for Ukraine. In a few hours, the Polish clouds – that looked a bit like dumplings – would give way to the sky of his home country. The Ukrainian sky.

He remembered all too well the night when that sky turned firm from all the iron bursting through the windows and children's dreams. That winter morning had begun so abruptly, like preterm labour. The sky, filled with howling and flashing, turned fiery red. "Close the sky!" the people cried out, as if the sky had become a knocked-down door.

Nobody did close the sky. Instead, it brought forth more hard strikes – again and again, and more often – targeting cities, houses, and lives, driving people into basements and underground metro stations.

He met a little girl once. "How old are you?" he asked. She raised three fingers. The girl's father took him aside and explained that she was actually four but they were not telling her that. On her birthday, there was supposed to be cake and a party; instead, bright and early, came missiles from the sky. She spent her special day in a basement – with a low concrete ceiling as her sky. Those missiles didn't kill the girl. Just her birthday.

> Then we embellish our missiles with stars and pride
> Sprinkle on them holy water 'cause that's the rite

Lower them ever so gently onto the ground
Point to the sky vicious nose cones of every round
Scribble some words, paint our sigils and seals on them
Pat their all-cast sides, admiring their newfound glam
Tell them: That's it, fam! And now it's godspeed, g'bye!
Surely, we'll miss you, but it's time for you to fly.
Dryly respond to us missiles from way up high:
Over community show we'll do a fly-by
Shoo little pooches and peeps not so far away
Drop by the party for that little girl's b-day.[1]

That experience of light he had in the Dutch town was still strong as he drew closer to the war again. The Ukrainian army liberated town after town, and the locals began to emerge from their underground hiding places. After a prolonged curfew imposed by the invaders, people ventured out onto the streets, wandering amid looted stores and burned-down gas stations, stepping over ripped wires and dead dogs. By the entrances to apartment towers, people lit campfires just to cook their meals. As Russian troops retreated, they left in their wake a land filled with mines and cities filled with hunger.

He sat in the cab of a truck with humanitarian aid right at the entrance to one such town. The day was sunny, warm, and quiet. Tanks had already left, heading east, but due to the lack of gasoline, no local cars were on the road, which was littered with burned vehicles. At the entrance was a checkpoint set up by the Ukrainian army. Beyond it was a small patch of woods and some residential buildings. He stopped the truck just past the checkpoint and stepped out, carefully watching his every step. The cell service was still out, so he had to figure out where to go next to deliver his cargo. There was no rumbling, no death falling from above – the sky was gorgeous, clear, and peaceful. He walked ahead towards some refrigerator trucks parked by the woods. There were some police cars there. Around the corner, there were more military SUVs and some vans. People in white protective coveralls, gloves, and masks climbed out and entered the woods.

He walked closer – and was stopped by police officers. He wasn't allowed to go farther. But he could see well enough: dozens of oblong pits, mounds of dirt and sand, people in coveralls shovelling and pulling human bodies out of those opened graves.

---

1. An excerpt from a poem by Slava Malakhov, a Russian poet currently imprisoned for his anti-war position; the entire original poem in Russian can be found on Malakhov's personal Telegram account: https://t.me/slavamalah/680.

A lot of bodies. A lot of shovels. An eerie silence in those ghastly woods. He saw the graves of tortured and murdered residents of that town. Pictures of these shallow graves in the quiet woods would soon spread all over the world. But until then, he stood there and watched a tiny body being pulled from the sand and placed in a black body bag. Behind him, the doors of the refrigerator trucks were opening and closing. Above him, the Ukrainian sky was swiftly turning hard and rigid – stiff, like the arm of a dead child.

On his way back, he stayed in Kharkiv. During the night, the welkin rang hard again as a few missiles struck near his hotel. He lay on the floor, listening to the hammering and pounding getting closer and closer. Walls were shaking, people were running up and down the hallway, yet he just lay there. The sky questioned him: "To live? What for?" And so it was. The second day.

Third Day: The Fruits

> And God said, Let the earth bring forth . . . the fruit tree yielding fruit after his kind . . .
>
> Genesis 1:11 (KJV)

The tree branches bent low with all the fruits, yet there was no one to eat them. Water was the first to run out – after shelling struck first the waterline and then the repair team that tried to fix it. Next, the city was hit by cluster munitions. So the people left, taking their children with them. Cherries, apples, and apricots were ripening under the hot southern sun; the branches were bent low to the ground, but there were no hands to pick them. Trees were broken by blasts and pierced by shrapnel; overripe fruits were strewn underneath, starting to rot. Trees were dying, yet still standing upright, ever faithful to their calling – to yield fruit.

People who had stopped building, trading, growing trees, and raising kids a long time ago – they, too, stayed true to themselves. Those people chanted "We can do it again!" so often that one day, they made war again. They started the killing. It was inevitable.

Once, he was part of a panel discussion – an attempt to figure out why the Russo-Ukrainian (2014) war began. He sat on the stage and looked at the audience with their watchful eyes and craned necks. Those Americans, representatives of the southern clans, were sincerely trying to understand what had driven the Russians to start this terrible war. "They could not do otherwise," was all the answer he could give them. They could not do otherwise.

Residents of one liberated village told him about the time they had spent under occupation. Soldiers – Russian boys – didn't mess with the locals, except for beating two local drunks who had tried to take pictures of armoured vehicles. But there were many, many hungry soldiers. They slaughtered the villagers' cattle. By the time they left, there were no sheep, no cows, and no goats left in the entire village. The walnut orchard was burned down. The fields were strewn with mines. That village reminded him of African settlements he had seen, where people simply sat for hours on brown, barren ground. "What do they do all day?" he remembered asking their guide. "Nothing. Waiting. A Christian mission comes in with food on Mondays. A Muslim mission comes in with clothes and hygiene items on Thursday. Sometimes, a truckload of government humanitarian aid comes in. This morning, some tourists ran over a wild beast on the road – so the locals will be dressing, cooking, and eating it."

Ukrainian villages became much like those African settlements – hardworking Ukrainian people with nothing left to do except wait in line for food aid distribution. These are the fruits of the tree of Russian statehood and the army knives of the Russian "boys." Why did they do this? Because every tree yields fruit according to its kind.

The Tajik taxi driver who took him all over Warsaw had his doubts: "Bro, maybe it's Americans warring with Russians in your country? Perhaps they started it?" No, brother, it's the Russians who are warring with us, Ukrainians. The Americans might be helping us, but they're not fighting in our stead. Sure, China and Iran are helping the Russians, but it was not the Chinese people who destroyed the waterline in his home town, nor was it Iranians who slaughtered all the cattle in that village. It was the Russian boys – these are the fruits from their tree. What the Americans did do was to drill deep wells and install water purification systems in his town.

Joining him on this food distribution trip is Pastor Zhenia – a kind, chubby man, who was placed on a kill list by Russia's Federal Security Service.

Pastor Zhenia rolls out of the truck filled with food, hygiene items, flashlights, and other items the villagers might need. His smile shines brighter than Kherson's southern sun. People instantly begin to approach the vehicle – boys arrive on their bikes, women help grannies in colourful kerchiefs. The pastor has a real – and rare – gift of talking to people. He doesn't preach at them. He doesn't rant or proclaim. He simply talks to them. Zhenia tells of his experiences – about living under occupation, about evacuating his elderly mother through the fields, and about driving across a bridge under fire with a car full of orphans. When Zhenia speaks, he clasps his tanned hands over his chest. An old lady beside him cups her hand over her ear to hear him better. Her head is adorned with a patterned kerchief as splendid as a peacock's tail. A boy, chubby like the pastor himself, stands right beside him. Dogs sprawl in the tree shade. People don't just listen to Zhenia, they talk to him, too. They tell him of slaughtered cattle, of water shortages, of a neighbouring village that is even worse off than they are. Zhenia is one of them, one of their own – not some UN or humanitarian aid worker. Every time this pastor comes through the village, people ask him to stay just a little bit longer. As a result, he has no set schedule – and is always late for everything. Zhenia's car is stuffed to the brim with food boxes, sanitary pads, and bagged apples – and he gives them out freely to whoever has a need, with no paperwork required to prove it.

People don't leave even after they receive aid packages from Zhenia. Today, a singer came along with the pastor. She's performed on stages all over the world, but today she's getting hugs from two village girls. People sing along to the "Red Viburnum" song and pray the Lord's Prayer along with Zhenia. They listen to the story of Jesus Christ, who was a refugee: Jesus was not born in a house but in a stable, and he did not die peacefully in his own home. People stand there, by the shrapnel-battered wall of a village hall, only a short drive from the front line. And he stands there with them.

In the middle of a southern village ravaged by war people come together, also ravaged by that war, to pray to the Father who is in heaven. There are no stone fingers of Dutch temples here, nor are there doors that can be locked. There's but the fruit that the tree yields after its kind. And so, this is the church. The third day.

Fourth Day: The Stars

> And God made two great lights; the greater light to rule the day,
> and the lesser light to rule the night: he made the stars also.
>
> Genesis 1:16 (KJV)

"So how does it work then? God creates the light on the first day and the luminaries – sun, moon, stars – on the fourth. Where did that light come from if there was nothing to give that light?" his father asks him with a condescending smile. His father is a member of the Communist Party of the USSR. A thick Atheist's Handbook lies on the desk. His father doesn't mind arguing with him, an eleven-year-old, about the existence of God. But it's less of a debate and more of a decimation – the young son has no good answer for his father.

The first day described in Genesis is indeed a conundrum. The light is there, but there isn't yet anything that could shine that light. How that is possible, he doesn't know. And if it is impossible, then Genesis is a badly crafted fairy tale, and so is God. A fairy tale. Checkmate.

The years pass. By the time he figures out how light can exist without a source, the answer is far too late. His father has already passed away.

So his father isn't there when this realization sinks in, but his father becomes one of those stars that keep shining even after they disappear. That's what stars do – they shine long after they're gone. Their light is the experiences and stories of other people in your life.

One such story was about a certain captain. His grandma shared it with him shortly before her passing. She told him of a man whose words had stayed with her for life. His grandma's large family had been deported to the Far North of Russia after having all their possessions confiscated. In Soviet newspeak, they were "enemies of the people" and so had to be "dekulakized." There in the Far North, in the small village of Teriberka, some of their children died and had to be buried in that cold, rock-hard ground, while others dug into that northern soil and survived. Years later, right before the start of the Soviet-Finnish War, people with weapons and service dogs came for the survivors. "Enemies of the people" might turn traitor and join the Finns, so they were "dekulakized" once again, stripped of all their possessions and shipped off into the unknown.

One day, as he was hanging out with his university classmates, they talked about Stalin's role. "Sure, there was a cult of personality. But what a personality it was. What a magnificent epoch it was. Victims? Well, chop a tree for wood, lose some to splinters,"[2] one of them said. "Well, would you have liked being one of them splinters?" asked another.

Maybe someone else can be that splinter. Not I. I'd rather watch the expanse of the logging and marvel – from afar. I won't bother anyone. I won't interfere. Should the splinters from chopping wood fall at my feet, I'll step over them ever so carefully. That's what many people had been – and still are – thinking. Until the moment that axe falls on their own heads.

His grandma didn't want to be a splinter. That cold morning, she, along with other "enemies of the people," was hurried out of her home and escorted to the shore of the Barents Sea. The guards forced them into the ship's hold and closed the hatch – and the ship set sail. Rough waters had those "splinters" thrown about the hold. The air was thick with the fumes of chemicals that the ship must have transported previously. Women and the elderly began to feel unwell; children began crying; cold, seeping from the depths of the sea through

---

2. This is a loose translation of an old Russian proverb, similar to the English saying "You can't make an omelette without breaking eggs."

the ship's hull, sapped life from their bodies... Then suddenly, the horror was over. Grandma remembered very vividly and told him how someone from the outside opened the hatch and called the people out – towards fresh air and sunlight. As they were climbing out onto the deck, the ship's captain addressed those shivering "splinters" – and his words stuck with Grandma her entire life: "Comrades, do come out. I don't do slave transporting here."

After that, they were quartered in cabins to warm up and transported to whatever destination the captain had been ordered to take them. He had no power to change the fate of these poor folks who were, for this grand country, not actual human beings but "dekulakized enemies of the people," splinters of the grand logging operation.

Grandma didn't know what happened to the captain afterwards, whether he was punished for his actions and words. Nor did the captain know that he had become a star. The light from that star travelled through Grandma's life and keeps shining. It shines even now, the light of a story about courage, dignity, and mercy. Yes, the captain had no say in the fate of those to whom he returned freedom and dignity, albeit for a short while. But his story became the light of a long-gone star, a story that changed the lives of those who heard it.

Courage to make decisions and be merciful. Readiness to set the oppressed free. Ability to choose the words that restore human dignity. When he does these things, too, the captain's star shines again.

But can a not-yet-existing star still shine? Can an invisible luminary give guidance and comfort? Yes, it sure can. This light is faith – believing in the seemingly impossible. This light is a dream – longing for the inconceivable. In such instances, a star shines even when it doesn't exist yet. Hope and dreams are its rays.

His daughter once asked him, "Dad, what's your dream?" He didn't know how to answer. His life had known the light of long-gone stars – the stories and experiences of others – that had helped him by providing comfort and support. But a dream? That was missing. Nothing glimmered on the horizon; nothing lit his path. He lived gazing into his own shadow, stumbling in the dark.

Of course, he'd had a dream a long time ago. He had imagined where he wanted to go and what he wanted to be down to minute details. His first dream job was as a groundskeeper at a preschool. He swept the walkways and collected rubbish. In winter, he would clear ice patches and sprinkle sand so that the ground wouldn't be so slippery. In summer, he'd sweep decks and porches, taking in the morning's calm and looking forward to the moment when kids would rush out onto clean wooden floors, shouting, "Hi, Mr. Yardman!" Autumn would bring wave after wave of fallen leaves he had to row through and rake in, swimming in the billows of white smoke as he burned them. He'd visit a metal scrap dealer (who looked a bit like a crab) to get back shoe scrapers stolen by junkies, drink coffee, and talk about God. He swung his broom, shovelled, dragged old sheets full of leaves . . . and dreamed, and dreamed, and dreamed.

And all those dreams came true! He pushed forward, pressed on, climbed higher, and took leaps . . . Then, finally, he understood: he had arrived. In some way or another, whatever he was dreaming of came to pass. But a new dream didn't arise. He'd lived for a few years in a kind of lull, as if he'd dozed off for a nice afternoon nap. Then one day, the blast wave from a missile that hit a nearby military base rattled his bedroom windows. War broke out.

So the war had begun, and one day, in a barracks, with a military ID in his pocket and an assault rifle by his headboard, he felt the light coming from nowhere. Rays of a star yet to exist touched his tightly shut eyes.

He began to dream again. He saw clearly – as in a picture – his entire family and himself standing on a walkway by a house that didn't look familiar. He imagined himself behind the wheel of a truck, moving down a bustling road. He dreamed of picking just the right words, ones that would sprout in his head like seeds so that he'd be able to pass the tender sprouts along to those who'd plant them in their own ground.

That's when he took a step out of the shadows and started preparing to go. His journey would take him to where his fears lay and to where the ray of that not-yet-existing star came from. This ray was the dream – proof of the existence of the inconceivable, faith in what he hadn't yet seen. And so he stepped out of the shadows. It was the fourth day.

Fifth Day: Dolphin

> And God said, Let the waters bring forth abundantly the moving creature that hath life, and fowl that may fly above the earth in the open firmament of heaven.
>
> Genesis 1:20 (KJV)

Loud children's voices woke him up. He was quite astounded as there were no children in the house he was staying in. The rooms were empty, tea towels draped over a kitchen chair and cups on a table. A toy box was shoved under a desk in the nursery, clothes hung neatly in closets, and books were arranged on shelves. But not a single child. It was as if they'd left that morning to go to school and would return in the evening to their books, jumpers, toys, and tea . . . except, they didn't come back. In those days, many houses in his homeland looked awfully like old photographs of the ghost town Prypiat, which was abandoned after the Chernobyl disaster.

Befuddled with sleep, he had mistaken the chirping of birds for children's voices. That spring, flocks of birds arriving after overwintering moved in the opposite direction of flocks of refugees fleeing. White storks flew back to their old nests, which were still on the same utility poles, except now the wires were snapped and the roofs of nearby houses were full of holes, like old beaten-up shipping boxes.

Ukrainian children were learning to speak Polish, English, and Dutch. Ukrainian birds were still chirping in their bird language. Ukrainian fish swam silently among mines.

The house was empty, awakened by birds, not children. He drank a glass of water and checked his phone. His Signal app had a message from Dolphin, asking for help with buying a wetsuit. Russian soldiers had fled from occupied Kherson, but had made fortifications on the other bank of the River Dnipro, from where they shelled the city daily. Dolphin's unit was under orders to cross the river and take out the enemy's firing posts. Humans had to turn into fish – which required appropriate gear and clothes.

He had met Dolphin a long time ago, when the trees in his home town weren't yet withering, Russian soldiers weren't yet slaughtering cattle in the surrounding villages, tap water was fine to drink, and father was there, willing to read bits of the story of this peculiar Jesus Christ to him. At 11:00 a.m., he had been baptized in an Orthodox temple, but later he began visiting a local music school where a Baptist congregation met on Sundays. Dolphin – a quiet, smiling boy – came there with his grandma. The boys often walked home together after youth group services, talking about God and bicycles. Poplar fluff wafted in the breeze, folks huddled around guitar players perched on benches, dates were happening at the corner café "Coolness," and local maternity wards discharged happy parents and fussy newborns every day.

Much time had passed since then. Then came a day when all that was over. Crimea, overtaken by "polite people," marked the beginning of the Russian army's invasion of Ukraine. People on the streets were falling victim to cluster shell bombings, the trees were felled to reinforce dugouts, children were evacuated, and Dolphin went to war. He made a good soldier, earned a good reputation with his commanding officers, and even became a commanding officer himself. That's when he and his unit received dolphin patches as part of their insignia.

They met up a few times. There was that time when Pastor Zhenia led a makeshift communion service – for Dolphin, two other soldiers, and himself – by pouring bought wine into plastic cups and breaking a baguette with his bronzed hands. He had thought Dolphin looked great, fit and kitted up. But now, almost a year since the full-scale invasion, he noticed that Dolphin had grown tense and that his laugh was shorter and choppier. Now, Dolphin would send him messages about brothers-in-arms killed in actions in the waters of the Dnipro. They didn't talk about God and bicycles any more. Still, Dolphin stayed true to himself – a courageous, honest, and upright person. The war couldn't turn him into a vicious, prehistoric predator swimming in muddled waters among the mines. Today, Dolphin had messaged him about a wetsuit.

This request should have sounded strange – yet it didn't. Even though war had festered on the peripheries of the country for several years now, the army still lacked modern weapons and gear. So it is now, and so it was back in 2014, when, down south near Russian-occupied Crimea, he met a few good men. They seemed rather overwhelmed, wearing forest camouflage uniforms that stuck out on the Southern plains. Still, they worked hard, digging trenches for themselves and pits for old Soviet military vehicles in dry, rock-hard steppe soil. These were Ukrainian soldiers hastily deployed from Central Ukraine to the South. Logistics were all awry: no water, no rations, and not even enough shovels or sandbags to build those entrenchments. People from nearby villages and towns came to help. Residents of southern Ukraine are usually Russian-speaking and often considered to have Russian leanings. However, the Ukrainian army was met with a grassroots volunteer movement that had already begun to sprout. Members of local government, business people, students and faculty of universities, farmers, and priests all offered their help. Pastor Zhenia approached the soldiers with an offer to pray for them. When met with, "Would love to, but right now we got to dig, not pray," he picked up a shovel and started digging.

Back then, at the very beginning of the Russo-Ukrainian war, many people rushed to meet the numerous needs of the Ukrainian army. Inexplicably, many cared so much that they came to the aid of struggling soldiers who lacked gear and were forced to fight with outdated Soviet weaponry. At the time, he, too, was collecting aid for solders on the front lines. What really caught him off guard, though, was the diversity of people who approached him with offers to help: a woman who had fled Nagorno-Karabakh years earlier and made her home in Ukraine; a skinny young couple whose single-room flat was stacked with boxes upon boxes of hygiene items; a wedding officiant who spent hours in a cold storage warehouse digging through second-hand clothing to find warm, dark-coloured clothes in men's sizes; successful lawyers who bought several hundreds of Kevlar helmets from Balkan thugs; a group of friends, just meeting for a beer, who pitched in to order several bulletproof army vests online; and, at a clandestine warehouse storing military supplies that looked like they had been squirrelled away from NATO aid shipments, a dealer asked, "What kind of chest rig do you want? I just had somebody from a church pick out ones with pockets for grenades."

The army's military equipment was largely embezzled. The country was weathering a serious economic crisis. The Russian subversive agent Strelkov's thugs were active in the East, while the Russian army was amassing troops in the South. The future of the entire country seemed extremely uncertain. There was almost nothing: no military equipment, no weapons, no solid government, no stable economy. Yet out of that "almost nothing," people made something incredible – they made "everything." All over his country, people picked up whatever little they could and passed it along to those in dire need: to villages ravaged by war, to cities liberated from Russian occupation, to dugouts and trenches, to hospitals, to orphanages, and to nursing homes.

All this reminded him of the story he'd read long ago with his father. In it, the day was nearing its end, and the disciples spoke to their teacher, saying something along the lines of, "Well, sure, there are a lot of people seeking your help, but it's time to wrap it up so they can get to the nearest villages and find something to eat." In response, the Teacher asked the disciples to share their food with the crowd. What they were able to gather was very little: five loaves of bread and two fish. After the Teacher pronounced the Jewish prayer of blessing over that paltry sustenance, the disciples began passing it out to the people. Bread and fish kept multiplying as more and more hands received their share of the gift offered by the disciples. Matthew describes it like this: "The number of those who ate was about five thousand men" (Matt 14:21), adding, like a true son of his times, "besides women and children" – who, very likely, were many.

Genesis tells us that on the fifth day, God created in the water "the moving creature that hath life" (Gen 1:20 KJV) – the ancestor of the very fish that would be multiplied by Jesus's disciples to feed the hungry crowd. And so, the story unfolded right before his eyes – in his own country, multitudes were doing the same thing Jesus's disciples did. They gathered up what little they had to give to those who had even less, and as they passed it forward, they realized with awe and wonder just how much they actually had. During the few meetings he had with Dolphin on the outskirts of their home town, which is now the front line, they talked very little. Usually, it was just exchanging a few phrases while standing next to Dolphin's camo-painted SUV. Wordy chaff fell away easily;

the weave of complex semantic constructs could not hold grand questions that didn't yet have an answer. During those meetings, the talk wasn't as important as seeing that Dolphin remained true to himself, that the war hadn't changed him into a shark, or a piranha, or an amorphous, limp jellyfish.

Sometimes, words of praise and honour are written about fallen heroes. Yet he wills and wants this mention of Dolphin here to be a prayer for protection and a long life: "Oh Lord, you have created life in the waters and multiplied fish in the hands of your disciples. May the life of Dolphin always be in your hands, and just as the fish were multiplied, may the days of his life increase. Amen."

As he stood there with Dolphin, he began to realize that for questions about life, death, and destiny – questions as heavy as waterlogged cabinets in flooded houses in Kherson – the answers would not come in the form of words but through his own decisions. Ukrainian birds were returning to their nests, and their chirping filled the void left by absent children's voices. The Ukrainian fish, Dolphin, went to war so that the children could return, too. The time had come to respond to the pressing questions of who he was and what he was there for. "To live? What for?" the Ukrainian sky had asked him on the second day. "To be yourself" was his answer. And so it was the fifth day.

The Sixth Day: Creation of People

> And God said, Let us make man in our image, after our likeness . . .
> Genesis 1:26 (KJV)

All that was left to do was to buy a bowl. The last time he'd held a bowl was during a camping trip in Crimea with his father. They had spent a week cave-crawling, sleeping in a tent, and, at the end of it, a few days by the seashore. During that trip, his father had a fling with a lady – a speleologist who was part of the group. The entire group watched this romance unfold. The lovebirds would take off into the woods for a while, and he – only ten years old at the time – was left by the campfire, unsettled and confused, fiddling with his bowl.

Right now, too, holding a bowl with a Krauff stamp on the bottom, he was perplexed. Trying to fit it into his backpack, he tried to think about other things he might need to add to the mix. The next morning, he'd have to make an appearance at the enlistment office and be off to the army. He packed a change of undergarments, some toilet paper, a book, and a stash of medicine. His last backpacking trip had been thirty-three years ago, and he had trouble imagining what it would look like to enter a barrack, drop his backpack, and become a soldier as a forty-four-year-old man.

"My Mykhailo got drafted." The message for an ex-colleague came through when he was in the fancy bathroom of a Hilton hotel. American consultants and Japanese journalists were hanging out in the hotel's lobby. The religious persecution in the territories occupied by Russia was the main topic of conversation over breakfast. Japanese journalists would conduct interviews, then turn off the cameras and go get coffee and orange juice. Air-raid alerts blasted throughout the night, compelling consultants, glasses of whisky in hand, to take refuge in a bomb shelter. On the outskirts of the country, the war raged on. Large cities suffered from missile and kamikaze UAV attacks, but restaurants remained open, street musicians busked, and forums were held on rebuilding the country after the victory that would come oh-so-soon, in just a few months . . .

At the enlistment offices, new groups of men kept forming. Fewer and fewer of them were warriors of light, bright-eyed and bushy-tailed; more and more were men with shoulders bent by the years and legs riddled with varicose veins.

"My Mykhailo got drafted . . ." That's when he realized that he needed to get ready, too.

So, one early morning in May, in the courtyard of an enlistment office, he stood smiling, the bowl nestled in his backpack. For the first time in his life, he marched in formation with other recruits, was compelled to show off his umbilical hernia to a captain of the medical corps, and received his uniform and weapons. Around him, other men – cussing at times – struggled to put on their stiff new military fatigues. All of a sudden, everyone looked the same, save for a few bearded or bespectacled men. The fatigues and AK rifles instantly transformed a motley crew of recruits on a smoke break in a courtyard into neat squads of identical soldiers. He stood there in one of the squads and kept smiling. Freedom was forfeit. Instead, he got a top bunk bed, perpetual exhaustion, a sore throat, and a hole in the bathroom floor. Yet faith remained: as long as he keeps on smiling, he stays true to himself.

At 4:00 a.m., a month later, he was in a dugout, surrounded by uniformed armed men sleeping in whatever odd positions they could get comfortable in. He just couldn't sleep, so he stayed up, tending the fire in a pot-bellied stove. He was struck by a strange feeling – as if he were surrounded by soldiers of the Terracotta Army, frozen in time, buried deep underground, just waiting to be unearthed. They all stayed ever so still, except for him, sitting there and throwing more wood into the underground stove. Above them, on the surface, wars, empires, hunger, and disease raged on. But they were beyond it all, safe – at least for now – though already changed. Logs crackled in the stove, everyone lay perfectly still, and he didn't want to make a single move.

There was no need for drinking booze any more, nor for the perpetual working up of dead mud-dough roads that always led towards war. No need to prove anything to anyone; no need to tell yourself that really he's not one to get taken into a concentration camp and wiggle out of it a pay cheque and living arrangements. So many debates inside him ceased, so many questions got answered as soon as he realized what he had to do. The army didn't become an answer in and of itself but, rather, became a space where he could see himself as he was meant to be. "Let us create man," said the Lord. Sure, at times, he still thinks that he's the one who creates and shapes himself, the way a piece of clay might think in the hands of a master potter. But at the end of the day, he knows that everything is in the hands of the One who, at times, is as hard to see as the light of a not-yet-existing star.

His shoulder marks had no stars that signified a higher rank; he was just an ordinary soldier. However, there was now one star – the most important one – shining for him. And now, ahead of him was not just the unknown but also the glimmer of light for a luminary yet to exist. He smiled, for everything had been done right. And that was the sixth day.

The Present Day: City at the End of the Road

> And I saw a new heaven and new earth:
> for the first heaven and the first earth were passed away; and
> there was no more sea.
> And I John saw the holy city,
> new Jerusalem, coming down from God out of heaven . . .
> Revelation 21:1–2 (KJV)

Imam Mohammed, junior lieutenant of the Chaplaincy Service, carefully portioned out rice pilaf into plastic plates and gave them to Father Oleh. Father Oleh, chaplain and priest of a chapel within the walls of this hospital, passed the plates to the men sitting in the shade of sprawling trees. Shura, a Jewish lady volunteering at the hospital, alternated between helping Oleh and Mohammed. A thought crossed his mind that this could be paradise as imagined by some liberal-leaning theologians – an Arab Muslim, a Jewish Christian, and an Orthodox priest feeding rice pilaf to wounded soldiers. Mohammed was so friendly, smiling gently into his beard. Shura would have a plate and a kind word for each one of her charges. Father Oleh would take time to sit and talk and offer hugs to everyone. Is this not a picture of paradise – except real, not painted – with beaten men being served by Love itself?

"There is no road back to Eden. There's only one that calls us ahead to the New Jerusalem," Andrii, a Jesuit, had once told him. Perhaps the heavenly Jerusalem will not resemble a hospital courtyard with angels named Shura, Oleh, and Mohammed. Perhaps everything will be drastically different there, but there's no way to go back to the lost paradise, where dusty mirrors, empty cribs, and dying poplars now linger. There's no way but forward, he thought to himself. Don't give up; push ahead, get used to uncertainty, and keep going like a dog that's following an army marching band. A dog's ears perk up, hearing the music, but it cannot tell the melody from the clamour. Still, what's important is that there is a melody – and that it has an author, too – and that on this road to the Heavenly City, he walks together with Jesuit Andrii, Imam Mohammed, volunteer Shura, and Father Oleh.

Jesuit Andrii had told him:

> Military chaplaincy is the church's mission to the military community. This mission begins with presence. A chaplain is a sign of God's presence and care. He must be seen, must be close. Through this "sign" – a chaplain – soldiers will "glean" the meaning of his presence here: to create opportunities for service men and women to receive spiritual care. A chaplain cares for the integrity of a soldier's spirit, a platoon's spirit, a CO's spirit . . . The mark of being real as humans is the ability to feel pain: if we feel pain, we're alive. But pain is not a reason to stop but, rather, a drive that pushes us forward towards the place where pain is no more. And that's what needs to be accomplished today: to take collective responsibility for a future without pain and to strive towards new horizons for Ukraine, which has been in all our dreams.

When Russian "polite people" took over Crimea, he and his friends were going to the southern parts of Ukraine to support Ukrainian soldiers. At the time, very few were calling themselves "chaplains," but the Lord was already multiplying the bread and fish – people went to share with the soldiers far more than what they could gather on their own. At one of the truck stops – a café for drivers – a tipsy woman blurted out, "I'd sell Ukraine if I could. I'd sell it for six dollars." A Lutheran priest, a German with the Ukrainian surname Shevchenko, replied, "I'm buying then."

Shura, Mohammed, Andrii, and Oleh are buying Ukraine right now. Each one of them, along with many other chaplains, men and women alike, are serving as signs of God's presence for the soldiers amid this great war. Each soldier whom they care for – they, too, are buying Ukraine. And the price is not a measly six dollars; it's six litres of blood running through each of their veins. The chaplaincy movement in Ukraine today is precisely about that: the blood, the struggle, the presence, the way. And an imam, a priest, a rabbi, and a pastor – all united by and around a Ukrainian soldier.

So, he had to stop drinking, weep at the locked doors of a temple, put on a uniform, and join the army . . . to find, amid the darkness and fear, the way towards the New City.

He will remember for the rest of his life the train station in Kyiv in March 2022 – the dim lighting, the wail of the sirens, the crowds of people. He overheard a woman next to him, who leaned over to her son and asked, "Is it too dark for you here? Are you afraid?" He spent the entire trip from Kyiv to Lviv in the vestibule of the carriage, hiding his face in his hands. Since their carriage was the last on this train, he could look out the back window and see the rails, checkpoints on the roads, and military vehicles. Everything he saw through that window kept getting smaller and smaller before disappearing from sight. So did his previous life – an Eden to which the road was forever gone. Their house was empty, their office in Irpin was occupied and burned, and their family – along with the two cats stuffed into the carrier – had crossed the border into Poland, just like many other refugees. For the next two years, those questions voiced by that woman from Kyiv's train station kept popping up in his mind: "Is it too dark here? Are you afraid?"

He witnessed the exhumation of bodies in Izium and was caught in the shelling in Mykolaiv, Kyiv, and Kharkiv. He stared into the night sky, clutching the cool metal of his weapon, and made his way among the people who burned campfires in the courtyards of apartment towers. Was he afraid? Yes. The darkness that swelled in March 2022 didn't leave him by daylight. Often, waking up in abandoned houses, he'd look at dusty mirrors decorated with stickers, wilted flowers, and dishes left on a table and realize that he was once again dreaming about falling into dark waters, sinking deeper and deeper. Was it dark there? Yes. Life had become a mishmash of war, darkness, and fear. Yet amid this fear, darkness, and war, he saw the light of the not-yet-existing star and felt underfoot the way to the city that awaited him at the end of that road.

His life turned out to be longer than he had ever imagined. He celebrated his forty-fifth birthday in a soldier's uniform, but the change that happened to him was not just on the outside but also on the inside: he has learned to have hope and to be patient. And now, he's grateful to God for his family and the people who didn't vanish into the darkness. But most importantly, he's no longer afraid.

"Mission means going the same way as your people and leading them to God. God himself knew no other way to bring salvation than to leave everything he had to become a part of this world in a particular place and time, to live through what his people were living through and bring them to the Father. He had no other way – and neither do we" Yevhen Yazvinskyy (p. 169)

7

I Will Follow You: Where Will You Lead Me?

Yevhen Yazvinskyy

Sergeant, Armed Forces of Ukraine; Communications Officer, 115th Mechanized Brigade of the Armed Forces of Ukraine

A Little about Us

I'm a fourth-generation Baptist. My great-grandfather, who lived in Ukraine, became an evangelical believer before the Bolshevik Revolution. He was searching for God but could not find him in the traditional church. God gave him a dream, directing him – if he truly was searching for God – to go on Sunday to a specific address in another village, a long way from home. My great-grandfather believed the dream and went there. He found a gathering of evangelical Christians, a denomination relatively new in Tsarist Russia. And that's how he became an evangelical Christian. My great-grandfather was "dekulakized": they took away all his property and destroyed the mill he had built. They imprisoned him for his faith and, before he was taken away, ripped the roof off his house, leaving his wife and five children without a breadwinner or a roof over their heads right in the middle of winter. But God took care of them all: his wife and children all survived, and miraculously, like the apostle Peter, he was released from prison. But that's a whole other story.

When I was very young, my parents were not believers. Even though my father came from a large Christian family, he did not attend church. However, when I was about seven or eight, he became a Christian, and my mom followed suit a few years later. As a child, I attended Sunday school, where my teachers took children's spiritual growth very seriously. We had to memorize not just Bible verses but entire chapters of the Bible. I wasn't happy about this back then; but thirty years later, amid war, I was so grateful for the lessons I was taught there.

That was my childhood. Children generally believe everything they're told and perceive the world much the way their community paints it. As a teenager, I lived a double life – being one way at church and quite different at school. I was shy about my faith. Eventually, however, I decided to surrender my life to Christ. I didn't want to be shy about my faith – I wanted to be an approachable, contemporary Christian. I had a passion for Jesus and wanted to share his message with people around me. While attending university, I witnessed to my fellow students and organized outreach events. Later, I joined Campus Crusade for Christ and became its local leader. After graduation, I decided to be a full-time missionary to university students.

My wife, Olena, comes from a different background. Her parents were not believers. Although they identified as Orthodox, they hardly ever went to church and practised a sort of "folk Orthodoxy."

After the collapse of the Soviet Union, Ukraine faced a major economic crisis. Many people were unemployed, and many men turned to alcohol. Olena's father, too, started drinking heavily. God orchestrated events so that Olena's mother began working at the same place as the pastor of a Baptist church. He talked to her and repeatedly invited her to church. I imagine he was also praying for the family. Eventually, Olena and her mother did go to that church, and so began their journey of seeking God.

A Christian summer camp left a profound and lasting impression on Olena. Her mother began attending that Baptist church regularly and eventually accepted Jesus into her heart. Around the same time, Olena, who was in her first year of university, also surrendered her life to God. Her father was vehemently opposed to them attending the Baptist church because he was in the grip of communist propaganda about Protestant churches. Olena tried to witness to her father, but he adamantly rejected her words and took to drinking heavily. Olena and her mother began to pray that God would reveal himself to her father through dreams. And God did. Not long after, her father began reading the Bible secretly and watching various Christian broadcasts on TV. Then, one Sunday morning, they watched him respond to an altar call at their church and repent.

Olena also volunteered with Campus Crusade in her home town, became a local leader, and, after graduating from university, served as a full-time missionary to students. I met her at one of the outreach summer projects where our organization gathered volunteers from all over Ukraine. Over the next few days, I saw her heart for God and ministry – and I fell head over heels in love. Two years later, we got married.

We were involved in student ministry for seven years in Odesa, in the south of Ukraine, and then another seven in Dnipro, in the east. For six of those years, I was the leader of the Dnipro team. During that time, the Lord blessed us with two amazing sons, Danyil and Matvii.

And then the war began.

The Lord Is My Light and My Salvation: Whom Shall I Fear?

> The LORD is my light and my salvation; whom shall I fear? The LORD is the stronghold of my life; of whom shall I be afraid?
> When evildoers assail me to eat up my flesh, my adversaries and foes, it is they who stumble and fall.
> Though an army encamp against me, my heart shall not fear; though war arise against me, yet I will be confident.
>
> Psalm 27:1–3 (ESV)

I kept whispering this passage under my breath, over and over again: "The LORD is my light and my salvation; whom shall I fear? The LORD is the stronghold of my life; of whom shall I be afraid?" For a good twenty minutes, I recited it on repeat, trying to memorize this psalm. An involuntary twitch of my leg knocked over my assault rifle. I leaned over, picked it up, and clutched it tightly. I had never fired one before – this one had been given to me mere hours earlier, right before being deployed to the combat zone from the last transit station on the border of the Donetsk and Luhansk regions. We received those weapons only after I threatened to call the Armed Forces hotline and complain that we were being sent completely unarmed to be stationed at the very front lines of Ukraine's defence – the infamous city of Sievierodonetsk.

"Why do you need an assault rifle? You're a communications officer," said one of the men in charge of issuing weapons. He spoke quite seriously, with no shadow of doubt on his face.

"We're not just going to war, we're going to the very edge of a sixty-kilometre-long, twenty-kilometre-wide strip, surrounded by enemy forces on three sides. And the city itself is at the very end of this strip. That's why we need weapons, just like everyone else. If you don't give us weapons, our platoon won't go anywhere, and I'm calling the Armed Forces hotline."

I knew that there were major issues with weapons at the time. I also knew that the army was facing turmoil because of the full-scale invasion of a magnitude that no one had expected. Few people knew the types or quantities of weapons available or how army logistics operated. Hundreds of thousands of people had been drafted and assigned to positions they had never held before – so they had no idea how to do their jobs.

After hearing my unequivocal statement, the guy grudgingly picked up the phone.

"You're not leaving yet. You'll have to wait a few hours – we'll find weapons for you, and then you can catch up with the convoy."

I was looking out the window. The school bus we were travelling on to the war was incredibly quiet. Not a word was spoken. There was no music playing. Now and then, Leova and Sorelto would cough, and others would echo their coughs... It had been almost a month of sleeping on the floor – most of the time on concrete, without bunks or sleeping bags – at various transfer stations while our brigade was hastily formed. The guys had all been ill multiple times, with high fevers and even pneumonia. It was most likely COVID-19, although we never did test for it. The treatment was very simple: antipyretic pills by the handful. Padding your sleeping spot with a piece of cardboard helped, too. Some guys got lucky – they found old, grubby, padded mats and slept on them, huddled in hallways, basements, or gyms. The even luckier ones settled in rooms, sleeping on whatever bedding they could find. Usually, those rooms were crammed full, with people sleeping packed like sardines in a can, leaving only a narrow path to clamber between bodies.

People were too afraid to leave those mats unattended, so they'd either carry them around or ask someone to keep an eye on them. At that time, since no one really knew each other, there was little trust between them. Still, everyone was worried about those who were coughing and barely able to stand.

"Chief, at this rate, kicking the bucket seems quite likely. Gotta get a doc to look at that."

I was probably the only one who didn't come down with a fever during that entire period. It was simply a miracle. I, too, had a nasty cough, but I didn't have a fever, while other guys got sick three or four times in less than a month.

We sat on the bus and stared silently through the grimy windows with a mishmash of horror, disgust, and hatred, surveying those blasted Donbas spoil tips and villages obliterated by artillery fire. The schools that had been destroyed by rockets drew our attention because we had spent the last few nights in schools just like those.

I clutched my rifle tightly. Yes, it was a rifle, not a Kalashnikov. It was a bulky and cumbersome Belgian FN FAL automatic rifle, made sometime in the 1970s or 1980s. A heap of these had been delivered to us in the back of an old dump truck, but most were rusty or had bent muzzles. Still, we were delighted beyond measure to have weapons at last. None of us wanted to go unarmed into a war we'd already glimpsed online. Molfar and I climbed into the back of the truck and started picking out the best-looking rifles from the pile of scraps and handing them out to the guys. Everyone immediately started cleaning, disassembling, and reassembling those wonders of NATO weaponry circa the previous century.

So there I was on the bus, clutching my long rifle, with Gypsy next to me, feisty Molfar somewhere nearby, Leova and Sorelto still coughing. I sat and watched the Luhansk region roll by my window – after all, I'd never been to this region before. The funny thing is, a year later, when we were sent to Donbas again, I was actually able to enjoy the incredible beauty of its landscapes. But that moment, I couldn't fully appreciate it. I was reading a small Gideon *New Testament and Psalms* that one of my civilian friends had given me. Summoning all my faith, I repeated these words like a mantra, a prayer, and a supplication: "The Lord is my light and my salvation; whom shall I fear?"

My eyes must have reflected the uncertainty and perplexity of an unclear future, the horror that I tried to hide, my fears, and my failure to grasp the reality that I was going to war – to the very heart of it – to a place that was practically begging to be encircled by the enemy.

We arrived at the distribution station; this would be our first time heading out to the combat positions. It was absolutely chaotic. People were randomly assigned to different cars, regardless of unit formation. Someone would shout out the number of available seats – and people were herded in regardless of whether they were scouts, mortar gunners, riflemen, communications operators, or whatever. Molfar, Tsyhan, and I decided to stick together, so when we heard that three seats were available in the same vehicle, we quickly grabbed backup ammo and hopped in.

Our minibus was speeding past destroyed houses and burned-out cars. Outside the vehicle, an eerie silence reigned supreme; inside, Marilyn Manson was blaring. There was a short stop under a bridge. There was hollering as some of the guys we came with hopped over into the car that was waiting for us. We helped them load the ammo and shells. Then off we went again, the city behind us, a village just ahead. Most of the houses were reduced to rubble. The landscape was dotted with the fins of Grad and Hurricane rounds. The ground was strewn with broken windows, bent gates, downed power poles and wires ... The driver deftly manoeuvred around all this without slowing down. Eventually, the road took us out of the village. Just ahead, I saw an abandoned ramshackle retreat centre. It looked deserted and lifeless, but as soon as we stopped, two officers popped up out of nowhere.

"Disembark, quickly! Move, move, move! Take your things and combat gear inside. Don't loiter outside – the drones are on the prowl."

We quickly got out of the minibus.

"Could I go out for a smoke?" asked Molfar, panting.

"Starting now, no one can go out without an order. Stay indoors even for smoking. Use indoor toilets. If you must go outside, stay on the paved paths – we've got landmines everywhere, even the entrance you came in through is wired to blow up. For now, get settled. You'll be on duty at the observation post in a few hours."

Soon enough, darkness fell.

And there I was, decked in full gear, heading out to my first-ever duty detail with absolutely no clue what I was supposed to do.

"Your partner will tell you everything," they said.

We walked quietly in the pitch-black darkness, stepping over, and sometimes on, broken glass, rubble, and metal fragments. Glass shards crackled and crunched under our feet. I couldn't see anything at all, so I grabbed on to my partner's back, tailgating him as he'd been there for several days already. Our observation point was located on the fourth floor of this retreat centre, and it had already had a taste of what the Russian world is all about.

We got to the fourth floor, but before the previous unit had a chance to hand over duty detail, I heard a long whistle and a rumble about five hundred metres away – it was unlike anything I had heard before in my life.

"Quickly, to the floor below!" came the command.

Everyone rushed to the third floor like bats out of hell. I was last, all the while trying to figure out which way to go by sound alone as I couldn't see a thing. The long whistles of flying mines merged into a continuous howl. Then came high-pitched hisses, followed by an explosion of a 152-calibre shell. A cluster round from a Russian BM-21 "Grad"[1] topped off the cacophony. Rumbling echoed all around, the walls and ceiling were shaking, dust was flying everywhere, and the guys were swearing loudly. And I didn't know what to do because no one had explained how to behave during a shelling. So I did what I already knew how to do. I knelt down and began to pray loudly, "Our Father, who art in heaven . . ." It felt as though this would be my first and last duty detail. That's why I prayed so loudly, thinking that this would probably

---

1. Self-propelled 122-mm multiple rocket launcher system (MRLS).

be the end of us. I wanted the guys to hear at least a word about God. And if we survived, they would remember this moment and this prayer.

Indeed, later on, Molfar and I often reminisced and laughed together over our first combat experience. We would tell this story over and over again, whenever we had lunch or dinner with those who had served at Salamander. I became known as the one who prayed loudly during the first shelling. The guys kept recounting how it happened – and laughing. And then, some of them talked about their own first shift on duty and their first combat experience, while others shared even more horrible and disturbing stories.

Yet, because of this occasion, our motley crew of units of our battalion now knew two things: who Santa (my call sign) is and that Santa is a believer. Everyone found it funny; still, no one was laughing when it was their turn for duty detail. Almost everyone had been reminded of God and faith again, but very few were willing to talk about it openly; the rest only mentioned this in private conversations with me.

I decided I wasn't going to be ashamed of what had happened. When the going got tough, I'd tell this story to those who had not yet heard it or even those who had but could use a laugh to lighten the mood. In the wake of this experience, I decided to officially tell my commander about my faith in God and ask for a fifteen-minute time slot between his morning orders and breakfast to speak a few encouraging words and pray for the troops stationed at the Salamander strongpoint.

This commander and the team did not know me at all, so, at first, they were hesitant to trust me.

"I'll give you three minutes," said the deputy commander, Tokha. He had seen combat back in 2015, so he was the most experienced of all these mobilized soldiers. Tokha looked at me with a hint of suspicion, probably thinking I was going to do some Bible-thumping, so he added, "Your time starts now."

I did not expect to have so little time. After silently asking God for wisdom, I opened by telling them that their families – and I, personally – were very proud of their service in defending our land and saving our people. I said that even though we were on the far end of this thin strip of territory surrounded by Russian troops on three sides, we were not forgotten by God. Because God's Son did something quite similar: he left heaven and those he loves to come to a terrible place, our world, for the sake of defeating evil and saving those who are perishing. I read a short verse from the Bible and said a quick but sincere prayer for them. The guys stood there looking at me for a moment, then started to come up to hug, shake hands, and thank me.

Tokha came up, too, and said, "Next time, you'll have your fifteen minutes."

I began to speak more openly about my faith and about Jesus, but I strove to do so in brief, relevant, and encouraging ways. Under the barrage of mines, punctuated by explosions of high-powered 152-calibre shells, when the wall would shake and rain dust and concrete debris, I'd read a passage from the Bible and pray. The guys would listen gladly.

After some time, Tokha took me off duty detail and assigned me to man his radio. He said, "You're a communication specialist, right? I need someone good on comms; there are enough people to do duty detail without you."

We became very good friends. He was probably my closest friend outside of the signal platoon. When I was transferred from Salamander to the battalion headquarters, we came to an arrangement with Tokha and everyone at that stronghold: I would keep in touch with their families and let them know they were doing fine. They gave me the phone numbers of their family members, and I texted and called more than twenty people every so often because I was the only one with stable access to the internet, while others experienced major difficulties with signal stability.

Sometime later, Kadyrov's Akhmad battalion reduced to rubble the town of Rubizhne right next to us and began targeting our left flank, where the first battalion was positioned. After the battalion commander was fatally wounded, the defences crumbled, exposing the flank. The guys from Salamander strongpoint were surrounded. I had transferred out to another location a mere week before.

I heard the radio transmissions as it went down. I heard the horrors of hell taking place there – it was my shift at the comms. I was terribly worried and prayed hard for those guys.

To escape the encirclement, they had to break through – not towards their rear but towards the enemy line – and travel through minefields. Their move took almost a full day, but everyone made it out! Molfar got a light leg wound, but that was it. It was truly a miracle. When we saw each other, everyone went in for a hug and a handshake, just like those we had shared after my first prayer at Salamander.

Fleeing

Fear. It's so sticky, so contagious. Paralyzing.

Everyone – big and small, young and old, weak and strong, brave and faint – feels fear. Christians, too, feel fear. However, what matters is how this fear affects us and what it reveals about us. It is like a storm that rages against a house built on a rock or on sand and, in doing so, uncovers our truest foundations. It exposes things we haven't considered or realized before.

I remember hiding in the basement during a shelling and wondering how so many Christians in Ukraine had just one reaction to the full-scale war: to flee. I remember the kilometre-long traffic jams at petrol stations on 24 February – all those cars full of people fleeing. I wasn't among them only because I had anticipated and carefully prepared for the war. A good two months before the full-scale invasion, I began making sure that my car's tank was always topped up and that I had two full spare canisters in the trunk (those once leaked badly, and I got an earful from my wife for being so imprudent). A month before the invasion, my mission team and I developed a contingency plan in case of war. We had a detailed protocol on how the entire team could leave the city within an hour, what route to take to get to the western regions, and so on. Everything was thought through: who would pick up whom, what to do if the war began at night-time, what to do if it began during the daytime, what to do if you were out and about when it happened, what if cell service was down, and so on. Each team member had cash on hand, both Ukrainian hryvnias and US dollars, just in case. Every one of us had a predetermined destination to head to if war broke out.

And this plan worked. I remember waking up at 5:00 a.m. to explosions; and by 6:00 a.m., our team was already in cars and outside the city limits.

Although we were afraid, too, I'm surprised by the extent of the fear that prevailed at the time. I'm also surprised that the only plan for many was to flee. Sure, the plan to take your family to a safe location is a good thing. But then what? It is surprising to see just how many men – believers and unbelievers alike – rushed to cross the borders. When they found out that men were not allowed to leave the country, their fear prompted remarkable – how should I put it? – creativity. Sadly, Christians got a bit creative, too. At first, men would bribe border guards to help them across the border. When that no longer worked, they came up with other schemes. I know people who, upon seeing unknown disabled people, simply picked them up and carried them across the border, pretending to be their escorts or helpers. I also know people who forged birth certificates – because fathers of three or more children were allowed to cross. This was easy to do, and papers weren't checked very closely. Still others forged documents claiming that they were students at universities abroad. There were all sorts of, ahem, creative ideas. For example, some fearful Christian men went to Russian-occupied territories while checkpoints were still open. They would show their papers to Russian soldiers to prove residency in Mariupol,[2] then ask to be allowed to pass to return to the city under the wing of "liberators." Once let through, they would go through Crimea to fly to Turkey or Georgia and then to Europe. To me, this is the most humiliating way to flee mobilization that I have heard of from some Christians in my circle – to escape at the price of covering up the utter horrors happening in Mariupol . . . Everyone has heard of the terrible massacre in Bucha – the horrors of Mariupol are fifty times worse. And sadly, it was Christians who fled this way and later claimed that God had blessed them by helping them to succeed. All this disgrace was driven by fear.

One lady, a counsellor, took care of my wife while I was fighting in Sievierodonetsk during operational encirclement. This city is situated on the riverbank. The enemy forces moved in on three sides, skirmishes were taking place within city limits, and all the bridges across the river – connecting us to free Ukraine and the supply lines – had been blown up. The plan was to fall back by crossing the Donets River. My distressed wife checked daily for updates on our location – and the news she saw, the hopelessness of the situation, and the emotional turmoil wore her down to the point she could neither sleep nor eat. Finally, she decided to seek Christian counselling. This counsellor told my wife how God had "blessed" her own family: some woman had forged their documents (probably for a fee), and they were able to cross the border. This oh-so-caring lady also tried to persuade my wife to seize any opportunity, pay anyone any sum of money, and do whatever it took just to get out of Ukraine. This was the advice of a Christian counsellor to a woman whose husband, at that very moment, was calling up his friends in the rear and giving them his unit and battalion number so that they could search for him among the POWs. This is just one of many examples of how fear paralyzes, shocks to the core, and destroys everything we believe . . . And I'm talking about Christians here.

Why was the first reaction of most Christians to flee rather than serve people who were unable to leave? Why was I, too, among those who made the long twenty-six-hour journey west to escape instead of mobilizing for ministry? Yes, not all believers fled. There were those who immediately began to serve people who were facing certain doom – in Mariupol, Melitopol, Irpin, and other cities – but they were few and far between. Many began to serve a month or two later – perhaps because they came to their senses and remembered their

---

2. Mariupol is a large Ukrainian city and port on the shores of the Sea of Azov. It was captured by Russian forces in March 2022, although fighting for parts of the city, including the Azovstal steelworks, continued until May 2022.

responsibilities, or because they were stuck and unable to cross the border, or because they felt ashamed for not fighting in the war.

I was surprised that the church was fleeing its very mission – the mission to serve and minister. This fleeing was prompted by fear. Perhaps the reason was that in recent times, at least in my circles, the focus had shifted from ministry and service to self-realization, personal growth, and a career in Christian organisations. We talked at length about measuring our effectiveness. It almost seemed like people were not choosing how to serve God but how to set up a comfortable life and how ministry could help with that goal. Perhaps that was why, in a crisis, some ministers left the ministry and those they served, choosing to build a life for themselves somewhere else, in less trying circumstances.

And then, I was fleeing, too. More precisely, I was travelling by car with my family and another colleague. Our plan was to get to Lviv, drop off my colleague, and then head to our friends in Uzhhorod. Another five hours, and we were there. Then came a week of the ordeals of being newly displaced. It began with searching for a place to rent at a time when prices had skyrocketed to New York City levels. The first few days, all four of us slept in one bed. We were constantly doomscrolling – and the news kept getting worse each day. The Russians occupied my home town – the city where I had lived, graduated from university, and where my mother and my brother's family still lived. Kharkiv, Chernihiv, and Mariupol were surrounded. Fierce battles were ongoing near Kyiv. Bucha and Irpin were taken over by the enemy forces. These were small suburbs of Kyiv we had considered moving to a year before the war – we would have lived in Hostomel, and the children would have gone to school in Bucha. But that offer fell through for some reason, although with many apologies for the cancellation of the move. Now I realize that it was God's grace, but at the time, I couldn't understand why God would close that door, and I was even a bit upset with my bosses for asking us to wait another year.

While staying in Uzhhorod, we did not know the extent of the horror and crimes Russian soldiers had committed in these towns, even against civilians. I only saw on the news how the invaders targeted residential buildings in Irpin – three or four hits per building in an apartment complex. I remember watching a YouTube video of a burning high-rise building in Kyiv. I saw another report from the Sumy region, showing how Russian tanks shot and ran over an elderly couple who were simply trying to get out.

All this triggered deep indignation and anger in me. I called my brother and mother, who were living in besieged Sumy. My brother told me how he would drive his car around Russian tanks on the roads while delivering aid to needy people in the villages. My mother told me how the men from our village (where I used to live) had gathered at the school (where I used to study) to dig anti-tank ditches, even though enemy tanks were already in the area.

Meanwhile, my family and I were living in peaceful Uzhhorod, going out to cafés for food and our favourite lattes . . .

That's when I decided that I couldn't continue living like this. It went against my convictions as a Ukrainian and as a Christian. How could I sip on this latte while such horrors were taking place in another part of my country?

At the time, I had no confidence that Ukraine could resist the Russian invasion. I was very pessimistic, fearing that we would soon lose our sovereignty and that Ukraine might disappear from the world map. Nevertheless, I felt that I had to do something. This was a tragic moment – but also a historic one. What was I supposed to do at this crucial hour: hide, flee, or respond? I felt that I could not let this injustice slide by without doing something. I felt God calling me to walk into this horror . . .

On the ninth day of the war, we attempted some sort of celebration for our youngest son's ninth birthday. The next day, I went to the military enlistment office. It was like a child's nightmare: you jump into the darkness and keep falling into the endless abyss.

Looking back on that particular season and my state of mind at the time, I can now see that this sort of spiritual paralysis occurs when a person focuses on themselves and on what they think is happening and will happen. We become fixated on our own perceptions and feelings, especially our fear. And fear is deceptive. It creates exaggerated and false pictures. Yes, on the one hand, fear is a God-given emotion meant to protect us from harm. But when we allow fear to control us, this can lead to disastrous consequences.

To overcome this fear, you must shift your focus away from self to what is causing this fear in your mind. It helps to simply do what you believe is right and what you have said you would do, trusting God with the outcome. It helps to recall your commitment to serve God here and now. My decision was to follow God – not to ponder, not to pick and choose, but to follow him wherever he leads. It's like the marriage vow to love one another for richer or poorer, in sickness and in health. And now is the time of poverty and sickness. So, this is the time to follow God wherever he leads and to love and trust him in the darkest hour.

The first thing that helped me overcome fear was to focus on God. I realized that our relationship with him and our love for him and our trust in him were being tested. I realized that I had to continue to follow him. Just like always, he calls, and I follow. I just have to look around less. Instead, I need to look at him and listen to his voice. I need to close my eyes and follow him, entrusting the outcome to him, just like in the film *Bird Box*, where the main character had to travel blindfolded – because outside, there are all sorts of chimeras that can kill you the moment you open your eyes.

The second thing that helped me battle my fears was principles and words. The time had come to put into practice everything I had believed and said. On 24 February, on our way westwards, I remember passing through a town with thick smoke bellowing from a missile strike while military aircraft were rumbling in the sky. We were terrified. Then I suggested that, as a family, we do what we believe in and pray aloud. I was the first to pray, followed by my wife, our colleague, and then the children. We began doing the right thing. We turned on worship songs and spoke truth to our fearful hearts. Little by little, we felt better. Every time the fear would come flooding back, we repeated this exercise. Looking back, I can say that life is a precious gift, but it is not the most precious thing. There are things that are far more important – like following God, like your faith, like your beliefs. In times of upheaval, we need to switch from fear mode to conviction mode. Do what you believe in and what you have proclaimed.

The third thing that helped me overcome fear and find strength during the war was to focus on serving others. I began to help others and give myself to serving them.

Let Your Will Be Done

What I struggled with the most was admitting honestly that I didn't want to die. I grew up in a culture where, for a long time, it was taught that the end goal of a believer is to go to heaven and that this is the greatest good and the main meaning of life. That's what we should want and strive for. We live to get to heaven. Christ is waiting for us there, and he will wipe away every tear from our eyes. But walking around the partially encircled city of Sievierodonetsk, taking cover from shelling, I realized that I really wanted to live. I was so ashamed to admit this to myself or to others, and it was even harder to admit it to God. There wasn't a single believer around to share this with, which made it even more agonizing.

It felt like I was betraying Jesus, as if something else had become more important to me than seeing Christ face to face. I could repeat the words, once again, that for me to live is Christ and to die is gain or that my desire is to depart and be with Christ. Although there were occasionally situations where dark thoughts and urges rose up within me, God stopped me, time and time again – and I'd unload my rifle or put away a grenade. But that's a whole other story.

Yes, I went to war to save those who could not defend themselves, but it was also to save myself. In one sense, it was something similar to what Christ did; yet I had to admit that I couldn't really do what he did. My entire stay in Sievierodonetsk – my first combat experience – became my Gethsemane: the place where Christ accepted that he had to die, even though he didn't want to.

While on our way to Sievierodonetsk – and even earlier, when I first went to the military enlistment office – I was quite pessimistic about the war situation, the state of the Ukrainian army, and my own future. I was pretty sure that Russia would take the whole of Ukraine east of the Dnipro River, and that was one of the reasons I decided I must fight in this war. Initially, I thought I probably wouldn't make it home alive, but then I reflected that even though World War II was more intense and extensive, people still survived somehow.

So, I simply entrusted – at least in theory – my life to God. I would recall Christian songs with lyrics like "I will follow you, where will you lead me?" And I thought that now was indeed the time to give another layer of meaning to these words and finally do what I sing about and what I have come to believe in. In Sievierodonetsk, however, I faced another dimension – a practical aspect – of what it means to lay down your life. Each day, I learned who had died and how. I saw with my own eyes the evacuation and how the situation kept getting worse and worse. We were slowly being surrounded, the guys were dying, and somehow, miraculously, I was alive – but I knew there was no guarantee that I'd still be alive five minutes later.

I remember being tormented by the thought that I really wanted to live and did not want to die at all. I wanted so badly to return to my children. I wanted to hug my little raccoon (that's my youngest son) and hold my eldest son tight. I wanted so much to enjoy life with my wife. And I was afraid and ashamed to admit this to God. It felt like I was betraying him. I couldn't give myself up for the sake of others like Jesus did. I wanted to – but I did not have such strength. It seemed like he had chosen me for this, but after a heavy shelling, I saw that even the body itself moves reflexively to survive, and I was ashamed before God that I wanted to live, rather than to die and to depart from this life to be with him.

I was tormented even more by the fact that everything God had given me – life here with Matthew, who loves animals, with Daniel, who is now a teenager, a head taller than me, and whom I have already taught to shave, and with my wife, who reveals to me the myriad of interesting things in this world – was more important to me than dying and being with Christ, who is the "goal of life." Oh, the anguish caused by the realization that living with what God had given me made me happier than dying and being with Christ. In short, I wanted to survive and return to my family. I was floored by this discovery. I discovered that I want to live here on earth. I want to hug my children and kiss my wife. And the shame of that desire gripped my heart in the face of God . . .

Our headquarters at that time was located in the basement of a funeral home. The yard was filled with various kinds of monuments, tombstones with inscriptions, and angel statues. On the ground floor, there was a kitchen and a room used for memorial dinners; on the second floor, there was a showroom where customers could select a coffin; and in the other rooms, among the coffins, there were various suits for the dead. Everywhere, there were icons, big and small.

I remember after the first three-hour-long shelling of our quadrant with 152-calibre shells – a rather powerful round – the building was in shambles. The guys, knowing that I was a believer, called me to the dining room, where all the windows were shattered, the ceiling was smashed, the slabs from the third and fourth floors had fallen through in some places and were hanging menacingly. But the guys had noticed something else.

"Look, everything was destroyed, but the wall with the icons was not hit, and not a single icon was damaged . . . Was it God who protected these?"

"Yes," I told the guys, not wanting to go into a long-winded explanation.

And then I spotted it – a painting of Christ in Gethsemane. It was an old image; I think it was from a children's Bible. Christ is kneeling and praying – "If possible, let this cup pass from me" – in the very place where he wanted to live, wanted as he'd never wanted before. This thought resonated deeply in my heart. I came closer. Glass crunched under my feet. Scraps of curtains in the broken window openings swayed in the draught, water dripped from above, and there was a lingering smell of gunpowder and dust. The guys were walking around, exploring the nooks and crannies of the dining room, looking for intact canned stew, leftover food, water. I took the painting and brought it to my chapel, where I placed it in the middle, right across from the entrance.

More than once, after being on duty and enduring the evening and midnight shelling (the Russians were firing at us as if on schedule, with evening shelling usually beginning at 10:00 p.m. and lasting until midnight), I'd run with a ladder and large coils of cables to repair the damaged wires. Often, the shelling would resume, and we would blindly throw ourselves into any kind of shelter to avoid getting hit by shrapnel. By the time we'd return, it would be well after 1:00 a.m. With the next shift looming, the soldiers would rush off to get some sleep. But I would first go to the chapel, which was usually empty at that hour. I would sit in front of that painting, turn on the praise music on my phone, and silently gaze at this image, trying to figure out what was going on in Christ's heart at that particular moment. What was he feeling? Why did he pray and ask his Father to let him live longer? Did he really want to live, too? And could I tell him my darkest secret – that I wanted to live more than I wanted to leave this life and come to him? How would he take it? Would he be offended? Would he continue to love me and protect me from the shrapnel? No, I was not yet ready to share this secret with him . . .

What gave Christ the strength to continue in that prayer, "Not my will, but yours, be done"? Perhaps it was Christ's will to continue living among this wonderful creation, which God himself had declared "very good." But what I wondered most about was why he prayed – and what gave him the strength to continue praying – "Thy will be done."

I would have ended that prayer with the words, "Remove this cup from me." Because sometimes, I felt completely exhausted. For a month and a half, I slept no more than four hours a night (if I was lucky), and the realization that the encirclement around our city was tightening was also emotionally draining.

Jesus knew what a terrible death he was going to die. He did not want to die, but he willingly went through it. Looking at this painting, I felt the humanity of Christ. He was not only God – he was also a man. He loved life, and he loved this world. So what gave him the strength to take the next step? And why can't I rely on God like Christ did?

I remember how sometimes, before running out to restore communications during the shelling, I would go to my chapel and – if I was sure that no one could see or hear me – just gaze at that painting and cry. I cried because I wanted to live and didn't have the strength to say, "Let your will be done, not mine." The most painful thing was that I was afraid to admit this to Christ. He went through it, to the very end. But I couldn't.

While at war, I used to pray and give everything – really, everything – to God. But I could not admit to him that instead of wanting to "depart and be with Christ" (Phil 1:23), I wanted to survive and be with my family. I was afraid to even have such thoughts. I was afraid to admit them to anyone. But most of all, I dreaded expressing my true feelings to Jesus. How would he react if I said that my family and my dream of reuniting with them were more important to me than being with him? Is this really what my faith is?

Before the war, I thought I was ready to die at any moment, and I didn't feel afraid. But then, for some reason, I suddenly wanted to live. Sure, there were moments during the war when I wanted to die and dreamed of a quick death. For example, sometimes it seemed that the only way to get out of a particular location was if you were at least wounded. I remember once, during a shelling, I was carrying out a task on an open roof, with mines falling nearby, and I asked God to let me get wounded so that I would be evacuated out of this horror show.

But when you refuse a quick death, you realize that you want to live.

I was afraid to articulate these thoughts. I was afraid that if I said the words "No, God, I want to live, I want to return to my family!" I would be betraying Christ.

I was afraid that this would seem like I loved my family and my life more than him. I felt like if I said this out loud, even though he wouldn't turn away from me, he would be disappointed.

Would he stop loving me after that? Here at war, every second of my life depended on his grace, and I was afraid to say that there was something that I loved more than him or something that was more real to me than him. Maybe it wasn't true, but my soul felt something that it hadn't grasped before, and I couldn't find the right and proper words to express myself.

I had to admit that I was falling short, very short, of Christ. He is God, and I am flesh. I cannot do what he does. I am not him. Only he can be the Saviour.

I kept asking myself: Why is this happening?

And so, in silence, not understanding for certain what was happening in my soul, I would sit in the chapel and cry when no one was around. I really wanted to talk to someone about it, but there was no one. I knew that Jesus understood everything, but I was afraid to tell him. I just kept silent and cried, hoping he would help my soul find a way out.

I thought about it for a long time. I also read some books. And, the thought came to me that loving this world is not a sin. After all, God loved it. Moreover, God loved this world so much that he died for it. He recognized that creation is very good. To enjoy this world and to enjoy life is to recognize the beauty of God's design. God likes it when we love what he has made for us. He likes it when we care for what he lovingly created. Tending to the garden in which he has placed us and loving him is also part of God's plan to redeem the world.

The idea that heaven is an improved version of God's creation and this world is a failed prototype that God wants to destroy – or at least forget about – is not a Christian idea. God still loves this world and is trying to redeem it.

Will God, like an angry little child, tear up his own painting?

For a long time, I was troubled by this question. But after a while, I realized that I had the wrong idea about salvation. I was viewing salvation only as evacuation to heaven and not seeing it in terms of God's restoration of creation. If salvation is simply evacuation to heaven, then it doesn't matter where you are evacuated from – the main thing is being saved, and you don't feel responsible for the place from which you are being saved. This is a spiritual victim syndrome, and it results in a failure to take responsibility for this world.

Serhii

I met Serhii at the very beginning of the war, about two weeks after I was mobilized. He was always smiling, clean-shaven, well groomed, and in a good mood. He often laughed, joked, and sang loudly. During brigade formations, the same school classroom was supposed to house both the communications platoon – to which I belonged – and a MANPADS platoon (a unit that operates man-portable air defence systems that fire at enemy aircraft), to which he belonged. Up to forty people would be crammed into a single room. Molfar, Tsyhan, and I, having already experienced living and sleeping on concrete, immediately ran to the second floor, where it was warmer, found a classroom with a wooden floor, and settled down by the radiator. It was barely warm – but not cold! Then the MANPADS platoon came in. Among them was a smiling Serhii, carrying a machine gun on his shoulder. I don't remember what he sang, but I will never forget how he sang. It was immediately clear that he was a true pro. He had a smooth, strong voice, and he sang old patriotic songs of the Ukrainian Insurgent Army, like "Lenta za lentoiu." Hearing such beautiful singing, I could no longer stay in my sleeping bag. Amid the filth of war, he reminded me of something beautiful from the past, something from ordinary civilian life. I don't remember how we started talking, but after that, we became close friends – as close as you can be when you are in different units. It turned out that Serhii was a choirmaster in an Orthodox church in the village of Hoshcha in the Rivne region. He was a deeply religious man but without any prejudice towards Protestants. Besides, I looked a bit like an Orthodox cleric myself, with a wooden cross around my neck and an elongated beard like that of a young and trendy Orthodox priest! We became fast friends. However, war is a place that tests not only your physical strength but also your faith.

Before leaving this school and heading to the Donetsk region, a fellow soldier named Tapas, who knew about my faith and had probably already dealt with believers, asked me to say a prayer. It was a timely request. I had been wondering how I could start praying with the platoon, so this seemed like an opportune moment! I quickly turned to the last psalm I had read that morning, read it aloud, briefly explained what it meant, and then prayed for our safety as we departed to the combat zone. One of the communications soldiers – probably Tsyhan – immediately stood up when I started reading. I think we began discussing faith with him on the second or third day after mobilization. The MANPADS platoon remained lying down – all except for Serhii. He got up, came over to me, and made the sign of the cross several times while I was praying.

"Could I sing a short psalm?" he asked.

"Sure."

Serhii sang Psalm 90 in the traditional Orthodox manner. More guys stood up, and a couple of people from the MANPADS platoon also got to their feet and made the sign of the cross. The lieutenant of the MANPADS platoon, whose call sign was Zefir, pretended that nothing was happening and continued to walk around the classroom. I felt I should make the sign of the cross, too, but I wasn't sure how it was done in the Orthodox way – was it from left to right, or from right to left? I was embarrassed that I didn't know! I had to do it quickly, right then and there, so I followed the lead of those soldiers who had already done it and made the sign of the cross, which signalled to everyone around me that the prayer was over.

As I mentioned earlier, after the first weeks of fighting in Sievierodonetsk, I was transferred from the front line to the first defence line at headquarters. The MANPADS platoon was housed in the next room, which meant that Serhii and I could hang out again! I was excited, but he was perhaps even more thrilled. I invited him to meet and talk about Jesus in our dining room (that is, in the ritual wake room on the first floor) after his shifts, during our breaks. On one wall were hung an eye-catching hodgepodge of icons – including the Our Lady of Kazan, a Gethsemane scene from an old Protestant children's Bible, bearded faces of saints, and tapestries with an embroidered pudgy baby Jesus. This varied mix seemed an appropriate reflection of our assembly of two. I would read the psalms and share my reflections with Serhii, and he would sing Orthodox liturgical prayers.

There was a fierce battle going on close by. We could hear Russian artillery and mortars firing at our first battalion. But it was as though God had covered our small church of two people with his hand, and we were not hit. We read the Bible for a long time, and Serhii sang and made the sign of the cross. Then he asked if he could make his confession to me and opened up to me about his secrets and pain.

After that first session, we agreed to meet whenever we had overlapping breaks. He would bring a flashlight, I would bring a thermos that one of my mission colleagues had given me, and we would pray and talk like that for hours. Before long, I began to think about setting up a field chapel for Orthodox soldiers – a place where they could come, pray, and find hope.

This was before the Russians began to actively target our battalion.

The first massive shelling of the headquarters zone brought about a lot of changes. For over three hours, we were shelled by three or four 152-calibre SPGs.[3] There was often less than a minute between each round of shelling, which meant they spent half a railcar load or more of shells on us. After that, life began to resemble scenes from the film "Terminator," where Kyle Reese and other rebels are running around, guns blazing, in dark basements and tunnels. Our soldiers tried to avoid going outside without good reason. The shelling was getting more frequent and unpredictable. The mission of the day became trying to figure out when to go outside to the loo without getting shot at. Some guys, unwilling to risk it during a shelling, used the only available room – which was filled with junk from floor to ceiling – as a toilet.

Following those shellings, our basement was swarming with people. Such a large gathering of soldiers in one room should not have been allowed under any circumstances. But that's how things were. This building, forever etched in my memory, withstood an unbelievable number of shellings. Meanwhile, I looked out for a place where Serhii and I could continue to meet, but every room was packed with soldiers sitting or lying on bunk beds.

I went into the room where the MANPADS platoon was staying. There were a dozen or more people there. Serhii welcomed me warmly. I asked how everyone was doing. The response was a resounding silence. So I asked for ten minutes of their attention to read a psalm and pray for them, adding that Serhii would sing. The soldiers didn't mind. They all got up from their bunks, except for one young man in the far corner who continued to watch a video. After I said "Amen," everyone made the sign of the cross several times. For some reason, I didn't – and I still regret it. Zefir offered me coffee, and the guys took out the remainder of their secret stash of sweets from relatives back home. I accepted, not wanting to hurt their feelings. An older man with a long black beard and a smile on his face – call sign Boroda – handed me the drink he had just made.

I asked, "Do you guys mind if I come by like this from time to time, ask how you are doing, and pray for you?"

"Of course, we don't mind, you can come here every day! We'll bring out the goodies for you."

I smiled and thanked God for opening this door for me to witness to this group of people. To jump ahead a little, I will say that Boroda was killed in the action near Bilopillia. By that time, we had become quite close, and we had lunch together just a few hours before his death. He talked about his son, who

---

3. Self-propelled artillery gun.

had been mobilized, and about the fact that it wasn't his turn to go on duty. Serhii was supposed to go, but he fell unwell, so Boroda decided to replace his fellow-soldier. During this shift, at the cost of his own life, he sent an alarm signal, warning his fellow soldiers – who were resting – that an enemy subversive reconnaissance group from the Special Forces had infiltrated their position. He paid with his life for doing so. Sadly, our guys were taken prisoner, except for one who was wounded by a grenade, but Boroda did all he could for them.

The guy who didn't get up for prayer was eager to go into battle and always determined to do something more important. He was assigned to drive an armoured vehicle. One day, his vehicle was hit. He survived but was admitted to a psychiatric hospital due to severe traumatic brain injury from the explosion. I don't know if this acquired mental trauma was successfully treated, but the guys said that he wasn't doing well.

"You can come every day," they would say, addressing me with respect, even though I was much younger than them – and in the case of many of them, including Boroda, young enough to be their son. Every day ... That's easy to say, but I'm only human, a soldier just like them, with duties, combat missions, and my own emotional and physical limits. I also needed rest, sleep, sustenance, and solace. In addition, I carried the weight of my worst secret. I carried it with me everywhere.

But we did meet. The guys would treat me to something, and I tried to be a part of their lives. Soon, like in all communities, conflicts sparked. As I understood it, some of these were about Serhii. The men did not quite understand him, and since he had been active in the Orthodox Church, Serhii often felt out of place among the soldiers, with all their swearing and drinking.

One night, I went to visit them. The room was dark. Almost everyone was asleep. Someone was lying down, fiddling with his phone. Off to the side, on the top bunk, a flashlight was glowing. Serhii was kneeling on the second bunk, an icon in front of him. He was quietly praying, bowing before the icon. I had planned to invite Serhii to my usual church gathering, but then I changed my mind. "This time, I suppose, it was me who came to his liturgy," I thought. I quietly sat down on a nearby chair and began to listen.

To be honest, I used to be quite critical of Orthodox Christians, just like many other hard-line Protestants. Folk Orthodoxy, with its emphasis on icons and rituals, turned me off. I remembered hearing, as a little boy in a Baptist church, something along the lines of Orthodoxy being paganism. At that time, I took it quite seriously. But as I grew older, my perception of Orthodox Christians changed. However, given the choice, I was drawn more towards Catholics. I liked their architecture and art, and the Mass. But things concerning the Orthodox faith remained incomprehensible, and it seemed to me that, unlike Catholics, few Orthodox believers cared to explain their faith in simple language.

But Serhii's prayer and singing captivated me. It was beautiful, and I didn't want to spoil this mystical and mesmerizing moment with my Protestant literalism. I just wanted to keep listening to his chants. I could understand parts of them – others, not so much. But the overall meaning was clear. He prayed an old prayer that priests used to pray, probably in the days of the Ukrainian Insurgent Army. It was amazing... And then he started singing Psalm 90 again, followed by another psalm. It was as if I had been transported to an Orthodox church, into its air of semi-darkness. I could almost see before my eyes the icons of the crucified Christ and his mother, Mary, so revered by Orthodox believers. For a time, the depression and anguish of my great secret seemed to leave my heart. The atmosphere changed. I could no longer hear the swearing outside the walls, the gloomy radio transmissions over the walkie-talkies, or the shelling. It even felt like the guys had disappeared from the room, even though some of them were snoring loudly and others were probably watching some trashy stuff on their phones. It was just me, Serhii, and Jesus.

I had been sitting quietly for twenty minutes. I thought Serhii was about to finish, but he kept on singing. So, I settled down, took out my copy of the Gospel, and began reading silently. All this while, Serhii did not know that I was praying next to him. He would finish one psalm, bow, and immediately begin another. Then he would stop, recite a Scripture passage from memory, bow again, make the sign of the cross, and continue singing. I sat for forty minutes, trying to alternate between praying silently to myself and reading the psalms. Serhii continued. After about an hour, I left as quietly as I had come in. But the weary soul of the Orthodox choirmaster continued to ask for strength and help from his Heavenly Father. This was his spiritual battle in the midst of war, stress, misunderstanding, and conflict. We have much to learn from Orthodox Christians.

Later I found out that these prayers were partly the reason behind the increasing conflicts between Serhii and the guys. And it occurred to me that we should set up a chapel to help Serhii. The only suitable room was the one that was packed with junk stacked higher than a man's height – the room where the guys sometimes relieved themselves without the knowledge of the officers. Still, this room could be turned into a good place for Serhii's prayers.

I wonder why, in times of peace, we find it so difficult to accept other expressions of faith, even those that are just slightly different from ours. Instead of viewing these differences as a view of God from a different perspective, a view that can enrich us, we see it as something hostile and unacceptable. But in times of war, when there are no other believers from your own denomination nearby, this pushes you to get out of your box. You begin looking for common ground. You begin to cooperate. However, in our missionary work, we tend to focus on the issues that separate us rather than the things we share. Why is it so difficult for us to make the sign of the cross during prayer and build a bridge to the heart of someone from an Orthodox background? Perhaps it's because when we do preach the good news, we do it in ways that are easier and more understandable to us. We have got wrapped up in ourselves.

Chapel

The idea of setting up a chapel had come to me some time earlier. But the energy to do so came only after my visits to an Orthodox liturgy in the basement of a funeral home in the midst of a shelling. I saw how Serhii was suffering, how he was fighting for his faith – and this gave me the necessary strength. We had to sacrifice our sleep to do this project, and it took us about a week to get it done.

At first, I felt I had no moral right to speak to any of the commanders about setting up a chapel or to seek permission from battalion headquarters. Nobody knew me. I had no unofficial access to officers and sensed that it would be better not to attempt anything like this without their knowledge.

Back when we were heading from the military enlistment office to the war zone and I was trying to process what had happened and what lay ahead of me, God somehow spoke to my heart. We had travelled all night. It was very cold. The wind crept in through every crack and chilled me. It was scary. I felt like my entire world had been shattered. I didn't know when – or if – I would ever return to my old comfortable world. It was as if I had jumped into an abyss and just kept falling and falling – but there was no bottom. My biggest fear was for my family, the ones I'd left behind. I can't say that my wife was having a breakdown – no, she's strong, even though she doesn't like it when I tell her that. But at that moment, she was definitely in shock. While we were on the road, I tried to get a few essentials done as quickly as possible: I gave her the passwords to various services, explained how to pay for utilities and school fees, transfer all the money, and top up her and the children's phone balances. In other words, I handed over all the tasks I used to handle in our family, which she now had to do. We didn't know what would happen next, but God somehow spoke to both of us at the same time with words from the book of Jeremiah, reminding us that God had a future and a hope for us (Jer 29:11).

Later, as the train carried me east, far away from my family, I felt God speaking to me again, this time, reminiscent of the apostle Paul's dream: Do not be afraid, you have a witness to give, so I grant you your life and those with you. I looked at those who were travelling with me and realized that I had to witness to them. This was my primary mission. This was the main reason I was here, and even the defence of my land and our people came second. It was time to leave the mission of serving university students and accept the mission of serving the military – soldiers and officers – in the midst of war.

Having become accustomed to "big time" ministry, I had forgotten that being on mission is often painful. Serving university students was, in many ways, much like the life of a middle-class educated person. You are respected. You are doing important work. When I think about ministry before the war, I think of trips, conferences, travelling abroad, strategies, coffee shops, sandwiches, speeches, nice clothes, and being neat, clean, and smelling good. Sitting in a dugout as I write this, in the second year of this war, things are very different.

Of course, ministry and mission are always marked by limitations and difficulties. But I was shocked by what happened to many ministers when the war began. Not all of them, certainly, and I would like to believe that it wasn't the case for the majority. Since I had gone to the battlefront straightaway and could no longer keep track of what was happening in Christian circles, I don't know everything that transpired. But I was stunned to see how many ministers failed the test for their calling to ministry at the very beginning of this war. Yes, many of them – including me, I suppose – thought only about themselves and their families. They abandoned those they were serving and, in doing so, revealed that they were actually serving themselves rather than the people in their care. But what shocked me even more was that they abandoned even those they had been serving with. The first priority became saving their own skin. It was even more surprising that, after the initial shock, many ministers never returned to their flocks – even where it was possible to do so – but moved on to Europe and the US. And they had no hesitation in saying things like "I see no prospects in Ukraine," "I will not be able to fulfil my potential there," "My children have no future there," and even "It was God who led us here, so we continue to serve here."

These statements were made by ministers, pastors, and missionaries. It's as if we've got used to the idea that ministry is about being comfortable and assume that God leads us to work and serve him only in pleasant places. But what about the early missionaries, who went to places where they faced death threats, wars, famines, and cannibals? Were they unwise? What about their children? Did their children have no future? And even if they see no future for themselves and their families, does that change Christianity? Christianity is following Christ, not seeking a comfortable life. And Christ himself, according to this logic, should not have come to this earth and died for us because he was better off in heaven, with all its comforts. Is comfort really at the heart of Christianity? I believe that Christianity is following Christ, which does not always lead to being comfortable. If the first Christians and missionaries had only gone where they felt comfortable and where there were good prospects for their children, there would be no Christianity in our country.

Lately, we seem to have gone too far in equating ministry with business, focusing too much on self-realization through ministry. While ministry, business, and self-realization often do go hand in hand, ministry must sometimes go in the opposite direction to where business tends to go. The way Jesus finished his life on earth shows that he was not always driven by self-realization. His service and obedience led him into misunderstanding, pain, and ultimately death on the cross.

I had never realized that mission could be so painful. I was used to hearing that for the sake of his mission, Jesus left heaven and God the Father gave his Son. These phrases had become clichés to me. But when I heard my wife crying on the phone and saw my children's confused faces during our video calls, I began to understand a little better what it means to give up someone you love for the salvation of others. This offered me a glimpse into the heart of God the Father and helped me to imagine what that separation was like for him and the immensity of his pain. It also became clearer what it meant for Christ to leave heaven, what it means to leave those who love you, and what the pain of being away feels like when you realize that there's a high chance you won't be able to return.

Mission sometimes, though not always, requires us to leave those we love behind. Mission cannot exist without pain. It also raises many difficult questions: Will this turn my children away from God? Will my wife fall out of love with me? Will I ever be able to return to them? Will I come back the same person and with the same body parts I had when I left? Will my children forgive me for leaving them and going to war?

The true Missionary – Jesus – knew the answers to these questions and chose to give himself completely, to give his life for the mission entrusted to him by his Father. The Father also had to endure the pain of separation, just like my wife and children are experiencing during this war. The true Missionary did not run away from his flock – instead, he died for his flock.

Mission is the way of Christ, and this way sometimes demands from us what it required of him – to leave behind the comforts we have created and enjoy. You may have to leave behind your cappuccino, your delicious steak and mashed potatoes, your warm morning shower, your clean and comfortable bathroom and be ready, quite literally, to sacrifice your life. For some reason, in our civilian life, we ask: What are the arrangements for ministry? Will I have an office? How many days off and holidays will I be entitled to? Many people refuse to serve if it means moving to a small town or, conversely, to a metropolis. Some people struggle to serve without a large church in the city, others refuse to do so because of low salaries or "the stress of having to work a lot," while still others say that "ministry makes things too difficult for my family."

Of all the things mission demands, the hardest is leaving behind those you love for the sake of those you are called to love and serve. The heart of God the Father – who sent his Son on a mission all the way to the end – can be best understood by those who will never see the return of those who left them to go to war to defend their country.

I prayed that God would open doors for me to witness meaningfully and share the gospel. Little by little, I began lending a listening ear to the guys, offering advice and hope – hope in God, that is. Over time, I found many opportunities to talk privately to people about God. But I realized that something more than private conversations was necessary.

The train whisked us farther and farther east. Then we were in a bus that took us closer and closer to the place from which, at best, only a third of the numerous yellow school buses would return . . .

The closer we drew to our destination, the quieter we got, each one engrossed in their own thoughts. I thought about those I had left behind for the sake of this daunting mission: Olena, Danyil, and Matvii. I thought about this mission that requires such great sacrifice. Had I been wrong to go to the military enlistment office? How would my family – my wife and children – deal with all this? How would it affect their relationship with God, especially the children? How would it affect them if I were killed or captured and the Russians demanded a ransom for my release? But it was too late for second-guessing. The die had been cast. The decision was made. All that remained now was to have faith and be faithful.

Looking at the faces of those travelling alongside me, I asked myself: What makes me better than them, that they should die and not me? Looking at Tsyhan, who was also silent and contemplating something else, I asked myself: Why should I, a believer, remain on the sidelines of this war, while Tsyhan goes into it without knowing whether he will return? He, too, has a wife and children. And what about all these soldiers, the six or seven hundred of them in the battalion? Are they worse than me, that they have to fight and God has to deliver me from this horror? Mission means going the same way as your people and leading them to God. God himself knew no other way to bring salvation than to leave everything he had to become a part of this world in a particular place and time, to live through what his people were living through and bring them to the Father. He had no other way – and neither do we.

The closer we got to our destination, the more I realized that I had limited time to proclaim the gospel to those around me. I kept praying for open doors – and for more than private conversations with a few people – to share the good news.

The last transfer station was in a village in the Luhansk region, which was still under Ukrainian control. The next day, we would head to Sievierodonetsk. Many of the guys tried to hide their fear. Some joked loudly. Others described in vivid detail just how much they hated the Russians and what they would do with them if they got their hands on them. But most were silent. The air was charged with unease and apprehension.

The village school had already been damaged by bombs. About forty of us were crammed into a small room. Everyone had to lie down in rows, practically snuggled together, taking up the entire classroom. To the side was a table, where a light shone faintly. A captain sat there, writing non-stop.

The guys were swearing, joking, and acting crazy. Suddenly, Tapas stood up and announced, "Guys, tomorrow we will be in the war zone. Instead of quarrelling, you would be better off preparing mentally for what might happen tomorrow. Yevhen, would you mind saying a prayer?"

Soldiers from the communications platoon and the MANPADS platoon fell quiet, but others kept talking loudly. Some of my guys voiced their support for Tapas's idea.

Although I was happy to be asked to pray, since there was an officer present in the room, I approached him.

"Evening, Captain. May I ask you a question? I am a believer, and the guys are asking me to say a prayer before they go to the war zone. Please could I pray for them and offer some words of encouragement?"

The captain got up.

"Of course, I have no problem with that. Guys, we're going to war tomorrow, so let's listen to what this man has to say."

Everyone quieted down. Some of my guys and some from the MANPADS platoon stood up. One of them started to make the sign of the cross. The rest lay quietly in their sleeping bags – some doing their own thing, some eating, some still swearing or laughing, but more quietly now.

I read a psalm, explained it, offered some spiritual encouragement, and prayed.

The captain turned out to be the deputy commander for Mental Health Support. He came up to me and started asking questions: Could you encourage the guys from time to time, like you did just now? If we assemble a group of people, would you speak to them?

So when I had the idea to set up a chapel, I knew exactly which officer to ask. The permission was granted.

After clearing the room of rubbish and junk, it proved to be quite spacious. Serhii and I installed the electrical wiring necessary to supply power. We brought in a table. Serhii found a carpet from somewhere, and we laid it on the floor. In the damaged building across the street, we found chairs and brought them to the chapel. I used some empty weapon crates as shelves to store the volunteer-donated goodies brought by my colleagues from the mission: good-quality European canned meat stew, Snickers, energy drinks, coffee, dry sausages, sweets, and more. We would joke that we offered "nourishment for both body and soul." There was no door to the room, so Serhii nailed a piece of fabric over the entrance to serve as a curtain. In the chapel, we enjoyed a true spirit of ecumenism. Serhii hung all kinds of icons everywhere. I placed a painting of Jesus in Gethsemane right in the centre. Both on and inside one of the empty weapon crates, I placed New Testaments and prayer books for the soldiers, along with "The Four" gospel bracelets[4] that my friends had brought in when they visited.

Initially, only Serhii and I went in to the chapel. I kept the curtain open so that the guys could see what was inside and come in if they wanted to. Since our chapel was located close to the entrance to the basement, everyone coming in from the street could immediately see the entrance to the chapel on their right. The hallway was dark, but we always kept a lamp on. I hoped that the light from the chapel would not only help the soldiers navigate the dark hallway but also spark curiosity about our room.

At first, I thought that everyone was deliberately bypassing this door and pretending the chapel didn't exist. Later, however, I noticed that there was

---

4. "The Four" gospel bracelet showcases the message of the gospel with four easy-to-remember symbols. The heart means that God loves you, the sign of division means that sin separates you from God, the cross means that Jesus has saved you, and the question mark asks you if you will trust him.

almost always someone there – usually smoking and laughing loudly. Whenever Serhii came there, he would scold them and demand that they stop smoking. But I was just glad that people came at all. Whenever I had time, I also tried to visit the guys. I gave out bracelets and shared the good news of the gospel. This often happened before a difficult combat mission, when the soldiers had to wait for a meeting with the commander and chose to wait in the chapel. Some of them would go there alone at the end of the day and sit in silence, looking at the icons and making the sign of the cross. Every morning, some of them would tell me that they had already visited the chapel and prayed. Many soldiers I had never spoken to before began to greet me, treating me with the kind of respect parents of students show to a teacher in a village school.

The chapel began to take on a life of its own. The food, copies of the Gospels, booklets, and bracelets began to disappear, which made me glad. I restocked the crates with new cans of stew, New Testaments, and bracelets. Since there was plenty of space in the room and usually very few people in it, the wounded were often brought in and laid directly on our carpet, beneath the painting of Christ in Gethsemane. Soon the carpet was covered with blood. Often, at the end of the day, I would find the floor littered with piles of torn and blood-soaked rags that had once been clothes, bandages, gloves, syringes, bloodstained body armour, helmets, and even weapons. As I cleaned the room, I would pray for those who had been there that day.

Sometimes, I would find exhausted doctors awaiting evacuation fast asleep on the carpet, on chairs, and even directly on the concrete. And from the Gethsemane painting, Jesus looked at them with sorrow in his eyes.

The combat situation was getting worse by the day. The harder things got, the more people came to the chapel. Some of the guys couldn't stand the strain and left the unit without permission – going AWOL. The Russian propaganda apparatus somehow found out about this and began broadcasting distorted information about our brigade and slandering Ukrainian soldiers on Russia's main channels. This made morale plummet even further. In response, a well known Ukrainian journalist came to us to do a story to counter Russian propaganda and support our guys. After he recorded his video, we were invited to take a photo with him. I approached him and asked, "Would you like me to show you our chapel? You might find it interesting." The journalist did find it interesting. He filmed the segment about the chapel and posted it on his YouTube channel.

This video about the chapel caused quite a stir. Almost everyone on our section of the front learned about me. Soldiers I had never met before brought me icons they had found. I didn't know how to react. I tried to explain this was simply a place of prayer, not an Orthodox church, but I could not stop the flood of icons. And, of course, I could not refuse to take them. So I thanked them and stacked the icons in the corner. Serhii chose some – which were apparently more important than the others – and hung them on the wall. Some people brought handfuls of crosses, others brought prayer books, and still others brought small laminated icons inscribed with Psalm 90. I placed many of these items on top of the crates so that the guys could take them if they wanted.

One day, Nisan brought me about a hundred and fifty crosses and a drawing. "These are not ordinary crosses. They were blessed in Jerusalem! This is your domain, Father, you know best what to do with them," he said.

He kept calling me "Father" the whole time we were on combat missions, even though I was young enough to be his son. He was a burly man, who snored so badly that he usually stayed alone in another building so as not to disturb the others.

"Well, all right. I'll give them to the guys," I said. And I thought to myself that it was a good thing he didn't bring more icons because I wouldn't know what to do with them now.

A few days later, he brought icons.

The war situation was deteriorating. There were many wounded and dead. We had to go to Bakhmut to bring reinforcements. It was night-time. I was on twenty-four-hour duty at headquarters. The commander called out to Nisan.

"Nisan, we have to go to the city to get more men. You have to leave at 3:00 a.m. so you can cross the bridge and the road to Bakhmut before sunrise."

By that time, the Russians had already destroyed two bridges. Only one bridge remained, connecting Sievierodonetsk, like a peninsula, to the mainland across the Siverskyi Donets River. Somewhere on a hill, an enemy mortar unit was shelling the bridge and vehicles that were driving across it. The bridge was already badly damaged, and there were damaged cars scattered here and there.

"Commander, sir, the idea of going all alone gives me the creeps," said Nisan, looking at me. I was sitting at the radio. I quickly looked away from Nisan. Goodness gracious, what is this Nisan up to?

"If Father comes with me, then I won't mind."

"Father?" the commander had to clarify.

"Yes, Santa is a man of God, and I am ready to go anywhere with him."

Oh, no, Lord. Is he talking about me? I'm not a real soldier. Besides, I've just been on duty for twenty-four hours, and I'm terribly sleepy . . . and, if I'm honest . . .

"Father, gather up your things, you're going with Nisan," grinned the commander.

I was terrified. At that time, going that way seemed extremely dangerous. But what could I do? A little shaken up, I went to get ready. Perhaps the call sign "Santa" fits Nisan better than me – he is chubby, has a grey beard, smiling eyes, a deep voice, always laughs loudly, and never seems afraid. That's the thought that ran through my head.

I got into Nisan's car. As usual, he was cracking jokes. We drove slowly through the city, with the headlights off, steering clear of broken cars, downed power poles, and fallen wires. As we approached the bridge, Nisan got quiet. We stopped about eight hundred metres before the crossing. I prayed loudly. Nisan made the sign of the cross. Then he switched on the lights to navigate around the obstacles on the bridge and stepped on the gas. One landmine exploded in front of us, another behind us . . . The next thing we knew, we were on the other side. We drove along a road that kept going back and forth under our control or the enemy's. We needed to cross that section of the road as quickly as possible because it was often the target of anti-tank guided missiles and machine guns. Another moment – and then it was already behind us, and the road ahead was safer. Almost at that very moment, the sun suddenly rose! It was one of the most beautiful sunrises of my life. Everything around us, including the road, was flooded with golden light. We were the only ones on the road. No one was on duty – not even at the checkpoints. We were flying along as fast as the car and Nisan could handle. We were rejoicing and laughing like children. And there, on that road to Bakhmut, we finally had the opportunity to talk about all kinds of stuff, including God, who is so good to us . . .

It was the sixth hour of non-stop shelling of our headquarters quadrant. There were incoming shells almost every minute. Our building absorbed round after round, surprising us by how long it remained standing. There was so much dust inside that you couldn't see a person two metres away. One exit from the building was already blocked by rubble. The second, a wider one, was still passable. We were all sitting in a narrow hallway where there was the least likelihood of the ceiling collapsing. With each shelling, we tried to joke around and hurl insults at the enemy. But everyone knew that the building probably wouldn't hold much longer. The only question was: When would it collapse? Which fateful round would be the one to finally bring it down?

We had already made the difficult decision to leave the battalion's command and observation post and had found a place to move to, but we couldn't leave the building because of the ongoing shelling. I took a photo for my wife. I spent a long time scrubbing my face with wet wipes and trying to smile before finally snapping it. Then I messaged Olena to say that I loved them all.

Then I turned to the battalion commander, who was sitting across and slightly to the left of me.

"Commander, sir, permission to read a psalm and pray?"

"Permission granted. Not like there's anything else we could be doing."

I read a psalm, prayed, and just as I said "Amen," we were targeted again. But then, instead of swearing, I heard a unanimous "Amen." Everyone fell silent, waiting for the next incoming round. But it never came . . .

"Yevhen, the shelling stopped after your prayer," said the deputy commander for logistics.

"We must evacuate immediately!" the commander bellowed.

Gathered and ready, we were just waiting for this command. We had to run eight hundred metres to the evacuation point, where vehicles had been waiting for us for several hours.

When I ran outside, I could not recognize our street. Everything was destroyed. Houses and cars were on fire. There were deep craters left on the asphalt. There were piles of metal chunks everywhere, smoke, the smell of gunpowder . . . But we all came out alive.

The part of the city where the old command and observation post was located was a hot mess. Nearby, street battles were going on. Enemy subversive groups darted about all over . . . I was so surprised when Toha, Gnom, Vkusniashka, and Bohdan arrived at the new command post, laughing loudly and eyes open wide – probably from adrenaline. Bohdan was the youngest. In one of our private conversations, he told me that although he came from a Christian family and had attended Sunday school as a child, he stopped when he became an adult. He seemed to think that God had sent me to him. I suggested that we read the Bible together. Although Bohdan was agreeable, this was difficult to coordinate since we were in different units.

"Santa, we got a gift for you."

"What kind of gift?"

They took me to the car. In it were the icons from our chapel! The guys went back there, to that hell, to save the icons . . . How can I possibly get rid of these icons now? But what should I do with them?

Toha, Vkusniashka, and Bohdan were killed six months later in the clashes near the Donetsk Airport. Bohdan was only twenty-two. The icons they rescued from the fiery chapel are now in a suitcase in my empty apartment in peaceful Dnipro.

Faith

I want to write what people expect to hear when you say the word "faith" – that it will all be over soon, that I am strong and doing fine, that we will win, that God saved me and those around me, that war is a place for miracles and not just death, that I do not condemn those who are not fighting on the front lines, and so on. But the war has tested our beliefs and our understanding of what faith really is. And I think that the understanding of faith among those who are actually in the trenches is still different from that of civilians who have suffered due to the war, those volunteering in Ukraine, or those who live somewhere abroad.

Yes, there is a general understanding of faith as God's guidance to escape from suffering and difficulties – that is, faith as salvation from torment and trouble. My great-grandfather once had a dream – a vision from God, as in the case of Joseph – in which God showed him that he should move to another land – a rather unfriendly place known as the Kuban. My great-grandfather obeyed, moved, and survived the Holodomor.[5] What is this, if not faith?

But there is another dimension to faith – the kind of faith that sees the possibility of suffering and decides to dive headlong into it. For some, this may sound like foolishness, but for others, it is their choice in life and their relationship with God. This kind of faith does not try to flee or avert its eyes from harsh realities, hopelessness, and despair; instead, it chooses to share the burden of those who are forced to endure this journey. Such faith looks with eyes wide open at the horrors of war. It does not close its eyes to the hundreds of friends who have died. It does not simply scroll through a Facebook feed stained with the tears of young widows – widows of the men you once split a coffee cup with.

Faith does not turn a blind eye to the mutilated bodies of wounded fellow soldiers or shield its nose from the smell of rotting corpses, gunpowder, and smoke. Faith does not cover its ears when it hears that the group must go back and look for the head of a fellow soldier because, without it, he will be considered missing in action. Nor does faith cover its ears when a wounded fellow soldier, who is a stranger, is screaming in the bushes nearby as you run back from the contact line. Faith does not stand still when it is necessary to

---

5. The Holodomor was an artificial famine that took place in Ukraine from 1932 to 1933. It was organised by the leadership of the Communist Party and the government of the USSR. The Holodomor is considered a genocide against the Ukrainian people, resulting in an estimated demographic loss of approximately 4.5 million individuals in Ukraine during that period.

act, even though the odds of returning are slim to none. Faith does not sit idly by when help is needed, and you can help, even though it puts you in danger.

Faith does not pass by.

Faith is not just being positive. A positive attitude cannot be equated with faith. We have become confused in our understanding of faith. Our theology has become mixed up because we equate faith to positive thinking. Such faith is shown to be empty and helpless by the harsh reality of war. Faith means having your eyes wide open to witness horror, injustice, abuse, torture, murder, and rape while not simply accepting this reality. Faith plunges right into this reality – so that even in the midst of this horror, there is still faith. And faith seeks to process everything, to understand, to live through it. Faith brings all this to God and asks God honest and bold questions.

Before attempting to offer answers to the world, faith waits for an answer from God to the questions arising deep within one's own heart. But such answers come only after faith has been soaked in the horrors of war.

Faith is tears. Smiling is not a sign of faith. Faith goes towards what repulses us, and that is the opposite to who we really are. Faith perceives, accepts, and plunges into the filth of a stinking, sinful reality. Faith shares the pain and suffering of those around. Faith is permeated by what pierces real people in the terrible reality of war so that it can see everything through their eyes and feel it in their own skin. Faith is moved by their feelings and suffering. And finally, as a consequence, faith takes away the positive veneer. It completely shares in the suffering of a person (that is, it is affected by their suffering, empathizes with them, feels their suffering as its own, and comforts them). Just as God himself once did.

That is why faith weeps. Faith bleeds from the pain that permeates this world. That is why faith understands that this world needs God, this world needs rectification, healing, help, and salvation.

Such a broken faith in the midst of pain and suffering reveals the suffering God of Christianity. Such faith brings a person closer to understanding the suffering Messiah. Such faith can show a compassionate, active God who did not turn away from the distorted world, who did not abandon the broken world, and who did not start over, creating an alternative one with people with mended minds. A God who came into this horror to set things right and save us.

This kind of faith bears Christ, who left heaven (Europe, America, and even the comfortable atmosphere of his family in Ukraine) to plunge into the foul abyss of the consequences of sin and war. To share with people their pain, crying, and suffering. To survive torture and violence with them. To endure, like them, hopelessness and helplessness. To be by their side when there is only one path to take. To give yourself completely and not think about going back.

He, the suffering Messiah, went all the way to the end. And when it seemed that he had been defeated, he actually won. The faith that carries such a God – not exalted but belittled – strikes a cord in the hearts of all those who are suffering in Ukraine today. Faith resonates in the souls of those who were unable to leave in time, in those who didn't look for excuses but went to defend their country, and in those who allowed a loved one to go and do so.

Such a faith, which has shared the pain of creation's suffering, will understand that all creation, including human beings are not God's failed project, that heaven is not just an alternative to a failed project on earth, and that salvation is not just an evacuation to heaven. Such a faith realizes that redemption begins here on earth. And that is why it makes sense to fight for justice; to not put up with sin; and to care for creation.

That is why there is justification, a reason, for our desire to live here and now. During the war, I struggled for a long time with the realization that I wanted to live. I was ashamed to admit to God that I did not want to go to him. I honestly don't want to die. I want to live on earth and enjoy my own piece of heaven here on earth with my family. I believe that God placed this desire to live in our hearts – to enjoy life, to begin the process of redemption where we are now, to spread his design all around us, and to bring life to people and nature alike.

Humans and the earth are God's only project. There is no other. And it begins here on earth – where I am, in this span of time and space – and continue in eternity where nothing is distorted by sin. That's why believers have no right to remain on the sidelines of events unfolding around them. Believers must keep their eyes and ears wide open, their feet moving, and their hands working – even when there is suffering, pain, and war all around. We can't just sit around; we have to be actively involved – because the tragedy of war is all around us and we were created to bring redemption to this world and to embody God's plan in this sin-afflicted world.

I'm not suggesting that everyone should leave their homes and pay a visit to the military enlistment office. Although, today, God is calling some people to do so, just as he once called the disciples – who had just caught the biggest catch of their lives – to leave everything and follow him. The issue of believers in the ranks of the armed forces is complex and painful. However, being actively involved while the war rages on does not necessarily mean being at the very front of the combat line. But faith is definitely not merely talking about or reposting other people's stories. Talk is not assistance. Talk is not the gospel.

God did not just talk – he left behind, he came, and he saved. We cannot stop at listening to other people's terrible stories of pain and powerlessness and copy-pasting these on our social media. Faith is far more than this. It involves leaving something, coming somewhere, and saving someone.

Therefore, we must cultivate a faith that shares the pain of the world and looks honestly at the consequences of sin. A faith that reaches out to people who are suffering the fallout of sin. A faith that does not look back or rely on a way to get back. A faith that does not calculate the benefits to oneself. A faith that shares the sufferings of others. A faith that accepts and contemplates the harsh realities of our world and takes these to God, asks him questions, listens for his answers, and then communicates these answers to the world. A faith that, despite everything, wants to live on. Such faith brings hope. Hope for healing here on earth. Hope for eternal life. Hope for life on earth. Hope in God. Hope for salvation.

God Is Faithful

God is always faithful, no matter how terrible our human experience may be.

In my story, God has been very good to me and my family. I am still alive and have not been wounded even once. My family is also safe.

God has been with me, as well as with my wife and children, every step of this difficult trial. Sometimes, I'm troubled by this. I feel especially guilty when I think about those who were killed or about my fellow believers who lost their limbs.

Sometimes, I am able to stop thinking about these things for a while. But when I remember or look at those who have been killed or injured, I don't even want to think about why I am alive and well while others are not.

It is especially difficult when you are 95 percent sure that your brother is dead but, for some reason, his wife has been told that her husband is missing in action. She has been waiting for her husband for two years now, posting photos of their son and writing that they still hope to see him. Or when you see a brother in Christ with an amputated leg, then look down and see your own two feet in brand new sneakers – and you feel terrible.

There is also fear in returning from the front. It's not like in Hollywood films. Our war is so fierce that, sometimes, you have nowhere to go back to. Your country is still at war. Missiles and drones strike peaceful towns and villages almost every night. Cities might be without power and water for fifteen to seventeen hours a day. I myself cannot return to the city where we lived before the war. My children will never go back to their old school again. That familiar life has been destroyed. There's no going back to it.

And there is another dimension to this return – the civilians we have to come back to. It is especially difficult to come back to Christians and to church communities. They seem to be living in another plane – a plane of high philosophies but not practical theology. It is frightening to have to communicate with them. To listen to their sermons. To sing songs with them. To listen with them to Scripture texts that they do not understand at all, and to promises to God that they are never going to fulfil in their lives. They will ask me how I am doing, and I'm afraid that I will have to remain silent – or smile and simply say that I'm fine.

But all that still lies in the future. At every stage, we need faith and the power of the Holy Spirit. The war has taught me that if I have God, I have everything I need. I don't need anything else. And fighting is a normal condition of human life, especially for a Christian. If I fighting, I am living. And fear should not paralyze me but, rather, mobilize me.

Now my wife and I are expecting our third child. We are having a girl! We decided on her name very quickly. We weren't even searching for a name – it just came to us. Her name will be Vira, meaning "faith" in Ukrainian.

Faith. Throughout this time of war, faith has been with us. And now God, in his goodness, tangibly gives us faith through the gift of this baby, whose name will be Faith (Vira).

According to Ukrainian law, if a man has three minor children, he is discharged from the armed forces and may return home. So, very soon, I hope to hold Faith in my arms. Faith led me to save people from the "Russki mir," and now baby Faith will grant me deliverance from the war as I return to my family. Sometimes, things like this happen. It is a miracle. It is undeserved grace. Again, I don't know the answer to the question "Why me?" But, like salvation, I accept this gift from God.

The war is still ongoing. We do not know when or how it will end, or whether it will be a just peace or a short-lived truce that will simply give Russia time to amass forces and start a new and even more terrible war – just as it has done, time and time again, elsewhere in the world.

Either way, after the war, there will be millions of people broken by war asking themselves, others, and God: What's next?

This should mobilize us to act. It should mobilize those who are reading this.

But that's something for the future. For now, I look at photos of my family and smile, thinking about who my Faith will look like. I would really like her to look like my wife. To have sun-kissed skin and long hair – black and pin-straight – green eyes, and a wonderful smile. And that's how I want to look into the future – with great faith and little Faith.

    And you, please, pray for Ukraine.

    Do pray. And act.

"For me, as both a soldier and a Christian, it is extremely important to experience God and keep hope alive, even when it seems to be lost. Soldiers who are believers have a certain light in their eyes that distinguishes us from others, and this is because, for us, the end of life is not the end at all." Illya Flisiuk (p. 211)

8

A Christian in the Army: An AFU Officer's Story

Illia Flisiuk

*Junior Lieutenant and Platoon Commander,
28th Mechanized Brigade of the Armed Forces of Ukraine*

Greetings! My name is Illia. I'm a combat officer in the Armed Forces of Ukraine, and this is my story.

The full-scale war took us by surprise. We had just finished celebrating the winter holidays and were getting ready for the spring season in ministry. We were dreaming of a wonderful future together – Olena and I had been married for only six months, and she was two months pregnant. We were so looking forward to this baby, getting ready and planning, only to be blindsided by the war at the worst possible time, just as we were trying to find our footing as a new family.

I have not left Ukraine since February 2022. We decided that day we would stay, no matter what. We were strongly convinced that we had to be with those hurt by this war that had blasted into our quiet, settled lives.

I remember that morning. When we learned about the invasion, we quietly knelt and entrusted our future to the Lord in prayer. Then we packed my wife's things, and I had her go stay with her mother because I was worried about the baby and wanted them both to be safe. Here's why . . .

I was born and grew up in a city so ancient that the first mention of it in written history goes back over two thousand five hundred years. The city's current name is Bilhorod-Dnistrovski, but over the centuries, it has had more than forty names. The locals regard themselves as Akkermanians because, before the Soviet era, the city's name was Akkerman, meaning "white city" or "white stone." The city itself is located on the shores of the Dniester Liman –

an estuary formed where the Dniester flows into the Black Sea. Right by the water stands the famous Akkerman Fortress. The Odesa region is geographically divided in half by the estuary, and there are only two ways to so-called mainland Ukraine. One of these – our magnificent drawbridge in the resort village of Zatoka – was later destroyed by a Russian missile. When the Russians occupied Zmiinyi Island, I feared that Odesa might be attacked through our area. Since keeping my wife safe from potential threats was my priority, I sent her to safety and started packing my gear, getting ready for whatever came next. I expected a call from the military division where I had done my compulsory service and later undergone military training – but a call never came. Perhaps that was how it had to happen. I had neither the desire nor a strong conviction to head straight to the front lines. This wasn't through fear but because I didn't sense God prompting me to do so, perhaps because it wasn't the right time yet.

After spending several days alone at home, I realized that events were unfolding a little differently than expected. So my relatives and I began looking for ways to help. We began with something simple – offering free rides to women and children evacuating to the border. This didn't last long due to lack of funding, but we didn't give up. Instead, we cooperated with everyone we could, delivering humanitarian aid to both the displaced and the troops – everything from wet wipes to military gear and medical equipment. We took on anything that could somehow support our country during these times of hardship and pain.

However, we did encounter some harsh responses – some were judgemental or vicious, others were dismissive, accusing us of showing off and saying that there was no need for "heroics." But we were just hurting – hurting for our land – and doing whatever we could, heartbroken and teary-eyed. How deeply pained we were!

To be honest, at first, I felt resentment and even contempt creeping into my heart and mind towards those who criticized our actions, especially because these were people who had fled the country as soon as the war started or even before. These people fled and did not look back, and yet we were charged with lacking wisdom. Even worse, such judgements came from ministers who had abandoned their ministries and encouraged people to flee even before there was any real danger. In time, however, God healed my heart because I remained committed to my task and persevered in my efforts to help. Did God honour my step of faith? Yes, because our capabilities grew, our resources multiplied, and we found new friends – like-minded people with whom we were able to work together. God was blessing us. We were all convinced that now was our time to serve with our hands and our heads. We saw God's miracles again and again – groceries would be delivered at the last minute, or someone would give us just the right amount of money for fuel. We were inspired and felt empowered to change the world.

Later on, the shelling of Odesa and surrounding localities increased dramatically. For some time, we lived at my mother-in-law's house, but we couldn't even get a good night's sleep because we would keep waking to the sound of missiles, planes, and drones flying inland over our house. Eventually, Serhiy – my brother-in-law – and I decided to send our wives abroad to Moldova for a while. The churches there were happy to host those who were stopping over on their way to Europe. I moved closer to Odesa and lived with my wife's brothers in a church, where we set up a warehouse for humanitarian aid and continued delivering supplies to the needy.

My beloved Olena really had a rough time. A short stretch of marriage, a much longed for pregnancy, separation for over a month, constant stress, an uncertain future, and now, shattered dreams and plans – it all took a heavy toll on her. To our deepest sorrow, due to the lack of proper conditions, limited access to medical care, and the constant stress, we eventually lost our baby. One Sunday morning, just before the service, my wife called me and said that there was nothing that could be done . . . The earth may have kept spinning, but my world stopped. Prayers, preaching, psalms, and people – they all passed by me. All I wanted was to hold my wife close and cry out to God, searching for the comfort that could only come from him. I was grieving, and my grief was so deep and intense that only God was able to pull me out of it. I remembered King David and the death of his newborn child. Although our circumstances were drastically different, the pain was all too similar.

To say that I was in utter despair after hearing this news is an understatement. I was furious, confused, and crushed. I was overwhelmed by hatred and resentment, longing for retribution and revenge. Yet one thing struck me to the core – I had no complaints against God, not even the slightest resentment. Just a simple understanding – which came later – that all this must have had some purpose. I did what David did: I knelt before the Lord, accepted what had happened, and thanked my God even for this painful experience.

After we lost our baby, my beloved wife, seeing no reason to remain in Moldova, came back, along with Serhiy's wife. So we were reunited. We put our heads together and tried to figure out ways to expand the scope of our work. After much thought and prayer, we decided to start a charity. Fast-forward through registration and organizational details . . . we were successful and received documentation confirming our status as legitimate volunteers. We now had opportunities to cooperate with well-known international organizations. During this time, I made friends with several outstanding chaplains and Christian leaders. Later, during my time in the army, I leaned on those connections time and time again to meet the needs of my men. Even now, my wife and I remain in touch with some of these ministers, who continue to support our soldiers.

Army

As the months went by, I had my papers checked many times at various checkpoints, yet nothing came of it. I always carried my passport and military ID with me, just in case I was told that my time had come to serve in the army. That year, my travels took me all over Ukraine – but there was still no call to military service. I asked myself repeatedly if it was time for me to join the army. I had served before and had received good training. I didn't consider serving in the army as something strange. In fact, my father had served, too, and I was interested in it and had a knack for it. But I suppose it wasn't my time yet. I often stayed awake at night, wrestling with the realization that many of my friends have been on the front line for a while now, while I hadn't even enlisted yet. My world view as a Christian did not prohibit serving in the army or bearing and using arms. I am no pacifist. The conflict in my head was not a theological question but a matter of timing: When would it be my time to enlist? The news that the army currently had no need of new conscripts brought a measure of relief. I figured that God had a different plan for me. Still, whenever I wasn't too busy, I'd be troubled by nagging thoughts about the question of my army enlistment.

I have always respected those who bear the sword in order to uphold justice (Rom 13:4), and our country's law makes provision for the punishment of wrongdoers and the use of appropriate force – without abusing our status or position – to stop evil. Sometimes, I'd judge myself for sitting in a warm apartment by my wife's side while others were out there fighting and defending the country. However, I took comfort in knowing that I, too, was contributing in other ways, especially by bringing in substantial amounts of aid and supplies for the military, police, doctors, and volunteers.

Yet I was also searching for answers to troubling questions: Will I be able to look people in the eye? What will I tell my children in the future? When I saw people in military uniforms walking around the city, I couldn't just keep walking. I felt shame and self-loathing because I wasn't in uniform, too. I never ended up in a theological debate with myself over whether it is permissible for a Christian – it was crystal clear to me. I never disregarded a summons to the Territorial Centre of Recruitment, even if one came over a phone call, so I have earned a solid reputation there, particularly as a believer. It's worth mentioning because not all church people are treated in this way there, and unfortunately, the believers themselves are to blame.

However, on the inside, I was agonizing over the fact that I was still in the rear, going on with my life and occasionally delivering humanitarian aid, while my brothers-in-arms were risking life and limb on the front lines. My wife Olena could see how I felt, and she understood that, sooner or later, she would have to see me off . . .

I have always been convinced that defence is not a sin. When I got married, I resolved that, as a husband, I would never allow anyone to hurt my wife or family. I have always been ready to make sacrifices for those I cherish and love. But apart from my family, I also have a country, a culture, and a freedom I was born into and have always valued – aren't these worth defending? This freedom came at such a high price. I had a lot to think about. The idea of "running away" has always bothered and offended me. David didn't run away from Goliath. I have always been inspired by the way God's people fearlessly confronted evil. Think of David's three soldiers who took turns standing in the gap and ventured out on their own even in seemingly hopeless battles (2 Sam 23:15–16). Why do we sometimes choose fear over trusting God and living expectantly?

After much thought and prayer, one day, God gave me a sense of peace with this thought: "When your time comes, you will be confident and calm." I clung to those words. For a few more months, I continued to serve people – both the military and internally displaced persons. We celebrated another Christmas and New Year. Then God showed me that my time had come. On the anniversary of the full-scale invasion, I found myself walking towards the Territorial Centre of Recruitment and Social Support (TCR). This institution collects and stores information on men and women serving in the army and deals with conscription and discharge from military service. I had taken my military ID with me that morning, and this was not an accident . . .

So there I was, at the TCR. A man at the entrance asked, "Are you coming in here?" I answered, "I think so." And I went in. To be honest, I don't think anyone has ever been treated the way I was treated there. They greeted me politely and escorted me in. Everyone shook my hand – because some of them had been working there since I did my compulsory military service and had been there to see me off back when I was a young recruit. I felt like I belonged there and was pleased to hear good reports about my time in military service. I had never had any problems with the military institution since I had never evaded a summons and had always reported on time for all checks and completed all my training. When they found out that I had a university degree, they immediately suggested that I work towards becoming an officer. I agreed. Shortly thereafter, I received my call-up papers, along with permission to travel all over Ukraine until March, when the next deployment would take place.

Then came the hardest part – telling my wife the news. We live on the third floor, and as I was climbing the stairs, I thought about how to break the news to her. But not surprisingly, I didn't have to say anything – my beloved Olena was quick to catch on. She knew that I'd end up enlisting because I had been preparing for this moment for a long time. I had a stash of military gear by our bed, which I had been accumulating piece by piece since 2018. I'd kept up with my training and stayed in shape, taking courses and doing drills – both by myself and with a team. I had got paramedic certification and even a full set of training weapons. I had never spoken about this to anyone in my church because of the traditional views on military service.[1] But my military leanings often showed in my clothing and in habits typical of someone who's served in the army. Later, when I went for training, I packed the biggest suitcase I could carry, with a backpack to boot.

When I got home, my wife could see it in my eyes. She asked me directly if I had, perhaps, been to the TCR. My eyes lit up, and my face bore no trace of regret or sorrow. That's when I grasped the meaning of God's promise that I would be confident and calm when my time came. We knelt together and thanked God, entrusting our future into his hands. The twenty days we had left before my deployment were spent together – serving, visiting friends, attending church, and helping children and military families.

And then the check call came to go for training for military service. It was time. I had everything ready, packed and waiting for the right moment. Although I can't quite describe the state I was in, a certain inner trepidation and excitement was definitely part of what I was feeling – not fear, but the anticipation of something unknown and exciting. The paperwork was done quickly, and then I was off in the car – first, to one of the training centres for two weeks, and after that to the military academy in Lviv.

Those were some very interesting times. I found like-minded people and also made some good friends at the centre – not many, just two. We still keep in touch, even though we all serve in different locations. I hope we all return to our families safe and sound and remain friends even after the war.

---

1. Historically, Evangelical-Protestant churches in Ukraine have mainly embraced pacifist ideas.

After a ten-hour bus ride, I walked into the training centre, laden with tactical gear. The locals were stunned and immediately asked if I'd served in the army before. When I said yes, they relaxed and quipped, "That explains it; the best-prepared man is here." It was nice to hear but also awkward because many men came with almost nothing, as if they were going for a casual stroll. I've always been perplexed by the lack of discipline and focus in some people – and it's a pervasive phenomenon. Some men even seemed to be using minor health issues as an execuse to avoid active service. I had four serious injuries, but I kept quiet about them so that I wouldn't get kicked out. I would have been ashamed to lean on a lame excuse just to get out of the army. I had served in the Airborne Forces,[2] so I can't even imagine what it's like to back out in this way. Then again, my expectations might have been too high for this group of about fifty people who had never served in the army before. Later on, I instructed them on how to march, how to figure out "right face" and "left face" when we did our drills, how to address their superior officers properly, and many other things. Sadly, this also revealed an unfortunate reality about this war. When I joined, I was ready – I had refreshed my skills and kept up with the reforms in the army to stay up to date. But since most people hadn't done the same, I guess I had unduly high expectations of them. While there was still time, I shared my insights and skills with others. As they say, you could smell the military air about me from a kilometre away. I jumped in quickly and soon earned a certain respect and trust. It is important, especially for believers, to step up and be where you need to be and do what you have to do properly, regardless of others' attitudes. I didn't want these men to be clueless when they arrived at the academy because this would only have made things harder for them. There weren't many experienced guys among the recruits at the training centre but, before long, we found each other and banded together to prepare the rest for the proper taking of the oath of enlistment. I took this oath with great reverence because I realized that from that day on, the country had entrusted me with protecting its interests. Today, I still feel that same sense of awe.

The days dragged on, with each one feeling just the same as the day before. The first priority was to establish proper discipline among the new recruits and get them accustomed to life in the barracks. Having been in the army before, I was used to living in barracks, forests, fields, or tents. It didn't matter too much to me as long as I had something to rest my head on and doze off. This

---

2. The Airborne Forces are one of the elite military elements of the Armed Forces of Ukraine, where highly professional, well-trained, and motivated soldiers serve. They perform combat tasks in the most difficult situations.

two-week camp for grown-up boys was nothing special: drills, guard duty, and so on. But it was here that I made friends with some good guys. We got along really well and – thank God – were later assigned shared living quarters at the academy. Since we were also sent out on duty together, we were constantly together. They had it easy with me because I had already served and was able to teach them many tricks. For the record, they are now excellent officers, serving in various capacities.

Two weeks later, we headed to Lviv on a bus. Unfortunately, we couldn't enjoy the journey as we were travelling at night and couldn't see a thing; so most of us slept. Lviv, my wonderful, welcoming Lviv, where I once studied at the seminary but could not finish my studies because of the war. As usual, Lviv greeted us with heavy rain and cloudy skies. Rain is what we remembered most about that two-week training course. The constant rain added another layer of difficulty to our training but, looking back, it was probably for the best. On the whole, the training at the Hetman Petro Sahaidachnyi National Army Academy was both interesting and intense. Every day except Sunday was spent learning and training, with most of the classes held in the field and most nights punctuated by air raids and mandatory evacuation to the forest.

The first week was difficult. We had to master a four-year full-time programme in a little over two months. My head felt like it would explode because the amount of information we had to absorb was simply insane. The teachers gave us access to electronic archives for further self-study because it was impossible to cover all the required content properly in the allotted time. Mostly, we learned only the basics – just the fundamentals – and studied the rest on our own as we went along. After a little over two months of intensive training, we had our final exam . . . and that was it! We were now considered tactical level officers – ranking as junior lieutenants – and were sent back to our training centres to receive assignments to combat brigades.

I also want to write about something that happened during the short time between my departure from the training centre and my arrival at the military base. This experience left me with a terrible impression of our bureaucracy. In my opinion, these bureaucratic procedures violate basic human rights and show no regard for human emotion. My wife and I later referred to this incident as a "three-hour date." Yes, it was merely a date and not meaningful time spent with my family before I left for the front. The memory remains a painful flashback, stirring resentment and frustration against a system that failed us. I don't want this to become standard practice. Every person who defends this country should have the right to visit their loved ones, and this right must not be taken away from any soldier or from their family. So there I was, travelling by train from the Vinnytsia region to Odesa. At the end of my training, I received orders to report at the military base there within twenty-four hours. I was given a mere twenty-four hours to get there. Most of this time was spent on the road – except for just three hours in Odesa, waiting for a connecting train to Dnipro. Goodness gracious, I hadn't seen my wife for three months, and all we were given was a measly three hours! I was frantic. I had forgotten what it meant to simply enjoy her presence! We spent those three hours strolling through Odesa, side by side, holding hands. We didn't even know what to talk about or how to make the most of those precious moments before we parted again, this time for nine long and difficult months.

Honestly, it pains me to see that our wonderful country still experiences so many problems and such mistreatment of its people. But at least here in Ukraine, unlike in other places, we are able to speak up, tell the truth, and express our dissatisfaction. The freedom we are fighting for will certainly be won, leading to liberation not only from the invaders but also from inept authorities. God is at work here.

We cried because I couldn't stay and she couldn't follow me. Those three hours flew by like three minutes. Then I was on the train again, distraught and dismayed by this injustice – I was a volunteer, so why such treatment, and why all these rules? And yet, despite all this, my heart clung to the hope that we would see each other again and share more than a few words. After all, we had been married for just six months when the invasion began, so we still had many things to look forward to, many plans, decisions, and dreams to share. The war stole our happily-ever-after. We had lived for a year always on the go – constant volunteer trips, lack of money, and lots of stress and worries. And now, having sacrificed whatever little comfort we had, we were compelled to live apart from each other – I live in ever-present peril, while she lives in constant fear for my life . . .

These were the thoughts circling in my mind as I made my way to the front line. For a long time, I couldn't fall asleep. I felt queasy. My emotions were getting the best of me, and I was miserable. My precious wife, my dearest friend, was left behind on the train platform, weeping and waving while I headed off farther and farther eastward, to the place where life gets extinguished . . .

Combat Experience

I made my way to the Donbas, the city of Kostiantynivka – or, as I sometimes call it, "the Barrack Town." There were military vehicles and soldiers everywhere. I had to wait a few hours until they came for me. I was taken not to the unit's location but to a training ground to meet the troops. Let me tell you, it's hard to walk into a team that's already established and has been working together for a while. When you're the new guy, the team usually judges you based on your appearance, not your qualities.

I was transported in a dirty, dusty minibus to an unknown destination. Dozens of thoughts were going through my head. Naturally, I was nervous. The ride lasted about an hour. My first impressions were mixed. Everyone who joins the service has certain ideas about the whole process, but 95 percent of the time, expectations and reality differ. This was certainly true for me.

We walked up to a dense tree line at the training ground. First, I was introduced to the company commander. We were both surprised. In front of me stood a skinny, red-haired guy, about twenty-two years old. He had graduated from the academy in March, and I had started my course in April. In other words, we had both got to the war at practically the same time. Neither of us said much; our conversation was short and to the point. He immediately took me to the platoon I was to take command of the very next day.

So there I was, standing in front of the soldiers as the commander introduced me. The men were looking at me strangely – they had never had a commander before, and I was their first platoon commander. It felt as though they were looking for something specific. At first, I thought I saw contempt in their eyes, and I wondered if they resented another officer coming here to tell them how to do things. But then I realized that it was hope I glimpsed in their eyes – hope that I was someone decent and that I would become the leader they hadn't had until now. Jumping ahead, I will say that this is exactly what happened later, and they all followed me into our first battle . . .

Then I was invited to speak a few words. As a seasoned paratrooper, and not just some rookie, I knew that soldiers don't like a lot of yakking around. So I addressed my unit briefly, saying that I wanted to build a good rapport with everyone and wanted us to work together as a unit. Perhaps these guys didn't expect such a clearly military approach from me – and I caught a faint sparkle in the eyes of some.

Then came some rather tedious introductions to several senior officers. Most of them barely paid attention to me. Another officer posted? A new officer has arrived — well, okay then.

That evening, I was taken to an old, cramped house. As an officer, I was offered a room to myself, but there wasn't even enough room for my belongings, let alone space for any kind of comfort. I thought, "Oh, my God, is there no better place? How am I to work here?" I couldn't even rest properly there. Nevertheless, I lived like that for three days.

My duties began immediately. Since we had already been warned that we would be launching an assault, I began preparing my men, and we trained intensively in landings – strips of trees and bushes along a road or railway. But I still managed to catch some sleep during the lunch break. I felt more comfortable on the grass under the bush – despite all kinds of crawling insects – than in that rusty, sagging cot in the shack where I lived.

But, thank God, my misery lasted only three nights. Some guys from my unit offered me a spot in a pretty neat apartment they were renting in the city centre. They approached me at the training ground and said something like, "Commander, you seem like a decent and reasonable guy. We don't drink, we're not troublemakers, and we have a nice apartment, with a shower, good amenities, and shops close by. Do you want to move in with us?" To be honest, this was quite unexpected but, naturally, I gladly agreed.

I had learned long ago to notice and be grateful for seemingly trivial things that are actually signs of God's care for me. I'm incredibly grateful to God for the way things worked out. Since then, those guys have been transferred to other units and moved out, but I still live in that apartment. Now that I have the place to myself, I've made it my own and it's become a restful place for me.

In my subsequent work with my unit, just as in the training centre, I was able to earn their respect through teaching them, sharing tips, and leading by example – which included getting down and dirty in the mud just like them and going through drills together. As the guys saw my attitude towards them and their training, they realized that I genuinely cared about them.

As the days passed, we continued our preparations. One evening, the company commander called for an urgent meeting of all unit commanders. We waited . . . The company commander came in and said, "Get ready, guys, in three days we're going to mount an assault." Our first reaction was silence as we processed this information. Then we began analyzing the task and determining each one's role in this mission.

The mission was not difficult. Some of the guys were familiar with that area, which was formerly under our control. We spent a long time studying the routes, exit points, and other aspects related to this operation. All the while, I was silently praying and thinking about my wife.

That would be my first combat mission. A great deal hinged on this – my reputation, as well as the attitude of my fellow soldiers and superiors. This would also reveal to me what I was and wasn't capable of.

We spent those three days preparing, and I tried to get the soldiers in the right frame of mind and figure out how to assign them to the various assault groups. Being relatively new, I didn't know them well enough to assess each one's abilities and capabilities. These men differed in terms of age, mindset, health condition, and the level of their morale. I don't know how I managed it, but I figured it out and obviously did so successfully because – spoiler alert! – every single person from my platoon returned from that mission alive and with no injuries.

Finally, D-Day arrived – the first real combat mission, not just for me but for most of my men. We had one final meeting, orders were issued, we were loaded into the trucks – and then we were off. We were taken to the position, where we got into armoured vehicles in small groups. As we headed out, it was early morning and still cold. I was riding in the front on the armour, wind blowing in my face. It's hard to describe what I felt at that moment...

We drove at an average speed, carefully avoiding shell craters, and passed through old villages that lay in ruins, even though they had not been under occupation even for a day and were still under our control. There was no life left in them, and every house had been destroyed by long-range artillery and bombs, and pummelled with shells. Scorched earth, trees slashed by shrapnel, damaged vehicles, burned barns and sheds...

As we rode on, I thought, "My God, why is this happening? We are now heading into mortal danger because someone wanted to play conqueror. How frighteningly easy it is to go tearing down something you didn't build."

We arrived at the location where our foot raid was to begin. I didn't know then that this day would be the most intense and dangerous of my life.

At first, everything went according to plan. We disembarked without a hitch and split into groups. The first group marched forward on foot. It was a long way to the point of contact with the enemy. A little later, our group also moved out. And then the plan went awry. The third group went off on the wrong side and got lost. Meanwhile, my group caught up with the first one – and then we got stuck. Even though we were moving through very dense brush, an enemy drone spotted us. Then the shelling began. The first group pushed forward, but we couldn't do so because we were blocked by enemy mortar fire. The situation was getting dangerous. The first group pushed ahead alone, without support. The enemy targeted us and started sweep shelling us. I backtracked a bit to round up a few stragglers. Suddenly, a large-calibre shell exploded nearby, and a large piece of shrapnel flew near my face, so close that I felt the air move. At that moment, I realized a terrible truth: for many men, the first (and last) battle in their lives never happened, because they did not even see the enemy or where their death came from. It is very distressing... such losses always take the heaviest psychological toll.

We walked on. I took the whole group forward, going last to make sure no one fell behind. A whoosh, a flash, a loud explosion – a heavy 120 mm mine exploded about ten metres away from me. At first, I was surprised, then a little scared, but after a moment, I automatically started looking at my men to see if anyone had been hit. It was only when I saw that explosion right next to me did I truly realize that we were at war. Despite what anyone says, no one takes war seriously enough until it hits close to them. I wouldn't really say I was scared – it was more like I embraced it. This is war, and the enemy is afraid and hostile because they know we're coming for them.

When the intense shelling ceased, we moved forward. The two groups reunited, and we reached the primary line from which we were to launch the assault. The company commander took command over the radio, and we moved forward on his orders.

Everyone was waiting. Everything had gone quiet. But soon enough, all hell would break loose. A few minutes later, the order was given: "Move out! Engage the enemy!" Our group moved through the tree line, flanked by another group – and engage the enemy we did. We came under heavy fire – it looked like they had been waiting for us. We pushed them back pretty hard. Our commander was giving orders, and we followed them, making good progress – several enemies were killed at once and others began to flee, abandoning their positions. Suddenly, a desperate call broke through the radio chatter: "Help! One of our guys is seriously wounded!" It was a mortar mine. Unable to counter our attack, the enemy started shelling us with mortars.

We heard more cries on the radio: "Hurry up and send someone to get him out!" But it was impossible to do so as the battle was in full swing. A moment later, we heard the same voice again: "Please help me, I'm also hit . . ." And then, there was just static – the kind of noise you get when you hold the tangent of a radio and don't let go. Later, I realized that there must have been an explosion, causing another injury, and the wounded man probably clutched the radio in pain. Then the noise stopped, and the call went dead.

As it turned out, one of the salvos had hit a soldier from a different platoon, and he took the brunt of the shrapnel. A young guy named Sashko, the leader of that group, made the fatal mistake of running to help – which he shouldn't have done because that left his men without a commander. When he reached the wounded man, one of the retreating enemies threw a grenade – as an afterthought, really – and, tragically, landed a hit. The grenade killed the first soldier and wounded Sashko. Those were his last calls for help . . . and a minute later, he was killed by another incoming enemy mine.

When we realized that Sashko was gone, time seemed to stand still. My mind refused to accept it – wishing it wasn't true, wishing it wasn't him. Since we didn't yet have confirmation of his death, we hoped that he was only knocked out. But no . . . when the fighting eased, someone managed to get to that spot and confirmed both KIA.

During that encounter, we killed five enemy soldiers and wounded three others, but the rest managed to escape. But we could not enter their positions yet because the whole place was booby-trapped. And so our adventure continued. We sent a request for sappers, and while we were waiting, the infuriated enemy started shelling their former positions. For about an hour, they bombarded us with everything they had. We got our first wounded, and the commander ordered me to organize the evacuation. I moved forward to find the wounded. The first soldier was covered in blood, but, thank God, he just had small fragment wounds and was bleeding slowly. I tightened his tourniquet just enough so he was still able to walk and sent him off to the evacuation point. Next, I evacuated five people at once, all of them supposedly with concussion injuries from a nearby explosion. But I wasn't born yesterday – when they reached me, I saw that only two of them had real injuries and that the other three were just badly shaken and very scared.

All the wounded were evacuated, and we kept waiting for the sappers. Eventually, they came.

One of my sergeants approached me. He was a smart guy, in his fifties but very nimble. He and I will never forget what happened next. I heard a command on the radio: "Meet the sappers." An armoured vehicle came along and stopped a short distance from us. Four soldiers got out. Ten metres away from where they got off, there was a trench. They jumped into it – and then everything went quiet.

An armoured vehicle is a hot target, and the drone spotted it right away. Between us and the sappers there was a small but steep ravine, tricky to cross. For some reason, we had no radio contact with them. The sergeant and I shouted for them to come to us, but they didn't respond, although we could see their helmets peeking out of the trench – the blue duct tape on the helmets marking them as friendlies.

We shouted and waved, risking being spotted by the reconnaissance drone, but they still wouldn't come out of their hiding place. Then we decided to rush over and fetch them by the scruff of the neck if need be. We quickly descended into the ravine, and what happened next was one of the most dangerous moments of that day. We had already started to climb up the slope and had almost reached those sappers when I heard the whistling of an incoming mortar shell! Just as I shouted for everyone to get down, it exploded, just five metres away from me. I fell down . . . right next to three anti-tank mines! None of us was hit, but if that shell had landed within a metre of those anti-tank mines, they would have detonated and pulverized us into a red mist. Yet again, God's hand shielded us.

But that was not the end of it. When we returned after taking the sappers to the right place, we encountered an enemy tank in action. The enemy had seen our activity from a reconnaissance drone. With no cover available, we had to run in the open, risking our lives. We heard the first shot – and then an explosion . . . It's almost impossible to hide from a tank because shells travel at speeds of one thousand metres per second – and since the speed of the shell is greater than the speed of sound, we often hear the explosion before the shot itself.

At the first incoming round, we hit the ground. With the second incoming, we found a half-destroyed machine gun nest to hunker down in, hoping we wouldn't get buried there. We took fire – nine rounds, each hitting quite close. Since the enemy reconnaissance drone, Orlan, was circling right over our heads, I figured they wouldn't give up. I ordered my sergeant to dash for cover in the thicket, heading towards our group. He went for it, and I was left there alone. Then I noticed a small dugout nearby, just big enough for four people. I ducked in there and found five soldiers from another company already there. Well, I became the sixth to squeeze in there. The tank fired again. After its fourth shot, I saw light coming from above – the ceiling right above my head had been demolished.

I radioed my commander that we wouldn't be able to take fire for much longer, so he ordered us to pull back to the control point. Even though I was exhausted, I began to move because you gotta do what you gotta do. A mad dash over an open field under mortar fire – and I ended up in a thicket along the tree line, right next to our guys and their evacuation vehicle. Since this was a decent shelter, I stayed there. The firing finally stopped. That second tank had divided its fire between myself and my advancing group. Fortunately, other than getting showered with dirt from the explosions, no one was hurt. Soon enough, our artillery drove back those tanks. Relative silence followed, with just a few mine explosions here and there but nothing too serious. Overall, our attack had been successful, and we had gained a foothold.

A little later, we received reports of two confirmed killed in action. I received orders to arrange recovery. I got my team together, and four more soldiers came to assist us. Needless to say, I was part of the mission. Once the fallen bodies were recovered from the front line, we split into two groups to carry them so that we could move faster. Unfortunately, it began to rain, making our mission much more difficult. In addition, our route went through a ravine that was blocked by some trees felled by the shelling. We had to make our way through slippery mud. We decided to carry the dead out one by one. It was a trek of about one and a half kilometres down a muddy, blocked path through the thickets to get to the evacuation vehicle. Frankly, it was challenging. Since I had been tasked with transporting the bodies all the way to where the medics were, I couldn't leave any of my gear behind to lighten the load. So I decided to do a dry run by myself: hike in full gear all the way there, drop off whatever I wouldn't need, and then come back. It turned out to be a great decision as this allowed me to scout the whole path and identify any tricky stretches. After I returned, we headed out again, carrying the first body. It took us two hours just to get to the end of the tree line, after which we had to go uphill – a slippery, soggy incline. I don't have the words to describe the tremendous efforts we made to bring our fallen fellow soldiers off the battlefield. Half an hour later, the second group decided not to wait any longer and started their trek, carrying the second body. This saved some time, but we still had to hurry because it was getting dark.

So there I was, sitting at the bottom of the hill, staring at the dead body in front of me. A thought ran through my mind: What if he just got up now? I seriously entertained that thought, and I wouldn't have run away in fear if he had. For a moment there, there was nobody around but the two of us and the crickets in the grass, I felt I heard him breathe, and I even got closer to him, but it was just my imagination. It wasn't a hallucination or a breakdown, just a wild hope that there might yet be life.

Then I heard branches snapping. It was the other team, carrying Sanya. I put my weapon down near the first body and went out to meet them. I took over the stretcher, and we continued walking. Thoughts started pouring in: "Darn it, this young boy, only twenty-three, and here I am, carrying his body. Only two days ago, we were hanging out at the training ground, and he really wanted to join my platoon, and was trying to figure out a way to transfer. And now, I'm sparing no effort so that his body can be buried properly and quickly before the summer heat takes its toll."

We were utterly exhausted. An adjacent unit, while moving positions, saw us struggling to carry the fallen and helped us out. Those six soldiers picked up the first body and rushed up the hill, leaving Sanya's body to us. There we were, inching up the hill, slipping and falling on the wet grass, trying to keep the body from tumbling off the stretcher. Despair and desperation. The living fighting for the dead. Oh God, how do we get through this? Dragging, falling, getting up, and dragging again. Finally, we crawled to the top of the hill and made it to the road, a stone's throw away from the vehicle waiting to pick up our heavy load.

The medic asked if I was the officer accompanying them. I confirmed it and put my gear into the armoured vehicle. There was no place to sit because the bodies had been placed on the seats. So I just sat on my backpack between them as we slowly made our way to the medevac point, the place where the evacuation of wounded soldiers can take place. It was pitch-black inside. I was holding on to some kind of strap to keep from falling. On either side of me, I could feel the bodies of the two fallen soldiers jostling against me with every bump on the road. Even though I couldn't see them, I felt them brushing against me.

I can't quite put into words what I felt. It was not fear of the dead beside me – just an eerie feeling that I would be getting out of this vehicle on my own but they would not. As we rode, I prayed quietly, thankful to be alive. I had no idea then that I'd be returning here in three hours.

The medics moved the bodies in and out of the vehicle by themselves. I was completely spent. That's when I saw the seriousness of the wounds of our fallen fellows – beyond all help and hope. The first soldier's arm was blown to pieces, so he couldn't have been able to do anything to help himself; and his other wound clearly indicated an internal injury – his insides were shredded, and he had died of internal bleeding. As for Sanya, this young soldier's skull was cracked open from the explosion – all the way from the eyebrow to the back of the head, like a ripe watermelon. His skull was half-empty – bits of his brain must have fallen out as we scrambled through the tree line.

I looked at him and couldn't believe that he was dead. My mind rejected the thought altogether because I knew what dreams and plans Sanya had for his life. But as he lay there in a white bag, his head split open, this was it. After this – a morgue, a coffin, a grave, perhaps lots of flowers . . . and yet none of these things mattered to Sanya any longer.

I can still smell it at times – the smell of recent death . . .

Three hours later, I returned to my unit. The day was quiet and rainy.

I was in charge, and the plan was to leave the contact line in the evening. As darkness fell, the first group, carrying a pile of spoils, was sent towards our deployment location.

Once again, I had the hardest job – to personally lead the rest of the team out, getting everyone into vehicles and making our way out of there. I split the team into two groups. The first group headed out and radioed in once they made it to the evacuation location. We followed, but it was already very dark.

Soon after we arrived there, we came under heavy fire from Russian MLRS. I hurried everyone into the bushes to avoid being spotted by a reconnaissance drone equipped with a thermal imager. All around us, explosions shook the ground again and again. We lay like that for two hours, with nothing but some bushes for cover, hoping we wouldn't get hit. I prayed hard, telling God that nothing could save us except his hand. As soon as I finished praying, the shelling stopped. It had shifted to another sector – obviously, they were targeting areas systematically. I informed the commander that we had a little time. They promptly sent transport to pick us up. It arrived about thirty minutes later, and I got the men into the vehicles and made sure that everyone was seated before giving the command to move. Five or ten minutes later, the enemy again began razing the sector we had just left.

That day, I could have died on eight separate occasions . . .

We were given three days to rest. After that came more training and drills at ranges and training grounds. Although we were preparing for action, we didn't yet know what our mission would be, only that it would definitely be another assault. For about a month, we trained every day. In the army, there are no days off on weekends or holidays during war. I lost – and still haven't regained – the ability to consider time in terms of days of the week. I only think of time in terms of dates.

Eventually, after we were assembled and given a combat order, we were able to prepare for a specific operation. On the day of the mission, we loaded up on armoured personnel carriers and set off. As we passed through villages razed by the invading horde, I was lost in thought. My first reaction was to ask God why we were going through this, but then it dawned on me that the question was not "Why?" but "What for?" This wasn't a punishment from God. But evil and the spirit of bondage always come against freedom, against choices made by free will, against the pursuit of progress. We weren't here to pay for some wrongdoing – we were here to defend our rights. We were here to face the covetous, perverted, and diabolical mind that saw us as a threat, even though we had never been one.

When we reached a location that was still safe for armoured vehicles, we got off immediately and quickly moved out because time was of the essence. A guide met us, and we followed him along the tree line towards our designated spot. We almost made it there, but the enemy spotted us and opened mortar fire. Thank God, we managed to reach the halt point. It was a proper dugout, and relatively safe, so we took cover there and waited out the shelling. By then, darkness had fallen. It was time to move out to the contact line.

Some of my men were unable to go on, so I decided to leave them in the dugout and pick them up on the way back. We headed off into the darkness without them.

When we set off, I had no idea just how difficult it would be to get to the target location. The darkness was so dense that you could almost touch it. Our route ran through a tree line decimated by enemy artillery, with no trail or markers to guide us. We were literally groping in the dark. I had my men proceed in single file, each holding on to the backpack of the one in front so that nobody would get lost. Using a proper flashlight was not an option – we would have been spotted immediately and fired upon by the enemy lurking in the nearby tree line. The most we could allow was a tiny lighter flashlight held close to the ground to light our way just enough to stay on track.

Without speaking at all, we made our way through the ravaged thickets and the darkness. Our noses and lungs were filled with the thick smell of rotting flesh – the ground under our feet was littered with the corpses of enemy soldiers. Some of them were strewn about, torn to pieces; the remains of others were hanging from mangled trees that had survived the recurrent shelling. It was a good thing we only noticed these much later – otherwise, even fewer people would have made it to the contact line with me. We walked for about an hour, maybe two. Finally, we reached the target location, where we joined another group and assumed defensive positions. The nearest enemy was no farther than thirty to fifty metres away – so close that we could hear them talking to one another.

For two hours, we watched the enemy positions using night vision devices. The waiting was wearing us out. Eventually, I climbed up on the parapet to see what was happening, to see if there was any enemy movement in our direction. Everything was quiet, except for a fresh light breeze that felt especially nice against my face. We were very thirsty, so we drank some of our water, leaving enough for the return trip. I was quite heavy-eyed, so I looked up to the sky and offered a silent prayer: "God, I'm so tired. Could you give me just twenty minutes for a nap and not let anything go wrong while I'm sleeping?" Soon I was fast asleep. About twenty minutes later, there was some commotion ahead of our position. I woke up and called out to everyone to keep an eye out. Silence fell. Everyone stayed still, waiting for the incoming attack... Suddenly, there was a big flash about ten metres away from us where the enemy positions were. My ears were ringing, and I barely managed to turn my head in time to avoid both my eardrums being ruptured. An enemy soldier had tripped a mine that our sappers had planted before the group arrived. We opened gunfire, forcing the enemy to take cover and abandon any assault attempts. We stayed there for another three hours until we received the order to pull out. Dawn was breaking, so we could finally see the thickets we had been scrambling through in the dark. We returned the same way we came – it wasn't an easier trek, but at least it wasn't as dark.

We moved stealthily to the location where the rest of our team was waiting. I approached the dugout with the question, "Ready to go home?" The men perked up immediately: "Commander, is that you? Yay! Guys, he came for us, let's move!"

So now we few, we band of brothers, were back together and moving on. The enemy artillery had laid waste to the path we took the day before. So we trod lightly, looking out for mines. I could tell that the guys were quite unsettled, not knowing the way. I saw the edge of the tree line and told them about a path running through it. But we still had to make our way there. So off I went, while they yelled, "Commander, don't you go! What about the mines?" I began to pray, "God, I can't lead them all to safety on my own. Help me!" And I continued walking towards that path, clearing the way for them. Eventually, everyone made it to the path, which shortened our trek by an hour and a half. That meant we got to the evacuation location ahead of schedule. We even went a little farther, to a safer area.

I was so relieved that I didn't have to lead people through the thickets, where dead tree stumps were festooned with the intestines and limbs of enemy soldiers.

Once at the evacuation site, I radioed in my report. Soon enough came this message: "The box is moving. Fifteen little bits." That meant that a vehicle was on its way to us and would arrive in fifteen minutes.

After positioning all the soldiers under the bushes so that they couldn't be seen by a drone, I looked out for our transport. What a relief it was to see it coming – it meant that my troops would be able to rest.

That mission was a great success, and all my men and I made it out safe and sound. That time, God gave me the strength to be bold and confident – I could have stayed behind and given orders from a safe place, but I was there with my men, which made them more determined. On our way to the evacuation site, I heard someone say that there's no fear with such a commander around. But I knew all too well that if it weren't for my faith and my God, I wouldn't have been able to do anything on my own.

During that combat mission, not a single soldier was wounded and not a single explosion hit near us, except for that mine on the contact line. It was the single most uneventful mission we had experienced – in and out, quietly and smoothly.

Now let me describe the worst situation that unfolded a month after the events I have just recounted. As usual, we were preparing for a mission and had been assigned an area similar to the one we were going to storm. This time, I was not supposed to go with the group, so I focused my efforts on preparing my best people, training with them and going through each stage of preparation for the upcoming assault.

Finally, we were ready. The soldiers were energized, motivated, and confident that everything would be fine this time because the previous missions had been quite successful. The command drew up a plan, and we went over it and communicated it to everyone...

Except everything went awry. The first attempt to launch an assault failed because of vehicle trouble. We postponed our move until the evening. That didn't work out either. We rescheduled it for the morning. My deputy and I stayed up all night trying to sort everything out and make it run smoothly. But in the morning, we suffered another setback. Unfortunately, the vehicle that was supposed to carry another unit into position for a simultaneous assault was spotted as it exited the village. It was hit by an enemy Lancet drone and burned down. Thank God the crew and infantry got away with only minor injuries and burns.

The next day, plan B came into effect. I was on the road most of the time, trying to keep people focused. At last, the day came when we actually managed to move out. I stood by as my fighters got into the cars. They said, "Don't worry, commander, this time we will definitely make it."

That assault mission involved half of my platoon and a few men from another platoon. The rest of us stayed at base as backup. I watched on the monitor as our guys stormed that tree line. I was extremely worried that they might be wounded or killed. Although I was physically at our headquarters, mentally and emotionally, I was there with my men.

It looked as if the assault had been successful. My men cleared the trenches and dugouts and secured their new position. As usual, the shelling started. It became apparent that the enemy was trying to regain what they had lost. There was a bit of panic, so it was decided to send reinforcements, led by an officer, to handle the situation on the ground and set up a good defence.

The company commander did not want to send me there and instructed another platoon commander to head to that area with his men. But he refused. I couldn't figure out whether it was because of fear or simply because he didn't want to. The conversation got heated. I didn't care why he refused – I felt that I had no free pass and that I should go, regardless of whether I wanted to or not.

I stood up and addressed the commander: "Ivanovich, if no one else does it, then I have to." He looked at me and simply said, "Thank you!" I began to get ready. Since I had my gear with me, I quickly got changed and tried to get up to speed on the situation. The challenge I faced was leading a different platoon – not my own – to the front-line area where our company had recently carried out a successful assault.

We received our orders, piled into the Hummer, and went off into the night with the commander's blessing. I had a lot on my mind and very little time to spare. I quickly messaged my wife to let her know that I was heading out on a mission. Before long, we were on the road and heading towards the front line. God does indeed move in mysterious ways – and right then and there, he intervened. Somewhere along the way, our Hummer had a tyre blowout. Since we were far from the contact line, we had to wait for another vehicle to come and get us. I moved the men into the thicket for safety, where they could not be easily spotted. While we waited, these soldiers from that platoon began talking – and I overheard a few choice words about their commander. I decided to cut in. "Guys," I said, "excuse my interruption, but listen carefully to me. I want to ask you all not to disrespect your officer despite what just happened. You and I don't really know why he backed down. Let's just settle down. I am here with you now, and I don't consider you strangers even though you're not from my platoon. Since I'm in charge of you right now, you are mine. I'll look out for you just like I do for my own platoon. Just be careful and vigilant, and we'll get through this, all right?" "Yes, commander. If only everyone else were more like you – that would be nice." We chatted for a bit until I heard a vehicle approaching. It was a small pickup truck, and we doubted it could get us to the location. Still, we loaded it up with our weapons and munitions and got in. It was a tight squeeze – packed tight like sardines in a tin can. As we moved on, I radioed in that "the box was on the move" and hoped and prayed we wouldn't all get wiped out.

We didn't make it all the way to the drop-off point. With just about a kilometre left to go, we encountered another unit also heading there. They arrived before we did, disembarked, and moved ahead on foot – and were spotted by the enemy, who opened fire on the location just as we rolled in. A 120 mm mine exploded near our pickup truck, collapsing it. The men tumbled out of the back of the truck and ducked, keeping close to the ground. I wrestled with the jammed door of that clunker but finally got out and immediately commanded everyone to take cover in the bushes. We crawled into some old trenches, hoping to wait out the shelling. I didn't know our exact location, but thank God for the wash of moonlight – I managed to make out some landmarks.

We hunkered down, and I radioed our commander. More concerned with our safety than with rushing us onward, he ordered us to stay put and figure out where we were. With the help of the military app on my phone, I was able to pinpoint our location – we were 1,200 metres away from our intended position. That was a bummer because it meant we had to move very quickly and leave some of our supplies behind.

About thirty minutes later, my commander notified me that the enemy had shifted fire, giving us a brief window within which to move. After a quick headcount, we set out once again. Pressed for time, we moved quickly until we reached the planned drop-off point – a large dugout used for rotations, which had water supplies and some cots for resting. We were two kilometres away from the combat line. We paused to catch our breath, drank some water, and filled some bottles to take with us for the other guys. Just to be clear, out there, you get thirsty in both hot and cold weather because the heightened activity causes the body to lose water very quickly, eliminating the urge to relieve yourself and leaving you extremely thirsty.

Sitting in that dugout, I kept thinking, "Dear God, what are we doing here in this sod hole? The journey ahead of us is difficult and uncertain, no one knows what might happen. Why are we here? We haven't even made contact fire, yet we're already so exhausted. Will we make it? Will we prevail?" I was lying there thinking about my wife, wondering how she was doing, and asking God to have mercy on me for her sake so that she could hear my voice on the phone again and know that I was well and safe. I remember praying very often in this way, for God to save me for the sake of my beloved wife because of the closeness we shared and the great sacrifices we had made.

We decided to split into three small groups for the mad dash ahead of us across 750 metres of open, barren, mine-riddled fields. I said a quick prayer that we would be able to go the distance. I took the lead, showing the way, grateful to God for the moonlit night that enabled me to see everything clearly. We hardly paused, except for occasional checks to ensure we remained on the narrow path that the sappers had cleared for us.

Just as we reached the edge of the field and ducked into some ditches, we faced fire from an enemy grenade launcher. This went on for about twenty minutes. As soon as it quieted down, we made a run for it and completed that last leg of five hundred metres. We had finally reached our destination. We spread out in the dugouts, making contact with the other soldiers there. The guys from my own platoon, who hadn't known that I was coming there, cheered up a bit and became more confident upon hearing my voice. A few of my men had got a little banged up, and although all were walking wounded, they still needed to be evacuated. I requested that another group that was about to leave take them along.

We took up defensive positions. Everything was quiet for several hours. But in the morning, the enemy opened intense fire, pinning us down for quite a while. The shelling, which lasted almost until evening, was like a firing squad of mortars. Whenever I was not giving orders, I was praying silently, asking God to save us and let us complete our mission.

Eventually, the shelling stopped. We received orders to send out a unit to claim the trenches the enemy had abandoned and strengthen our position. The company commander radioed the list of soldiers in each group, and I rounded them up and explained the mission to them. Another senior officer, who was to lead the team, received further orders from the commander, who had a reconnaissance drone overseeing their movement.

What came next was deeply wrenching for me. Three people from my platoon and three from the second platoon were sent there. They moved together, but at a certain point, they split up: my men went to one side while the rest went to the other side, where, as it turned out, several enemy stragglers had been hiding. Their group commander's name was Vitalii, and he had a young wife and a little daughter. Sadly, he was killed in action in that encounter – their group fell just short of reaching a hideout.

I heard him clearly over the radio: "Contact, we have contact." Gunfire followed. They returned fire. The radio blasted with his yelling, "We're taking casualties! We're all wounded!!" My heart sank. I could still hear him over the radio, and I kept telling him to roll back. His replies were fading fast. "I can't... I can't... – I'm hit – it's bad – my lu – my lungs... send help... I'm hit... I'm..." Those were his last words. All I could hear after that was his wheezing. I realized that he was struggling to breathe, that he was dying, and that I could do nothing to help him. I can still hear his voice, shouting over the radio and pleading for help while I felt completely helpless and useless. I wanted to bring all those guys back safe and sound. We had overcome so many challenges on the way there and made it, and we had hoped to return to base joking about how, once again, we had dodged death...

Instead, these men were gunned down by an enemy straggler with a machine gun, who then promptly ran away. It all happened so fast. If only they had left a minute later, perhaps they'd still be alive.

Writing these lines stirs me up inside, like I'm stuck in that moment again. I have no words or the strength to explain in detail the tragedy that unfolded. I remember being angry at the time. All sorts of dark thoughts rampaged through my mind. But God kept me from falling apart. Whatever happened,

I had no grounds for griping, grumbling, or blaming him because he did save me time and time again. This is war, and we're in it. War claims the lives of good people. Each one has an appointed time. But even though you recognize this truth, every loss still weighs on you.

Despite suffering casualties, the first group, which was made up of three of my men, cleared almost the entire line of those trenches and took an enemy soldier captive. He was brought to me. At first, I was overwhelmed with anger and a fierce desire to tear this enemy apart with my bare hands. But as I looked at him and saw what a frightened wreck he was, deceived and tormented by his own superiors, I almost felt sorry for him. I remembered that we Ukrainians are not savages and resolved that no one was going to be cruel to him. We took the captive to the safest dugout and interrogated him briefly to at least figure out his identity and background. I offered him some water and gave him an old sleeping bag so that he could be a bit more comfortable lying down with his hands tied.

During the interrogation, he looked at me, all scared, even although I wasn't saying anything threatening or nasty to him. A little later, it dawned on me that I was sitting on the corpse of a dead Russian FSB officer, the Alpha chevron visible on his sleeve. I hadn't noticed the body at first because it was covered by a sleeping bag – but this sight must have made quite an impression on our captive. When I stood up, I accidentally stepped on the corpse's head and almost fell. The body, still fresh, was right in the middle of the passage-way, but because it was so huge – maybe 120 kilograms – no one could pull it out. The guys had resorted to just covering it with a sleeping bag. Yes, this kind of thing happens, especially when there's no time and no way to observe proper decorum.

I returned to my dugout. The reception signal was very poor, so in order to report to command, I had to go outside and hold up the radio. And right at that moment, a 120 mm mine exploded next to me. I was stunned – it felt like I'd been hit on the head with a stick. My eyes saw double, my ears were ringing, and I suffered concussion from that blast. To this day, I have continuous tinnitus.

I sagged forward, then backwards, and slumped into a ball. I might have blacked out, or maybe it was just the effect of the shock wave – I'm not sure. For several hours after that, I felt like I was in a fog, struggling with a headache and severe nausea. I would probably have vomited, too, but I couldn't because I'd skipped a meal in the rush to leave. I heard my unit radio in to report my condition and the commander's reply "++," confirming that he had heard them, and all was calm.

An hour later, we successfully repelled an attempted counter-attack.

It was getting dark. I was feeling progressively worse, and double vision had set in. My condition was so bad that it felt like an eternity... But when the darkness fell, we received an order to leave as a new unit was being sent to relieve us.

One of my soldiers – the commander of the group that had captured the prisoner – ran up to me and said, "Commander, good news, get up, we're leaving, get us out of here." He didn't know that I was injured as he hadn't been there when it happened. Without revealing that I was feeling very poorly, I stood up and ordered him to take a headcount of everyone who would be leaving. As it turned out, we had some extra soldiers, who had gotten separated from another nearby unit. Since I had double vision, I couldn't do a proper headcount.

In the meantime, to our surprise, things quieted down. Splitting into groups of four, we staggered our departure. We also had a captive whom we had to deliver alive.

We had run out of supplies – no food or water left, and we were really thirsty. We walked slowly along the same route we'd used to come in, moving a little faster on this time because returning from a combat mission puts a spring in your step, unlike moving towards the enemy. When we reached the edge of the tree line, I noticed that we were all piling up in one place, which was quite dangerous. I ordered everyone to disperse and take cover in some old foxholes for about ten minutes. Just then, I heard someone call out from the hole, "Commander, is that you?" "That's me. Sergeant, well, I'll be... are you still here?" I replied. I was extremely angry. I had instructed the wounded soldiers stay with him for evacuation – yet they hadn't left but were all still here. (This made it into my report later on.)

The sergeant continued, "Finally, guys, we're getting out of here. This is our commander – he always gets us out." We shared a little laugh, but we were not having much fun because we still had to cross the same minefield again. I was hurting badly, dizzy, and thirsty, and we had to dash across that field – the entire 750 metres – knowing that there was an enemy ambush party about 150–200 metres away to our left. I took the lead and ordered my men to spread out. We followed each other, keeping a gap of seven to ten metres to reduce the risk of being hit.

I had reached the middle of the field when I heard our drone in the sky. I stopped and watched it fly along the tree line we had just left. Suddenly, I heard machine-gun fire from the tree line occupied by the enemy. The bullets flew so close that I could hear them whizzing by. This is one of those moments that I recall with gratitude for God's protection: whatever compelled me to turn to watch that drone. I shouted for everyone to get down. We hit the ground. I waited a few minutes, but everything was quiet. So I continued to lead them out, despite feeling like I was about to collapse.

Finally, the perilous field was behind us. We ducked into some bushes and hunkered down. Someone suggested we rest, and I agreed wholeheartedly. In the bushes, we come across a single bottle of water, no more than a couple of hundred grams. What were we to do with it? We gave it to the captive, shocking him. But we had to stay human, even towards the enemy. Plus, we knew that there was a dugout with water ahead. We just had to press on, and soon we would be safe.

After a short rest, we continued. It was getting harder and harder for me to walk, but as the commander, I had to get every single one of my men out.

Finally, the most dangerous part of the route was over, and I could feel the last of my strength slipping away. Our wounded guys could not move quickly either. But stopping was not an option. We had to keep going. We decided that we would split up: I would take the first group to the evacuation location, and the second group would follow in fifteen minutes. Until they got there too, I agreed not to radio in that we were ready to evacuate.

So, the group led by one of the sergeants stayed behind. The rest followed me.

We walked for what felt like a very long time, although it might have seemed that way to me because of my concussion. At one point, I stopped and sat down. A soldier came over to check on me, and I reassured him that I was fine and just needed to sit down for a moment. I added that we were already on the road that led directly to the evacuation point.

A few minutes later, we slowly moved towards the pick-up location. I looked around as we walked. It was so quiet that I could even hear the crickets. I saw long-range missiles heading towards the enemy and watched their trajectory. A light breeze brushed against my face, and my legs just kept on moving despite the pain and exhaustion.

But when we finally reached the evacuation site, trouble hit. The second group had got lost somewhere – they had probably made a mistake with the directions. Without saying a word I took off my extra gear and weapons, grabbed only my radio, and walked back to where we had split up, which was about two kilometres away.

I walked back along the same path. I could still hear the sounds of explosions now and then, but I was calm and felt completely safe. I knew that God would not leave me and would help me complete my mission. As I walked, I talked to the Lord. I told him that I longed to do the simple, ordinary things –

to wash up, put on a clean uniform, go to a coffee shop and enjoy a cup of good coffee, call my sweetheart and tell her that I had made it through and that I just wanted to get into a clean bed and sleep for at least two hours. I told the Lord how grateful I was to be unharmed. Sure, my head was hurting and my strength was lacking, but I really, really wanted to get my guys out of that hole. I asked God for just a little more strength. Miraculously, my blurred vision cleared, my heart rate steadied, and I even quickened my pace.

It took me about thirty minutes to find the second group. I had tried several times to call them on the radio but was unsuccessful – apparently their battery had been dead. I prayed, "God, help me to find them," and in a few minutes, I did! They were sitting in an old, wrecked dugout, waiting. The sergeant with the wounded knees – the same guy I had been with while hiding from tank fire on a previous mission – asked in surprise, "Commander, is that you again? You're injured and yet you came for us? Wasn't there anyone else?" I told him I'd never leave my men behind. His reaction was a mix of relief and confidence that everything would turn out all right.

The two of us hugged.

On the way back, I was clearly running out of steam. So I let the guys go ahead, saying that I wanted to make sure no one lagged behind – although the truth was that I didn't want to hold them up. They went on, and I followed slowly. But I soon realized that I was falling far behind. They were getting farther away, and I was walking more and more slowly . . . And then I felt completely exhausted. I fell on one knee, then the other, and in an instant, I was lying on the ground out in the open. I don't remember whether I passed out, but I felt I had no more strength and could not go any farther. I knew there was a road nearby and that vehicles could be travelling with their headlights off for camouflage purposes, so I crawled to the side of the road and lay down, putting my radio by my head in case the commander came in. A car did pass by me, and I thanked God that I was not run over. I must have blacked out again . . . Suddenly, I jerked awake because I was feeling cold. It must have been five in the morning, and I was soaking wet with sweat. I don't know how long I lay there. Eventually God gave me the strength to get up. I walked another kilometre and finally reached the evacuation point. I heard my soldiers talking – no one even noticed that I had arrived. I just sat down next to my gear and leaned on my helmet as if nothing had happened. Then, the sergeant popped out of the bushes and asked, "Commander, would you like some water?" Of course, I said yes. I drank and washed my face. Just then, I heard the familiar and welcome hum of our vehicles approaching. The drivers who came to pick us up were very surprised that we had gone so far beyond the target evacuation location.

I pushed myself to the limit to make sure that all my men reached safety. I don't think I could do it all again. It only worked out because of my hope in the Lord and a simple but sincere conversation with the Creator right in the middle of the theatre of war.

When we arrived at the base, I was greeted warmly and almost immediately, shoved into a minibus and sent to the medical centre. The doctor examined me and diagnosed my concussion. After a shower, clean clothes, a hospital, and an IV drip, I was able to text my wife.

This entire story is filled with amazing miracles of God's protection. Never during my service and combat action did I doubt that God was with me. I could have died so many times while fighting this war, but clearly, God has other plans for me. I'm not special or better than anyone else, but everyone has their appointed time. My time to die hasn't yet come, and so I continue to serve faithfully. For me, as both a soldier and a Christian, it is extremely important to experience God and keep hope alive, even when all seems lost. Soldiers who are believers have a certain light in their eyes that distinguishes us from others, and this is because, for us, the end of life is not the end at all.

To this day, I can still hear the last words of the fallen soldiers, and I still remember how helpless I felt as I heard their voices yelling through my radio. I still see their faces, and I still can't fully accept that these brave soldiers are gone. These memories often keep me awake at night as I replay all those scenes in my head. They remain fresh in my memory – and perhaps they always will.

My Life after Active Combat Experience

Once I returned to the unit after undergoing treatment for a severe traumatic brain injury, I was no longer involved in direct combat. Instead, the commander assigned me to the company's command post. My duty followed a rotation: I spent four days of rest and preparation, followed by four days leading the defence in the proximity of contact line positions. Although still considered the contact line, this area was a little farther into our controlled territory. There was a small dugout, with a few cots for sleeping, a workstation with monitors and an internet connection, a communication station linked to the front line, and observation logs.

After a few months of diligently carrying out his duties and leading the unit in repelling enemy attacks, the commander decided to take leave for the first time in two years, leaving me in charge of leading the company and overseeing our defence.

During my command, all objectives necessary for the unit's survival were fulfilled, all materials required for constructing defensive fortifications were delivered in full, and all replacements and rotations were properly planned and executed. In the absence of the regular commander, there were no refusals to serve, no wounded, and total loyalty from the senior command. I am convinced that it was the Lord who gave me the wisdom and determination to do my job and do it well.

Moreover, we managed to cause such massive fire damage to the enemy that in the days before I handed over the company to the commander, there were no more shootings or attempts to storm our positions. I personally directed fire from our combat vehicles, making corrections in their aim as guided by the drone. We had a pretty good track record, and the success rate of our combat sorties exceeded 80 percent. One of our teams became quite popular among other units, and for a good reason – these guys truly excelled in their work.

One day, I went with the soldiers in search of a new location that would allow us to deliver fire even more effectively. We arrived at the spot and walked around, surveying the area. It looked like we had finally found the right spot. Using a modern navigation programme on my tablet and a digital rangefinder, we were standing there calculating our options when an enemy reconnaissance UAV spotted us. Of course, they opened mortar fire on us – it was very close to us, and they were targeting us purposefully. Suddenly, I had an idea. I told our driver to quickly get into the car and drive away, while we followed him at a moderate pace along the tree line. This way, we managed to move our vehicle to a safe distance. Then we ran towards it, one after the other, keeping about five metres between us to avoid crowding. When the car slowed down and rolled forward in first gear, we jumped right in. This simple move allowed us to save our vehicle and avoid becoming a stationary target. The enemy invariably targets transport because it is so important for logistics. However, we managed to complete our task and get all the necessary data for targeting the enemy; and thanks to this small adventure, we also gained valuable combat experience.

Once again, I realized that my quick thinking did not come out of nowhere but, rather, because I had prayed before we set out, asking the Lord to protect us and enable us to carry out our task. All credit for my competent performance goes to God, who sustained and empowered me.

My Relationship with the Church

Let me start from the very beginning. Before I joined the army, I was a member of the church board in our local evangelical church. The very next day after the invasion, the pastor called us all to a meeting. The first issue raised was that we were being asked to vacate our rented premises. This was a military facility – an officers' recreation centre – and it was going to be set up as the headquarters and barracks of the local territorial defence battalion. We were instructed to remove all our equipment because several hundred soldiers would take up residence in the sanctuary. Of course, we complied promptly.

The second issue was more complicated. It had to do with the first thought that crossed the minds of most of our ministers – that it was time to leave the country. Since I had served in the army before, I was the first person to be discussed. I found this extremely frustrating. I had only been married for six months – and that's what they focused on. Without even asking for my opinion, they immediately began pressuring me to leave the country. I responded bluntly, the way I usually do. I said that I was waiting for a call from the relevant authorities regarding the draft and that I was not going to run away. I was genuinely surprised that my fellow believers didn't support my decision since they had known that, since I was a child, I had been interested in the army. I have always disagreed with the draft-dodging views held by some of my fellow believers, and I still don't understand why, after all these years, this old pro-Soviet tradition has not faded from their world view. While I cannot condemn them personally, I can never condone what happened next.

Some board members and I proposed that instead of running away, we engage in volunteer work to help the soldiers now living in our sanctuary, ministering to them through Scripture and prayer and serving through both conversations and food. We received this answer: "That's just not our place."

But I didn't give up. My wife and I moved to Odesa and, together with my brothers-in-law, began volunteering on our own. As I have already mentioned, we began by helping people with children to get to the border. Then we began distributing food and helping to transport goods for military needs. We took on whatever we felt we were able to do. At the same time, members of my home church were leaving Ukraine. In a single move, people I had once looked up to were undermining the messages they had so often preached from the pulpit.

For almost a year, I was actively involved in volunteering, while also preaching and teaching from time to time. My wife and I were involved in the planting of a new missionary church, which eventually gave me its blessing to serve in the army. None of my fellow believers who fled abroad ever sent me a word of encouragement or blessing. Later, I found out that they were simply afraid or hesitant to contact me because they believed that I didn't need their support – even though I genuinely longed to hear from them.

Everything I went through compelled me to reconsider what it really means to be a local church. The war shattered my previously held views, and now I consider all believers to be my church. I lost my "home church" but gained something far bigger. Today, I have friends from different churches and fellowships in Lviv, Kyiv, Dnipro, Odesa, and Zaporizhzhia. And this is far more precious to me than what my soul once grieved over. I have new friends – including chaplains, pastors, and leaders of various ministries – across the country. Now, people who I thought were out of my league during my pre-war Christianity consider me a friend. Those who once formed my circle of influence have now been replaced by people who play a far more significant and meaningful role in my life. For this, I am grateful to God. Today, my name is remembered by people I have never even met – yet they sincerely support my family, pray for me, and love Ukraine with all their hearts.

Despite many frustrating experiences, I do not deny the importance of the local church. I will just have to find a home church that is closer to me in spirit and understanding. I long to find a church like this, and so I continue to build bridges with new people and new churches, casting aside stereotypes. I love the church. And everyone who welcomes me today, who sincerely tries to understand me and maintain some kind of relationship with me – I consider these people to be my church.

I believe that this war will do more than put an end to the madness of a certain neighbouring regime. It will also break down the walls between believers of various traditions and denominations, giving birth to new and genuine relationships centred on a single shared reality – the person of Jesus Christ. And that is all we really need.

"Loving is never easy. It is always demanding. But no matter how tired I am, I still have the strength to continue my service to God and my ministry to the people of Ukraine. And I intend to carry it on to the end." Andriy Polukhin (p. 236)

9

Loving Was Never Easy

Andriy Polukhin
Private First Class and Photographer, Public Affairs Service,
24th Mechanized Brigade of the Armed Forces of Ukraine

If you love me, you will keep my commandments.

John 14:15

Relationship with God

I'm not a fan of action films. When I was a kid, our family would have film nights. As I was still little, our time together in our one-room apartment felt warm and cosy. As a child, I craved peace and calm, and the staged shooting, explosions, and casualties among minor characters completely ruined those warm feelings.

My twin brother and I were born and raised in Kyiv. That's why I'm tempted to tell my childhood stories as a dual narrative – after all, we did have all our adventures together, even though we sometimes viewed them differently. And we had plenty of adventures. We were born in 1991, so our family experienced the hardships of the transition from a planned economy to a market economy after the fall of the USSR.

My dad is Russian. He grew up in Siberia – the city of Kiselyovsk in the Kemerovo region – and has an engineering degree and a handy knack for fixing things. One of the most precious gifts my dad gave us was a 16-bit game console he built himself. Until recently, it was still in working order. I also remember how he would bring Kinder Surprise – a chocolate egg with a toy inside – for my brother and me. At the time, those were a rare treat in our neck of the woods. But this was really the extent of the treats and joys our dad gave us. For reasons I don't fully understand, he was not very involved in our childhood and upbringing. Although he could have spent more time with us, either he didn't want to or thought that this was our mother's responsibility. He moved to Ukraine in search of a promising position at a factory in Kyiv. He met my mother through some mutual friends – I think it was at a birthday party for the lady who later became my godmother. Dad didn't share much about his parents or relatives. My grandfather on my dad's side was gone before I was even born, and my grandmother passed away when my brother and I were about six or seven years old. My dad wasn't in contact with his relatives, not even by letter. I found an old letter from my aunt to him, asking why he had disappeared and saying she had given up hope of receiving a reply from him. I still don't know if I have any relatives in Russia – not that it matters now. I try to maintain a good relationship with my father, even though all these missing pieces make me wonder if it's worth it. Even though he's not particularly interested in what's going on in my life, he's still my one and only dad.

My mother hails from Kyiv. According to my grandparents, they spoke Ukrainian when she was little, but after going to Russia to get her degree, my mother became russified. She's very creative, but she had to take whatever work she could find to support our family. My grandparents settled in Kyiv after World War II and met while working on the post-war rebuilding of the city. Serhii, my uncle, was born first, followed by my mother and her twin brother, Vitalii. On every holiday, we used to gather at my grandparents' house for a feast. My mother would take us to visit them often, and they took good care of us.

My grandfather and Uncle Serhii had a greater impact on my personal growth than my father. My grandfather was a World War II veteran, but he never told us – the young kids – about the war. It was only when I was an adult that he shared how, during the Nazi occupation, he and his friends found a machine gun in the woods. As they were shooting it near their village, they were detained by the German police and sent to do forced labour in Germany. After the fall of Berlin, my grandfather fought as an artilleryman on the Japanese front. He was wounded in action there, suffering a shrapnel wound to his head and partial hearing loss. My grandfather was a very hard-working man and, for as long as he was able, tended a vegetable garden near his apartment in Kyiv.

But the best storyteller was my grandmother. We'd cosy up in our bed in the evenings, and she would tell us her stories to get us to sleep. She would recount the Holodomor, describe how a local one-armed communist took down a cross from the local Orthodox church, and tell how their village was occupied by the Nazis during World War II. While she appreciated the Soviets providing free apartment housing, she rejected the Soviet anti-religious propaganda. "We didn't tell anyone that we believed in God, but we kept icons at home and prayed," she told us. Indeed, her stories – untainted by propaganda and simple enough for a child to understand – were the best lessons on the history of Ukraine I ever received. In high school, I could recall one of her stories to accompany almost every major chapter in the modern history of Ukraine. She was also an excellent cook, as is the way of most Ukrainian women.

Since Uncle Vitalii got married after my mother did – and lived with my grandparents until then – he spent a lot of time with us kids. I don't remember for sure, but I think he was the one who taught my brother and me to sing. It wasn't about singing well or properly but just singing out loud – that's what we started doing with him. He was a member of one of Kyiv's Messianic communities. Thanks to him, I visited a Protestant church for the first time. Shortly after their wedding, he and his wife moved to Germany. But that was the '90s, and I was too young to remember them very well.

I also don't remember anything about the economic crisis and its aftermath, nor the days when my parents skipped meals so that my brother and I could eat. My earliest memories begin with preschools – yes, plural, because I had to switch schools. For no apparent reason, I started having vision issues and underwent surgery to correct strabismus. My final preschool group was a therapeutic one – and this proved to be a turning point in my life.

It happened in the summer, as the preschool graduation celebrations were underway. A travelling amusement park rolled into our neighbourhood. We'd get on all the rides that kids that small could safely ride. At the end of our trip, the teachers asked if we'd like to go to the House of Horrors. Of course, everyone said yes – after all, this was an amusement park, and it was just another fun ride, right? Well, I sat through the entire ride with my hands over my face so I wouldn't see those scary dummies. Terrifying sounds had me jumping out of my seat. When the cart finally stopped at the end of the ride, I couldn't move until someone called out to me. One of the teachers looked at me and remarked that I was "a bit shell-shocked." I liked my preschool and my teachers, but what happened that day made me lose trust in people.

Around this time, I began sorting people into "good" and "bad" categories. The "good" ones were a small group: my family, a few teachers, and my friends. The "dark" or "evil" ones were people who had hurt me; and after the House of Horrors ride, strangers were also included in this category.

I started school. Naturally, my brother and I ended up in the same class, along with some mutual friends from preschool. First grade went well, but troubles arose in second grade. Whether due to my reserved personality or because I was taller than my peers, I was labelled "weird." Subsequent bullying shattered my confidence. That was my school life. Sure, I had some friends, a few buddies to play with outside school hours – mostly thanks to my extroverted brother – but at school, I was verbally bullied. The same thing happened at the first few summer camps we attended.

But one camp – a very different kind of camp – changed everything. It happened that my godmother came to church after being invited by Uncle Vitalii. She accepted Jesus, and so did her daughter, Masha. One day, my godmother came to wish my brother and me a happy birthday, and we all went to the nearest church. It was a Pentecostal congregation. I remember going up to the front during an altar call, even though I don't remember the words of prayer, the call itself, or the reason I decided to go forward. Although nothing really changed after that altar call, when summer rolled around, my godmother called my mom and asked if my brother and I wanted to go to a camp. This was a different kind of camp – it included tents and lasted only a week. I immediately began to imagine all the ways I could be bullied there. But my brother really wanted to go, and since our parents wouldn't let him go by himself, I agreed to go as well.

On the bus ride to camp, I realized that there was something strange about these people – both the adults and the kids. If someone made a joke, everyone laughed. No one insulted or hurt anyone. Since the weather that week was mostly rainy, many of the camp's regular activities were cancelled. Nevertheless, the camp became a landmark event in my life. This was the first time I had encountered authentic Christians. I was only twelve and didn't understand much about what it meant to have faith. I just learned some songs and memorized some Bible verses. But I really wanted to go back to that camp again.

The next summer, my wish came true. Even though only a year had gone by, I had a much deeper understanding and found the Bible lessons extremely engaging and meaningful.

I accepted Jesus on the first day of July 2004. It was a completely deliberate decision. I don't remember exactly how I felt in that moment – only that I wanted Jesus to be in my life as the friend whose love I had experienced through those camps. From that day on, I began to talk to Jesus.

At that time, I didn't go to church – I didn't quite understand the reason for doing so. Every night, before going to bed, I talked to Jesus about whatever had happened during the day. I hung the printouts from camp where I could see them often. I read the Bible on my own, although not consistently. It was a while before I began going to church – and when I did, I stayed for good.

We had to pay a fee before the next camp, so my brother and I had arranged to drop off the money at a Sunday service. I handed the fee to Pavlo, my future mentor – although I never used that term to describe him, that's exactly who he was to me. During the service, I realized that the church was where I belonged and that I needed to be there. A year later, I got baptized – curiously enough, before my brother, even though we were always side by side.

As I felt Christ's presence in my life, I became more confident around my peers at school. I was beginning to change. At some point, my mother agreed to go to church with me. She accepted Jesus on her third visit. In one of her testimonies, she shared that she had noticed how much I had changed – and that's where she saw God's hand. My mother and my brother were both baptized in 2007.

I got involved with the youth ministry almost immediately after coming to church. At first, I was just a listener, but later, I was given a small tech-related responsibility. Over time, my responsibilities grew. Eventually, I was entrusted with leading small youth gatherings. I came to love our youth group and this ministry, and I began to see how God was revealing himself in my life as love. This, for me, is still the most important part of Christianity.

For the final night at one of the camps, my brother and I prepared a song – "Grass by the Home" – which we performed to a karaoke track. Surprisingly, the performance went well and people liked it. When my mother found out about his, she connected us with our church's music leaders, who were in the process of forming a church choir. This was the beginning of my music ministry. Recognizing that my brother and I were good at music, the choir directors offered us one-on-one music and voice lessons. My brother began learning the guitar. Eventually, we were both invited to join the main worship team. Around the same time, our choir director, Yulia, suggested that I consider studying music at one of Kyiv's seminaries. I did so and, despite the fact that I was already dealing with PTSD (post-traumatic stress disorder) by that time, graduated in 2014.

The Revolution of Dignity in 2014

The Orange Revolution[1] of 2004 passed right by me. I was thirteen and sick with pneumonia, so all I saw was the news and orange ribbons everywhere.

---

1. The Orange Revolution was a series of mass protests and acts of civil disobedience that took place in Ukraine in the autumn of 2004. These events were triggered by widespread fraud in the presidential election, which resulted in Viktor Yanukovych being declared the winner,

Back then, if someone had asked me, I would have said I was an Orange supporter all the way, even though I wouldn't have been able to give reasons for my response.

At that time, church and politics seemed incompatible, even though many members of my church were actively involved in the Orange Revolution. However, when protests began again in the autumn of 2013 – eventually leading to the Revolution of Dignity[2] – figuring out how to regard the protesters was not complicated for long. The action escalated quickly. One day, scrolling through my social media, I saw a photo of a girl from my church – with her legs beaten and bruised. She was a student at the Kyiv-Mohyla Academy and had supported the protests against the then Ukrainian president's arbitrary decision to assimilate with Russia. The night the special police force unit "Berkut" beat up protesting students, she was among the victims.

I had never felt such a strong sense of injustice. This was a peaceful protest, and these were not criminals. This was someone from my own church. This struck very close to the heart because it was one of my youth group members, someone I cared about, who was hurt. I didn't want anyone else to get hurt.

After the students were beaten up, the Euromaidan protests grew stronger. An energetic group of Christians set up a prayer tent and held prayer services. Ministers from the New Life Church in Kyiv were among the organizers. One of them was Oleg Magdych, the youth pastor at the time, who later went on to minister to soldiers and now leads a team with the Hospitallers – a volunteer medical battalion that treats and evacuates the wounded. On hearing about these efforts, I joined the tent team. The prayer tent was a place to drop off donated food and items for the protesters on the barricades. I joined the security team and distributed sandwiches; on several occasions, I stayed overnight to keep watch. That's how I became involved in the Revolution of Dignity – until January 2014, that is.

---

causing outrage among supporters of his rival, Viktor Yushchenko. The protests lasted several weeks and led to a re-election of the president, which Yushchenko won. https://en.wikipedia.org/wiki/Orange_Revolution.

2. The Revolution of Dignity, also known as Euromaidan, was a series of mass protests and civil unrest in Ukraine that lasted from November 2013 to February 2014. The primary reason for the protests was the government's decision to suspend preparations for signing the Association Agreement between Ukraine and the European Union. February 18–20, 2014, were the most tragic days of the Revolution of Dignity, when mass killings of protesters took place on Independence Square in Kyiv. As a result of these events, President Yanukovych and his government were removed from power. The Revolution of Dignity resulted in significant political and social transformations in Ukraine. https://en.wikipedia.org/wiki/Revolution_of_Dignity.

Around the same time, I was invited to work at the Light in the East missionary society. As administrator of the missions department, I was responsible for organizing and providing material to support various events, which took up most of my time. The mission often supplied Bibles and Christian literature to the prayer tent, and I was involved in delivering these materials.

In January 2014, I was in the middle of seminary exams when I heard about the first protesters killed on the Maidan. I couldn't stay in class a moment longer, so I sought permission to leave and headed straight there. As I watched the smoke roll down Hrushevsky Street, I experienced once again that strong sense of injustice. Peaceful protesters had been killed by the authorities – how could this have happened? I began to realize that I was of little use just standing around our prayer tent. Sure, we were praying and helping the activists, but the protest was in its third month and there was still no resolution in sight. So I took to the barricades, too. In February, when the call to march to the Verkhovna Rada was issued, I took a day off work to join the march.

I arrived there just as protesters in Mariinsky Park were being beaten up by the police forces. The government quarter was cordoned off, so I stopped at the intersection of Shovkovychna Street and Instytutska Street and joined the other protesters in throwing stones at the Internal Troops. That was the first time I had ever used physical means to defend myself. Most of the stones we pulled from the pavement and threw didn't even reach the troops, but the sheer number of stones flying in their direction stopped their advance. I didn't want somebody else getting hurt. But then the Internal Troops began using rubber bullets and flash grenades. Before long, I had to help bloodied people get to an ambulance. From time to time, I helped move things to fortify the barricades. And so it went on – until the authorities decided to increase the pressure.

That was the first time I witnessed violent clashes. Stones, non-lethal weapons, tear gas, burning rubbish and tyres, yelling and shouting – a motley crew of a crowd opposing a black horde under criminal orders from the authorities against their own people. Eventually, they did manage to push back the protesters and drive them from Instytutska Street. I was one of the last to retreat and got hit on the head just as I had almost reached the barricade. Thanks to the hard hat I was wearing, I hardly felt the blow.

The incident responsible for my PTSD took place just a few minutes later. I saw my friend from church outside the October Palace. She was crying, could barely breathe, and was obviously very shaken up. Even now, it hurts me deeply to picture that scene. This girl and I had ministered together frequently through church camps and youth groups. Seeing a member of my church, someone from my own community, being so badly shaken up and mistreated by the authorities left a lasting mark on me.

The girl was taken to a first-aid station in the October Palace and given a sedative. I was given a cane – taller than me – because riot police were beginning to surround the Palace. As I held it, I realized that I was not a pacifist. I was ready to use that cane – but thank God, we were able to leave through the back door.

The girl's friends took her in, and since it was too late to catch a ride on public transportation, I started walking home. Once I got home, I discovered that I could not recall much about the roads I had walked down. After that night, I couldn't bring myself to go to the Maidan again. A few days later, the protesters were shot by the police. I began to blame myself for not going back. That's when my PTSD kicked in. I constantly replayed those events in my head, wondering what I could have done differently, what I should have done better. I kept praying and asking God why those people – who may not even have known him – had died while I was still alive. Sometimes, I'd be completely engulfed by these memories and tune out everything around me. When something irritated me, I would often react by turning aggressive.

Meanwhile, Russia began annexing Ukrainian territories. Within a few months, a girl I was in love with found out about my feelings from a friend. She sat me down and explained that she didn't feel the same way. A few months later, my grandmother passed away – and we had been very close. I didn't know what to tell God as I prayed. I just knew that if I stopped praying, things would get even worse. At times, my prayers were sharp reproaches against him for what had happened. But I still felt that to lose God would be to lose everything. I clung to Jesus, even when I was angry with him.

I was totally shattered by the events of the year 2014. But I'm also grateful to God that, in his infinite wisdom, he used all those experiences to rebuild me. It was a preparation for the future.

The War

The Lord touched my heart one night in a tent in the middle of the Zhytomyr region. I was on a mission trip, standing guard over our belongings in a large church tent. While praying to Christ and meditating on the One who took my place on the cross, I received a revelation – similar to that of Job. Who am I to question my fate? Am I not the one with so little control over my life? Who holds life and death in his hands? Isn't it he who was crucified for me and gave his life for me? And if he did that, then he surely does not intend to destroy my life. I repented of my accusations against him and entrusted justice into his hands. I cried all night long. I don't know if this would qualify as healing, but the PTSD was gone.

Around that time, I heard about fellow believers who were travelling to the east of Ukraine to serve as chaplains. I spent the entire summer of 2014 on mission trips, returning home to Kyiv in time to celebrate Independence Day on 24 August. For the first time in my life, I found this holiday truly meaningful. As I followed social media posts about those trips to the east, I began praying and thinking about joining. It turned out that one of the deacons of our church, Oleg Marinchenko – who later became the first chaplain at Donetsk Airport – was preparing for such a trip. I was very interested in what he was doing.

During my time off, my pastor reached out with an invitation to visit Druzhkivka in the Donetsk region. The city had recently been liberated, so this would be a mission trip. The local church, Light of the Gospel, led by Pastor Fedor Bespalov, was bringing in and distributing humanitarian aid and serving displaced people. That was my first encounter with wartime realities such as military vehicles, checkpoints, and ruins. Once again, I saw the threat to my loved ones and felt moved to join the defence campaign. I began praying seriously about this. Another missionary who went with us and also wanted to be a chaplain encouraged me to make that decision.

In December 2014, Deacon Oleg approached me about going to Donetsk Airport.[3] He knew about my adventures on the Maidan. His chaplaincy community wanted to establish regular rotations of ministers at the airport, but they didn't have enough people to pull it off. Oleg asked if I knew anyone who would be willing to go. I called up friends who had been on the Maidan with me – some were already involved, others were thinking about enlisting. And then I thought: Why not me? As it turned out, Oleg had been hoping that I would answer this call.

No one really seemed to understand my decision – not my family, for obvious reasons; the young people in my church were dubious; and my decision came as a surprise to most of my friends. Back then, the word "war" was far scarier than it is now, when we are well into the third year of the full-scale

---

3. After the victory of the Revolution of Dignity in Ukraine, the Russian Federation provoked a crisis in the border regions of Ukraine in the spring of 2014. This led to the emergence of separatist movements there, which seized part of the Donetsk and Luhansk regions. From September 2014 to January 2015, heavy fighting occurred between the Ukrainian army and Russian-backed forces over control of the Donetsk airport.

invasion. One of my good friends later admitted that when I announced my decision, he thought that would be the last time he'd see me.

The mission organization of which I was part was a tremendous help in getting together the necessary gear. On 10 January 2015, I set out of Malyn on my first rotation, along with Pastor Leonid Kravets. It was his second rotation – his first had been when we were in Druzhkivka. I began my service with the scouts of the 80th Brigade. They were ordinary guys, very much like those we'd see at youth gatherings and mission trips. I realized that those soldiers were indeed ordinary folk – just like our neighbours, our classmates, our friends. These were the very people our churches were trying to serve. These were my neighbours – the people here in this ravaged village just outside Donetsk.

We arrived at the rear station, but getting into the airport took some time. Only military vehicles could make that trip and we, as chaplains, weren't on the roster for the first round. For the first time, I saw the fear in the eyes of uniformed men – and that's what scared me the most. I found a quiet place and began to pray. In my prayer, I told God all I'd been thinking about the war and the reasons I had come here, and I asked him to be with me. As I prayed, I experienced a deep sense of peace. I felt calm and stayed calm throughout my entire time at the airport. I experienced first-hand the truth of the apostle Paul's words: "Do not be anxious about anything, but in every situation, by prayer and petition, with thanksgiving, presents your requests to God. And the peace of God, which transcends all understanding, will guard your hearts and your minds in Christ Jesus" (Phil 4:6–7).

This was my most challenging rotation. Even now, I consider it one of the worst hotspots I have ever been to. But at the time, I didn't realize this – I thought that was just how combat operations were. A full account of this trip would probably be too long, so I'll try to be brief. I ended up at the new terminal of the Donetsk Airport, where I was to relieve Deacon Oleg, who had been there for more than two weeks. He found me quickly. Then Pastor Leonid headed to the control tower. Earlier when planning this mission, we had agreed that we wouldn't just talk to the soldiers but also play a practical role. Since we had opted to provide medical care, our position was by the side of the combat medic. So, the first thing Oleg showed me was where the medic set up and what to do when the wounded were brought in. He introduced me to the "doc" himself – Ihor Zinych, whose call sign was "Psykh." Ihor's family attended a small Baptist church near Kyiv, so we hit it off quickly.

Intense fighting broke out the following day, with the wounded arriving every ten to fifteen minutes. There were four of us providing medical aid at the time, and we were able to help almost everyone – even the heavily wounded

"Fedya," who had pneumothorax and internal bleeding. Evacuation took place that evening, followed by another rotation later that night. Oleg was able to leave during that rotation. He asked me if I wanted to leave as well since only one chaplain had to stay on duty and Pastor Leonid was also there. Since I'd been there just two days, I thought to myself: Why did I come here if I'm just gonna leave now? So, of course, I stayed – and I have zero regrets about my decision.

I will remember the next day – 16 January 2015 – for the rest of my life. The enemy threw everything they could at the new terminal. They managed to get inside on the upper floors and pelted our positions with explosives. There were many wounded, but our troops stood their ground. The enemy troops then deployed tear gas and forced us out of our hideout. So there we were, about fifty people, standing in an open space, unsure what would happen next. Suddenly, I saw a repulsive green and yellow cloud forming near the upper floors of the terminal. This cloud began to move towards us. Instinctively, I started praying, and a fellow Orthodox soldier next to me did the same. I hadn't even finished the sentence "God, send even a small breeze" when I felt a rush of air on my face. The wind moved that cloud towards the enemy, who then started throwing gas grenades outside so that the wind would drive the gas cloud towards us. But this time, after our brief prayer, the wind stopped completely, and the gas just rose into the sky.

The battle lasted all day, with only brief respites. That evening, while trying to rescue a wounded man, I was hit by shrapnel from a mortar shell that exploded against the terminal wall, hitting several other guys along with me. I received minor wounds in both legs and in my left shoulder. At night, the fighting subsided, but the next three days were filled with uncertainty. It became clear that we were caught in an operational encirclement.

Three days is a long time. We felt trapped in the tight confines of the First Post. Two dozen wounded soldiers were awaiting evacuation – but that was no easy feat. The last two shuttles that made it all the way to the airport were hit by a rocket-propelled grenade just as they began unloading. This made it challenging to find a willing driver and vehicle to evacuate us. Every few hours, we received radio transmissions promising to pick up the wounded – but no one came. The more time that passed, the more I began to feel that I might never make it home. Everyone there probably had similar thoughts. During those three days, we had virtually no food or water. Sleeping was difficult because of the cold. On the third day, I discovered a warm sleeping bag and got inside it, finally feeling warm for the first time in days.

I am still baffled by what happened next. It was late at night. I was bundled up in my sleeping bag, but I could hear everything around me. After a short while, I saw a light in front of me – pleasant, like the dawning sun. I felt as if I were being lifted up and carried away. Surrounded by this golden light, I was approaching something that looked like a gate, with the source of that light just beyond it. As I did so, I sensed a question being presented to me: Do you want to live on? I began reflecting on all the things I hadn't done yet. At that moment, I realized that I wanted to have time to start a family. I decided to answer yes – yes, I want to live a little longer. As I was thinking this, I heard some movement and the sound of an engine. They had finally come for us!

I was picked up along with the wounded. As we were leaving, I heard bullets pelting our vehicle.

Two days later, the enemy blew up the new terminal.

Ihor was killed, along with sixty other soldiers. So, my ministry to the troops began with funerals. The bodies were returned over a two-year period, and each time, Oleg, Pastor Leonid, and I were invited to pay our last respects. There were so many funerals that I came to a point where I couldn't get myself together to attend. I was all right physically, but it took a huge emotional toll... Still, time and time again, I dug deep and went anyway.

The hardest part was the farewell to Ihor Zinych. The funeral was held at a local Baptist church I'd visited before. As I approached the coffin, his brother saw me, quietly took my hand, and held it until it was my turn to deliver the eulogy. We still keep in touch. Ihor's death showed me that soldiers sacrifice themselves for others and, in doing so, embody the sacrifice of Christ. They prove their love for their families, their people, and their country right up to their dying breath. And I wanted them to know what Christ has done for them. Ihor had the option to rotate out of the Donetsk Airport even before I got there, but since there was no replacement for his position, he chose to stay – again and again. He set an example for me. Even though Ihor had left the church shortly before the war, he clearly believed in the gospel, and he proved this by his heroic actions. He was the first sergeant and medic in the history of Ukraine to be awarded the highest national decoration – Hero of Ukraine. Sadly, this was conferred posthumously.

That was the beginning of my chaplaincy ministry. I can't officially call myself a chaplain because I'm not an ordained minister, which is a requirement for that position. Technically, I was a volunteer chaplain assistant, but regardless of my title, I was ministering to the guys. From then on, I began making frequent visits to the front. I'd bring my guitar and sing, talk to the guys, and share the gospel, and this continued until 2019. For the most part, the other chaplains and I spent time with the 36th Marine Brigade, but we also had a few rotations with the 57th Brigade. We ministered in Shyrokyne, Pisky, and the surrounding villages. What I went through at the Donetsk Airport made it easier to connect with the guys. And my experience in administering first aid came in handy during the full-scale invasion, enabling me to serve as a medic in 2022.

Full-Scale Invasion

I got married in 2018. The war is what brought me and Olya together. She also wanted to help people in the eastern parts of Ukraine. That's why she joined a team of missionaries in Svitlodarsk, a city near the front line. Around the time we were discussing where we'd live after getting married, we were invited to join a team in Svitlodarsk who were doing a lot of social work and needed more people. We lived there until the full-scale invasion. We hadn't planned to have children yet because we lived in a war-ravaged community that needed our help. We ran a youth centre and brought in international donors and volunteers from all over Ukraine – all to show that this city near the front line is still part of Ukraine and deserved to be supported. I found myself growing attached to the local youth and longed to help them achieve a brighter future.

But God had other plans for us. The full-scale invasion began.

The east faced the full-scale war two weeks earlier. The Russians destroyed utility lines: power stations, gas pipelines, and water supply hubs. Many civilians suffered severe consequences. Our neighbouring village, Novoluhanske, was already relying on power generators a week before the Russians breached Ukraine's northern and southern borders.

I had my bulletproof vest and helmet ready. Reports of troops amassing on the borders and intense shelling along the front line were clear omens. A call from my brother woke me up early on the morning of 24 February. I immediately set up a safe "workspace" sandwiched between hallway walls and started monitoring the news. When I learned of the enemy's advances in Luhansk, Kharkiv, Kyiv, and the south, I decided to leave the city. At the time, Olya was in Lviv, which is in the western part of Ukraine. Thanks to friends, I was able to join my wife in just three days. While travelling, I spent most of my time on the phone, connecting fleeing families with churches that could take them in for the night and figuring out how humanitarian aid could be channelled to Svitlodarsk and the Donetsk region.

I couldn't sit back and do nothing while war was sweeping across my country. My friends, acquaintances, and brothers and sisters in Christ were suffering. The nation I loved and belonged to was suffering. I wanted to help, but in those early days, neither volunteering nor social work felt like the right role for me. Around that time, the Lviv regional administration issued a resolution requiring all men who had come to the region since the beginning of the full-scale war to register at the nearest Territorial Centre of Recruitment (TCR). Needless to say, I did so immediately. The officer in charge of registration at the TCR was a former company commander with the marines, and I had served with him during a rotation in Shyrokyne. He spurred me on to mobilization by asking me if I wanted to join the fight. I said yes.

I didn't tell my wife about wanting to enlist. I hadn't told her even half of what had happened to me during my earlier six months of service. Olya and I talked about it only later, and seeing her reaction was heartbreaking . . .

I was assigned to the 24th Mechanized Brigade. It was evening when our bus got to the base. After a quick medical examination – which was more like a document check and questions about my overall state of health – unit assignments began. When asked about my education, I mentioned the seminary, my chaplaincy experience, and my tactical medicine skills. That's how I ended up in the medical unit on 7 March 2022.

Medical Unit

Those assigned to the medical unit got lucky with their living quarters. We moved into the empty wards, which were far better than the barracks – where dozens of people had to share one room. As I write this, I can see God's helping hand even in such little things.

Very soon, I was asked to conduct basic training in tactical medicine for the new recruits. Out of the three hours of training each day, one hour was dedicated to tactical medicine. Although one hour a day is not a lot of time for such a course, at the beginning of the full-scale invasion, people were needed – lots of them and quickly. Our brigade did all it could to get the recruits as well-prepared as possible. I taught about five hundred people over the course of that training. My call sign was settled quickly and predictably: "Pastor." I was open about my faith and chaplaincy experience, so this name came as no surprise.

Nine days later, we were sent to a hospital in the tiny town of Hirske in the Luhansk region. Our medical company had been stationed there since the brigade was deployed to the combat zone in the summer of 2021. Instead of getting right to work, we received additional training during the first few weeks. The Lord provided for us in that, too.

The medical company was a unique crew: highly skilled doctors, anaesthetists, and traumatologists. Those who did not have a medical degree absorbed the necessary knowledge as best as they could. We wanted to be helpful. One of the officers, who was a translator of tactical medicine protocols, expertly lectured on advanced tactical medicine. One of the mobilized men taught tactics, passing on the information he had learned at a Special Forces course. There was also a hands-on module. Our hospital was guarded by a separate company, consisting mainly of contract soldiers, and these soldiers showed us how to handle and maintain our weapons. All this training was self-organized, but even now, listening to stories of rookie soldiers who have been training for a month, I realize that we received top-notch training.

About a week later, our first rookies began going out with teams to the stabilization posts.[4] My turn came a few days later. At the time, our operational zone was the towns of Popasna and Zolote. Our mission was to stabilize the wounded and prepare them for transport to a rear hospital. This stabilization post near the combat zone was set up to perform simple surgeries and resuscitation. Medic teams were on regular rotation. The morning we arrived, a couple of mortar shells hit. We had no opportunity to set up or get our bearings because we had to seek cover inside. We had a radio, and we heard what was happening in combat. We heard Russian soldiers manoeuvring into the rear of our troops. We heard our command set up their withdrawal. Since I became involved in the war in 2014 I had never witnessed such intense combat. The situation changed dramatically with each passing hour.

Then our tanks fired from behind our position. The Russians countered – Grad multiple rocket launchers fired right back into our quadrant. So, just two weeks after mobilization, I sustained my first blast-related traumatic brain injury. But God protected all of us that day: the rocket exploded on the roof but without breaking through inside. Several others also suffered traumatic brain injuries, and the evacuation vehicle was damaged. As one of our officers said, "God let us get off lightly."

The stabilization post was relocated to the village of Pokrovske, between Bakhmut and Popasna. Although we were relatively safe for the next two months, those months turned out to be intense. We were incredibly busy, taking in up to a hundred wounded soldiers a day. Most had minor injuries,

---

4. A stabilisation post (also known as a stabilisation point) is a medical facility located in the frontline zone, where the wounded soldiers are evacuated from the combat areas. At the stabilisation point, first aid is provided, the condition of the wounded is stabilised before they are then transported to a hospital.

but some had suffered severe injuries or were in critical condition. Once, they brought in a soldier who was unresponsive and clinically dead. That's when I realized how amazing and talented our medics were. Our concerted efforts brought him back from the brink of death! He fought for us on the battlefield, and we fought for his life on a makeshift hospital table – two nightstands and a door leaf. This is our mission under God: to bring our guys back to life according to his will.

My list of duties was long and diverse: keeping the makeshift "operating room" clean, helping the wounded, and identifying the dead. Every day, fallen soldiers were brought to us. The other medics and I checked for any remaining live ammunition and tried to identify the bodies. Since not everyone had papers, it wasn't always possible to identify them. Some of those in our medical company couldn't bear to deal with the fallen, but I had become accustomed to dealing with dead since my time at the Donetsk Airport. Blood, mangled remains, and resuscitation all became part of the job. There were emotionally jarring moments – such as a fallen soldier's phone ringing, perhaps with a call from home – but I learned to take these in my stride.

The medics and I split the day in half for watch duty. I was assigned the night shift. It was usually quiet at night, with no wounded coming in. So I would read Psalms. Within the military context and amid combat, I saw this book in a whole new light. David had been at war, too; his words now carried a particular gravitas. I understood the pain he must have felt as he recounted the crimes of his enemies against him and his people. I understood the intensity of his cries to God and his joy when God answered.

Our team ceased operations at this stabilization post after our troops withdrew from Popasna. Thereafter, our medical company opened two new aid posts for the wounded and set up a medical supplies storage unit in the Bakhmut hospital. One day, heavy gunfire broke out in the village where we were based. We were alarmed and set up additional security posts. It turned out that a Russian reconnaissance drone had been spotted and our men had tried to shoot it down. Although our air defence guys downed it, the Russians had noted the military presence in that village. Grad rockets hit us an hour later. Once again, God protected us, and we were able to evacuate without a hitch. Later, we named that incident a "Kadyrov-style wedding" – referring to the celebratory gunfire traditional for weddings in the East.

A few days later, I was transferred back to the stabilization post in Hirske. But the enemy was advancing rapidly. Before long, the hospital was shelled, so the majority of the medical company withdrew to Bakhmut. Our post was shifted to another building – a large basement. This was probably the most active site I've worked in during my service.

The situation at that time was rather bleak. Popasna was already under enemy control, and the evacuation route from Hirske now ran alongside the contact line. Eventually, the Russians began to envelop the area with the intention of encircling it. Evacuations became very difficult, and you could always see and hear the impact of incoming shells. It was then that I made it a habit to pray constantly while on the road. Because you never knew when or how close a shell would hit – you have no control over it. But God is in control over everything, and that was my only hope.

One of our doctors – a very intelligent man – was having a hard time coping. His analytical mind saw that the situation was going from bad to worse. I asked him why he was so worried about things beyond his control. But he couldn't help it. Since he was an atheist, God was not part of his world view. Eventually, he was diagnosed with chronic anxiety, caused by these worries.

Usually, we tried to evacuate the wounded at night so that our vehicles would be less likely to be spotted by the enemy. Once, while evacuating the wounded – one seriously injured and the other two lightly wounded – we came under fire in the area closest to the front line. A shell hit nearby, kicking up dust, and the bottom of our vehicle clipped a rock, causing an oil leak. Eventually, we were forced to stop. The driver, Yaroslav, told us to abandon the car because we'd be sitting ducks there. So we took the stretcher with the seriously wounded man and began walking. The nearest checkpoint was about five kilometres away. The wounded man's condition was serious, we were wearing armour and carrying weapons, and it was an uphill trek. We couldn't go on like this for long. So I suggested that we split up: I would stay by the road with the seriously wounded and one lightly wounded, while the driver and the other wounded man would head to the checkpoint and call for help.

We went off the road to find some cover. I was praying constantly. I asked the lightly wounded man if he was a believer and offered to pray with him. I don't remember what he said. The Russians kept firing artillery and Grad rockets all the time we lay there. I even saw an aerial bomb fly through the sky towards the city of Lysychansk. The seriously wounded man literally had a hole in his back – his spine was intact only by the grace of God. He was under anaesthesia, and I kept him in the car, where he slept peacefully the whole time. Eventually, the guys returned in another vehicle, obtained from a nearby interception post. But we had to carry the wounded man to the car because the driver was afraid to pull up any closer.

After that episode, people in the medical company began to treat me and Yaroslav with more respect. I saw how faith can make a difference. Despite that shelling, he and I had kept going to complete the mission – no matter what. We believed we would win this war and did everything we could to push closer towards victory. The other driver's fear made things a bit harder for us.

The next day, Yaroslav and another officer were able to retrieve our car and tow it to a garage near the stabilization post. We went to repair it, but the shelling started – Grads at work once again. At first, it was regular rounds, but then came incendiary rounds – also called phosphorus rounds. But God protected us again: the regular rounds flew past the garage building, and the incendiary rounds landed nearby but did not hit us. We watched the phosphorus burning right outside the door. It was a good thing the roof didn't catch fire. After a while, we decided to leave – the car repair would have to wait.

The next day was my last day at that site. Tired out, I slept late, waking up at about ten in the morning. We had a separate room for meals, and there was also an observation point on the ground floor. Going to the dining room was not very pleasant. So, Yaroslav and I decided to have lunch later and went there together again. We were only five metres away when there was a powerful explosion. I saw a flash of light up ahead – and then darkness. A cloud of dust covered everything. Yaroslav lost his bearings and immediately shouted, asking where I was. I took him by the hand and led him back. The Lord saved us. If we had gone to lunch just a few seconds earlier, I would not be here today. There were people in the dining room at the time. Many lives were lost. Oleg Vorobyov, my brother in Christ from the Greek Catholic Church and the commander of the company that guarded our stabilization point, was also killed. I had got to know him after seeing him read the Bible. We sometimes discussed matters of faith and enjoyed a good relationship. Oleg had been at the centre of the explosion, and there was very little of him left . . . It was a terrible loss.

All these events took place within just three days. Nevertheless, my time at the stabilization point was pivotal. During those days, I knew what I was doing and why, and I experienced the war in its entirety. These events brought me to a focus. I constantly trust God with things that are outside my control. But I realized that I also have to take responsibility for the things that depend on my actions. I never knew if I will make it to the hospital while escorting the wounded – nevertheless, I had to go, believing what I was doing and why I was doing it.

That same day, our stabilization post moved ten kilometres away, while a mobile evacuation team remained in Hirske. We served there until the brigade was withdrawn to prepare for a counteroffensive in the Kherson region. After

Hirske, every other place where I served seemed much quieter. Although there were shellings lasting several hours and we came under enemy fire during our movements, it all seemed less dangerous. Since that time, I always pray before going to the front line, asking for safety and entrusting myself into God's hands.

The year 2022 took a lot from me. My grandfather went to be with the Lord in the summer, and we had been very close. In many ways, he gave me what my father couldn't or wouldn't give. I was granted my first leave to pay my last respects to my grandfather.

A week before the counteroffensive in the Kherson region, even before our brigade was transferred there, Oleg Marinchenko, the deacon of our church and my friend and mentor in chaplaincy, was killed. A mine hit the dugout where he was giving medical aid. He shielded the wounded with his own body, and they survived. I knew that it was inevitable that I would lose people close to me in the course of this war, but understanding this in my head and experiencing it with my heart are completely different things. Oleg's death was the kind of death he was ready for. I find comfort in knowing that he gave his life in the service of people, fulfilling the greatest commandment.

I remember the time of the counteroffensive in the Kherson region as a quiet one – in the sense that by that time, our team was well-coordinated and everyone knew what to do and how to do it. The wounded rarely stayed with us for more than half an hour – even the severely injured were ready for evacuation within that time. But our brigade suffered more losses in this operation than at the beginning of the invasion. One day, we received more than twenty bodies of the fallen at once – the most I saw during my entire service. But our brigade fulfilled its mission. Then we were transferred out again – this time, to prepare for the battle for Bakhmut.

The commander of the medical company was now an officer. We had been through the events in Hirske together, and he knew that I was a believer. On several occasions – such as Christmas Eve and Easter – he invited me to share a few words from the Bible with the soldiers.

Present Day

After the battle for Bakhmut, our brigade was transferred to Horlivka. Now we are back near Bakhmut, in the town of Chasiv Yar, where we continue to carry out combat missions.

A year ago, I was transferred to the brigade's press office, and now I accompany the journalists as they carry out their work. This also gives me the opportunity to get to know many people in my brigade. It's evident that everyone is tired. Although they sometimes complain about their long deployment, most of them are not going to just hand over our land to the enemy without a fight. And neither am I.

It's hard to wrap my head around the fact that it will soon be three years since the war began. All this time, my wife and I have been living apart. Although we have a strong relationship, we still feel the impact of such a long separation. I can't take proper care of my family. In addition, for almost three years, I have not been part of a church community. From time to time, I experience new voids in my life – as loved ones are taken away by Russian terror. Volunteers, civic activists, brothers and sisters from church – many of these people went to minister to people through military service. Some have already been killed by the enemy. The life I lived before the war was destroyed by the Russians. I won't ever be the same as I was, and I am mentally exhausted.

But love is not just a feeling. It is a decision and a willing acceptance of duty for the sake of those you love. And I love the people I live among. Sometimes, you just have to do what you have to do, even though you don't feel like it. This is why I continue to fulfil my duty.

Sometimes I find motivation by asking myself: What have I done today to bring the victory in the war closer? This spurs me on. I also notice how much Jesus sustains me in my service. Even as I write about these events, I can see how he cared for me – and continues to do so. Even though I am not doing too well with regular Bible reading, he remains faithful. Every day, I tell him what I'm going through.

Loving is never easy. It is always demanding. But no matter how tired I am, I still have the strength to continue my service to God and my ministry to the people of Ukraine. And I intend to carry on to the end.

> And one of them, a lawyer, asked him a question to test him. "Teacher, which is the great commandment in the Law?" And he said to him, "You shall love the Lord your God with all your heart and with all your soul and with all your mind. This is the great and first commandment. And a second is like it: You shall love your neighbour as yourself. On these two commandments depend all the Law and the Prophets." (Matt 22:35–40 ESV)

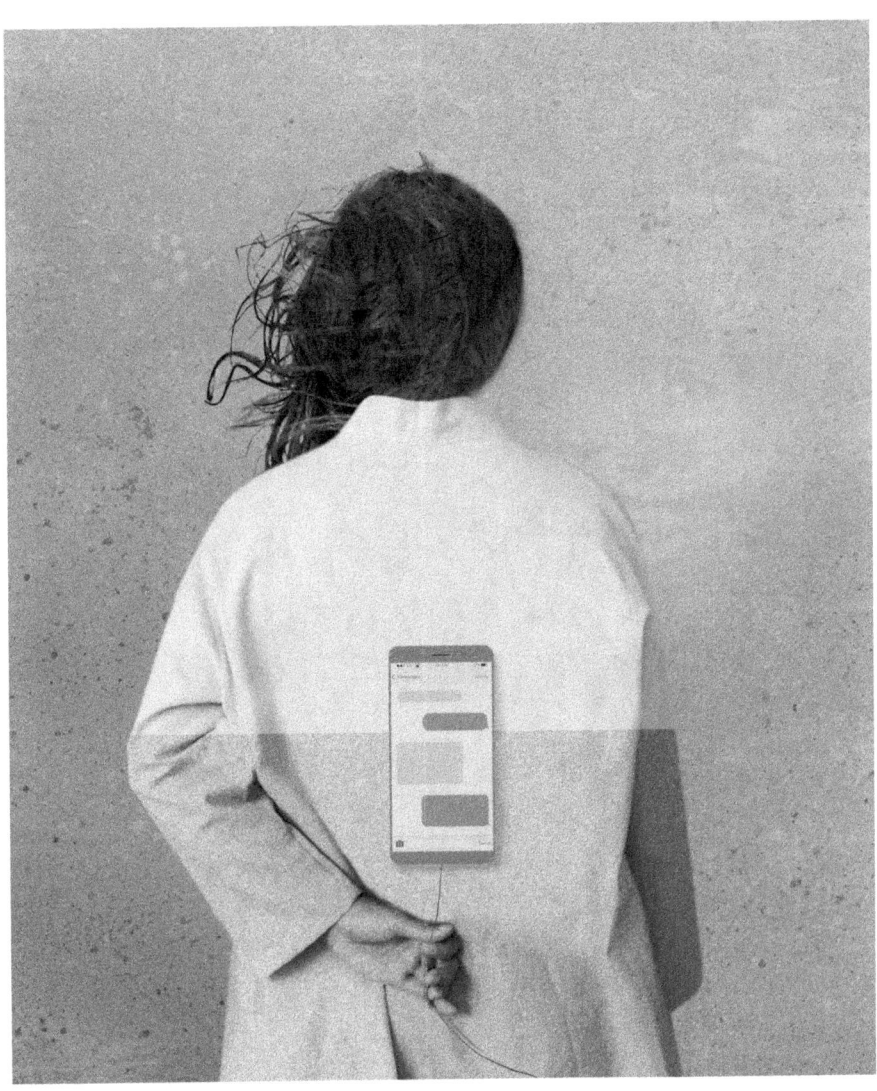

"I was taught that Christians should suffer with and bear the burdens of their people. I can't be responsible for what others choose to do – or choose not to do. But I thank God for my path here in the rear, working with the families of soldiers, while there on the front line, my husband became one of the best commanding officers. I wish I had a priest with whom I could share all that I'm going through. But I am grateful that I still have God who understands me completely." Alla Shyrshyna (p. 255)

10

On Being the Wife of a Soldier Fighting on the Front Line

Alla Shyrshyna
Wife of a Soldier

I'm often asked how I am coping with this situation. The truth is, I'm barely managing. I handle some things better, others – worse. Some things I don't have time to get to at all.

Along the way, I've come to realize and rethink a few important things.

I have to rely on myself now. I can rarely expect my husband to be there. He's reliable and wonderful. He's mine, and he's wonderful. But for most of these years, except for rare and fleeting moments, he's been preoccupied with survival: his own, his fellow soldiers', and our country's. He's engaged and focused on that, and only occasionally is he able to divert his attention to family matters.

I used to be able to tell him everything. Now, that's no longer an option. There's no way to call, no time to do so, or no energy to try. But the Lord is there for me through it all. Other people have their own lives and problems to deal with. So now, more than ever before, I wait for my children to fall asleep at night, and then I pour out everything to God – ups and downs, sorrows and joys, fears and dreams. My relationship with God has never been so deep.

My husband loves our children dearly. Unfortunately, he rarely gets a chance to connect with them. They don't know how to read or write yet, so video calls are the only way to stay in touch.

Every night, as I put the children to bed, I tell them that not only do I love them, but that their father loves them very much. I often buy and give them little gifts "from Dad." I record videos of them and send these to my husband. We're in that season where I'm the one answering all their questions and solving all their problems. I really miss my husband's advice, and I feel so blessed whenever I'm able to get it. But more often than not, I have to rely on myself.

Children have myriad questions and fears: What if Dad doesn't escape from the Russians? What if our house is destroyed by a missile? Is Dad wounded? I have to answer calmly, even when their questions hurt so bad that I can hardly hold back my tears.

Every day, I try to do at least one thing that refreshes me. I was brought up in a family where women displayed sacrificial selflessness. Giving up your own wishes for the sake of the family was considered worthwhile. I am learning to live differently. For the sake of our family, I have to be a calm mother, a sensible and grounded woman. We are living in a time of war, and this war will not end soon. If I want my strength to last, I must find a way to renew myself. So far, I've found only two ways to do this: God and self-care.

***

In February 2022, the war blindsided many people. But not my husband and me – war was where we first met.

I'm so blessed to have been born into a family that valued independent thinking and open expression of opinions. Of course, our parents really hoped we'd make decisions guided by their wisdom and experience, but they still gave us freedom – freedom of choice, freedom to make our own decisions. While they would always warn us about the consequences, they left the choice to us. Growing up, I was a rather unconventional Christian. I always wanted explanations. "Because the pastor said so" was never a good enough reason to me. I always had to know why and based on what. My friends would playfully tease me, calling me "a real Protestant" because I protested so often. It was my questioning mind that led to my slightly unconventional view of ministry. When I was seventeen, I dreamed of becoming a volunteer. Before starting a family of my own, I really wanted to spend a few months doing something for the good of the world and people. But then I went off to get a degree and after that a job, so this dream had to be delayed.

Then came the Euromaidan[1] – which led to a lot of volunteering. And then came the war in 2014. I dreamed of being in the thick of it. I longed to do something for my country. Around that time, I heard of Project Frontline. One of the churches had set up a missionary training programme that sent people to serve in smaller towns along the front line. To be honest, I really

---

1. The "Maidan Uprising," also known as "Euromaidan," was a wave of protests that began in November 2013 after Viktor Yanukovych, Ukraine's president at the time, decided not to sign the European Union–Ukraine Association Agreement. https://en.wikipedia.org/wiki/Euromaidan.

wanted to do this, but I was still afraid. Then came one of the hardest life lessons I've ever received. A close relative of mine died. He was very young, and this happened in his own backyard. As we paid our last respects, I realized that no one can live longer than what God has decided. People die for different reasons. People die in different places. It was at the grave of that young man that I decided to go to the war zone.

At the end of 2015, a few weeks after that decision, I showed up in Sloviansk with my travel bag. A month later, I ended up in Svitlodarsk, in the Donetsk region. This town was just a few kilometres from the front line. The only bright spot was its name, which means "giving light." But the situation was dark – so many street children and drug addicts. Now, Svitlodarsk is under Russian occupation. This was where I got used to explosions, stopped being scared of loud noises, learned about bomb shelters (although I didn't really use them), mastered the proper way to drive a car at night near the front line, and got into the habit of keeping money and personal documents next to my bed.

That's where I first heard the locals tell stories about their relatives being tortured by the Russians for supporting the Ukrainian army and about their nieces and sisters going missing in occupied towns. I saw shells hit preschools and witnessed explosions near schools. And yet, somehow, the war didn't feel as scary back then.

Nine months later, a guy from Crimea joined our mission team. His name was Oleksandr, and he had moved back to Ukraine in 2014 after completing his studies in Poland. He, too, wanted to serve his country. Our relationship began during the war. One night, on our way back from visiting friends in a nearby town, we were stopped at a checkpoint. The soldiers there told us we only had forty minutes to get home – that's how long it took to reload between rounds of shelling. We decided to risk it because we had to get back home to Svitlodarsk. The field by the road was ablaze, and thick smoke billowed into the sky. The town seemed deserted, and the sky was orange from the fires. We lost cell phone reception. The cannonade kept booming. It was so loud that I turned on the music to drown it out so I could get some sleep. We didn't know what to expect. We had connected with some families with children – mostly mothers. The shelling was so heavy that we thought we might have to evacuate the children. We parked our car right by the entrance to the apartment building so we could jump in and drive off quickly to help people if necessary.

We only slept for a few hours. In the morning, we went to check out the damage. Several shells had hit the city, but there were no civilian casualties.

After the shelling we had survived together, after witnessing his calm and collected manner and his willingness to help people even in such difficult circumstances, I began to view Oleksandr differently. And this feeling was mutual.

We got married six months later. It was a small ceremony – but full of warmth and deeply meaningful. A year later, our son was born. We continued our ministry in Svitlodarsk. During that time, we founded a youth centre for teenagers and college students. We hosted a variety of events, training sessions, and gatherings. The centre became a safe place for these youngsters. For some, their lives were changed forever. Five people who came there wanting to make a difference in this town ended up volunteering at our youth centre. We brought together a group of locals who loved Ukraine. It was a challenging yet exciting time.

In 2019, after our daughter was born, we moved to Chernivtsi. In this new town, my husband continued working with young people, this time with the Ukrainian Leadership Academy. I had my hands full raising two little children.

Then came the COVID-19 pandemic, which brought more changes. My husband was offered a new position in the Mariupol branch of the Academy. Do you know our biggest reason for turning down this offer? We had small children, and there was only one road out of the city. Instead, we packed up and moved to Ternopil – a new city to live and work in. That's where the war found us. I still consider Ternopil one of the safest bigger cities in Ukraine.

**

The full-scale invasion was not totally unexpected. I worked for a charity foundation supporting people near the front lines. Even six months back before February 2024, we had a strong feeling that something was about to happen. The tension in the air was palpable. I began following the news closely.

My husband decided to sign a contract and join the reserves. He wanted to have a plan for where to go and what to do if anything should happen if the situation escalated. A month before the full-scale invasion, his application was successful and he joined the reserve of the paratrooper brigade stationed in Lviv.

Two weeks before 24 February 2022, my brother sent his wife and child from Kyiv to our city. I can't speak for others, but we were certain that something major was about to happen. However, we believed that the escalation would unfold from the east.

Neither my husband nor I have ever been pacifists. Both of our fathers served in the army in their youth, at a time when conscription was mandatory. I am a fourth-generation Christian. We are both patriots who believe that our country must be defended – with weapons, if necessary. However, believing this was easier than acting on this belief.

The news reported that reservists would soon be called up. That was the first – and last – time I reproached my husband: "Why did you ever sign that contract?"

On 23 February, he received a phone call. He had to report to the military base. He wanted to leave that same day, but I asked him to pick up the children from preschool and spend some time with them, saying goodbye properly. That evening, we decided that I would take the kids to preschool the next morning and then go with him to Lviv. I hardly slept that night, and woke up to the sound of fighter jets flying overhead. I woke my husband, and we spent hours monitoring the news and checking in with family and friends.

The preschool was closed. So I could only go with my husband as far as the bus stop at 8:00 a.m. That was it. He didn't know what awaited him. I didn't know what awaited me. Neither of us knew what lay ahead for us. And so, our war began.

On my way home, I stopped at a supermarket and wandered around aimlessly for about fifteen minutes. I just couldn't think clearly. I browsed half-empty shelves and automatically picked up food that my husband liked. It was only afterwards that I realized that no one in our family eats fish except him. As I looked at that fish, it slowly began to sink in just how different my life would be from now on.

One of the first things I did in the days following my husband's departure was to donate blood. I'm not a regular donor because my blood type is very common. But I really wanted to do something to help our soldiers.

That same day, my husband's unit was sent to the southern part of Ukraine. I often hear it said that there is too little training for new recruits. The truth is, soldiers who went to the front lines in the early days of the war had no training at all. Whatever they learned, they learned through combat. There were delays in deliveries of both ammunition and food. Their chances of survival were slim. What those men did have, however, was very high motivation.

***

If you ask me now how I got through that time, all I can say is that I don't remember much of it. I worked a lot and took care of my children. I certainly had a lot more energy back then. Not any more.

Recalling those early days is distressing – the store shelves bare; nights spent in the bathroom, until I realized that shattered tiles could be quite dangerous; and air-raid alerts that didn't scare me but triggered panic attacks in my nephew. I was very much afraid for my children. But they weren't afraid at all.

My children knew two things about air-raid alerts. First, they had to shelter in the hallway. Second, they had to remember that while all this was happening because Russian planes and ships were firing missiles at us, Dad was protecting us from them. For children that small, it was the best way to explain things, by associating protection with a trusted adult. At the end of every air-raid alert, Sashko, our son, would announce: "Mommy, Daddy brought down all the planes. We can come out now."

Eva was very fond of racoons. She had four toy racoons, nearly identical. During every air-raid alert, my sweet, caring girl would bring these racoons to the hallway, pet them, and tell them not to be afraid because her Daddy was strong and would protect them, too.

I often worked at home late into the evenings. At the time, blackouts were imposed to keep lights to a minimum to reduce the risk of night-time air strikes. One spring evening, I was in our kitchen, finishing yet another report. There was very little light – just my dimmed screen and a backlit keyboard. Suddenly, I saw a flash of light. I rushed out of the kitchen but was unsure where to go next – my son's room or my daughter's. I had never felt such fear in my life. A moment later, I realized that it was just a lightning storm. But I was so shaken that not only was I unable to finish my work, I couldn't even fall asleep without a sleeping pill. For some time after that, I put the children to bed in the same room.

At some point, I ended up completely alone with two little children. Eva was two. Sashko was three. Some people left the country. Others moved in with their relatives. We had many friends abroad – people my husband had met as a student. They reached out constantly, writing and calling with offers to help. They wanted to take me and my children in. But I couldn't even get to a shelter on my own because waking up two little children in the middle of the night, calming them down, getting them dressed, and carrying them to a shelter was not something a person could do alone.

The truth is, I wasn't afraid of the explosions – because I'd experienced them before. During those days, I was afraid of only two things: that my children would be wounded and suffer and that there would be shortages of food and medicine. Only such shortages would have been a compelling enough reason for us to leave the country. It was extremely important to me to stay in Ukraine, and time would show that this turned out to be a wise decision. First, we were in the same time zone and environment as my husband. Second, whenever he managed to get some free time, I could visit him – even for a day or a few short hours – and this was one more way for us to keep our special bond alive.

My thinking was clear: while my husband was protecting us, I had to take care of the children here. So, I moved our sofa into the hallway and would move my sleeping kids there during air-raid alerts. While this wouldn't protect us from a missile strike, it was effective against glass shards.

I avoided spending money on my husband's bank cards. In fact, I stopped spending money on myself altogether. It just seemed pointless and superfluous. However, I now recognize that this wasn't a good thing. Far too often, money is the only support a husband can offer from the front line and one way in which he can still be involved in family life. It's important to a solder that his wife and children go on living. That's why he's over there, at the front line. War doesn't just destroy houses – it destroys families, lives, and health. That's why it's crucial to make the effort to build something, even if it's something small. Bit by bit, however slowly, we must keep building.

I found it hard to manage the children on my own. My husband had been in charge of disciplining; I was more mild-mannered. Now, I was with the children 24/7, with no breaks and no time for myself. Speaking from personal experience, the best ministry a church could offer would be one that supports mothers with children. Quiet time is essential to sort through our thoughts. Quite often, the greatest need is time to be alone with yourself and God.

During that first year, I stopped attending family holiday gatherings. Everyone else came as couples or whole families. I was the only one alone, with just the children and myself. This made me feel even more lonely, and the problems being discussed at those gatherings seemed absurd to me. The same thing happened at church, where, instead of being helped and supported, I was lectured about my children's behaviour. That really hurt. I knew my children were rambunctious. I knew that I couldn't always rein them in – and I already felt guilty about that. What I desperately needed was someone to help me out – not critical remarks that only rubbed salt into the wound. Just when I felt most alone, I had to face a string of difficult and awkward questions that were too exhausting to even try to answer.

A word of advice – never ask military families about their finances. First, most of their pay is spent on war-related things. Second, no amount of money is worth even a day of hellish combat action or the distress of a family worried about their loved one.

One day, my son confided in his aunt: "When my Dad went off to defend our country, Mom started buying me lots of stuff. I don't need that stuff. I just wanted my Dad." Hearing his words broke my heart.

My husband and I used to share parenting responsibilities. I spent more time with our daughter, while he hung out more with our son. He would take our son to preschool on his bike. They'd go to the park, exercise, swim, and do a ton of things together. For a very long time, my precious son could not understand why things had changed so drastically overnight.

I stopped working while the children were awake. Only after they'd fall asleep would I squeeze in some work.

***

On 24 February 2022, a worry crept into my heart. More than two years later, it still dwells there. I wake up and fall asleep with it. It follows me to breakfast and when I go out for coffee. It haunts my thoughts as I read or work. It's ever-present. This worry is about my husband. Some days, it's barely noticeable. Some days, it's so overwhelming I can't take a breath or live a normal life. Some Christians tell me that if I give this worry over to God, then I'd find peace. They have no idea how much I'm praying these days. This worry coexists with my unending prayers and supplications. I've been told that I ought to trust God and that then everything will be all right. I do trust him. He's the only one who knows how this will all turn out. He knows the number of my days, my children's days, and my husband's, too. He alone knows. I'm not one of those Christians who believe that if you walk with God, everything about your life will be fine and dandy. I know that if I'm with God, then he is with me – even when the night is dark and the desert is scorching. I know that he's the one who gives me the strength to live.

I'm deeply disappointed with the stance taken by some of my believing friends – who are now ex-friends. Some of them left to build up churches in Europe – perhaps that's needed, too. But I don't believe that God brings people to a safe place through illegal channels, using deception and bribes. I know that God is honest and just. He is the one who gives life. He is also omnipotent. He is able to protect the life he gives if it is his will to do so.

Our freedom in Christ is both a great privilege and a tremendous responsibility. We may be free to do anything – but not everything is beneficial and constructive, is it? Are we ready to bear that responsibility?

For a Christian, living in Ukraine is a gift. The Lord has never been so near. Never has he given us so many opportunities to minister to people. God has never shown miracles in such a way as now. We have a unique opportunity to influence what's happening in our country. We have a voice that's now being heard and an opportunity to influence society. But have we acted on these opportunities?

I find it difficult to go to church these days because I don't get the answers to my questions. Very few people in the church understand the daily challenges I face. For instance, I find it hard to hear about new opportunities for Christian men or to sit in a meeting with Christians where a well-known lawyer explains how to avoid mobilization. I long for sermons that would support men and women who have chosen to defend their country from invaders.

One day, as I was praying, I started thinking about what we, as Christians, could do to ensure our victory. And then I remembered the story of David. Compared to our enemy, our country is young and small, just like David; but our people are also strong and brave like David. If we had more "Davids" in our army, our prospects of victory would be much higher, and the voice of the church would be more powerful. Where, if not at the front lines, is the need for ministry greatest? Where is prayer more urgently needed? Where is there a greater need for words of encouragement and support? And I'm not talking about chaplaincy here – not the kind of ministry that involves a visit once every two months to a place thirty or forty kilometres away from the actual front lines by someone wearing an army uniform. I'm talking about a day-to-day and shoulder-to-shoulder kind of ministry. After all, there are many ways to serve in the army without having to take up arms.

***

The spring of 2022 was the spring of rallying together. We didn't know what would come next, but we remained steady in our work. Even before the full-scale war, the foundation where I worked had a project aimed at helping mothers of children with disabilities. We organized support groups in various locations in the Luhansk region, and a psychologist from our team led sessions with those women. That spring, our psychologist lost both her sister and mother in a little town called Shchastia – ironically, the name means "happiness" in Ukrainian. At the time, women and little children were fleeing the Donetsk and Luhansk regions and heading into the unknown. For a few months, I coordinated their travels, finding them safe places to stay along the way – places that would be suitable for children with disabilities – so that they wouldn't have to stay in camps. Those women passed on my phone number to their friends, and soon my phone was ringing day and night. This proved to be a great distraction and helped me cope – I knew what I was doing was very important.

Communications with my husband – calls and texts – were very brief. I hardly ever cried. This war has made me tougher and stronger. The first time I cried since he left was when I got this text message from him: "We're going into battle today. Most likely, I will not make it out alive. Tell the children . . ."

Needless to say, I stayed strong for my husband, offering him support. But after that, I cried all evening. For the first time, my dad had to come and spend the night with us because I just couldn't bear to be all by myself.

That day, my husband had moved about five hundred metres away from their position so he could fly a drone. While he was away, a mine hit the dugout, leaving six dead and six wounded. He was able to get them all out of there in his car. He often says that his guardian angel has now been mobilized and is on duty 24/7, with no holidays or breaks.

Summertime is when people usually think about going away on a holiday, enjoying things, taking long walks, and eating ice cream. But not in the summer of 2022. That was a very difficult summer. I learned all the military slang so that I could understand what little my husband was able to share without having to stop him and ask for explanations. Whenever he called, I would leave any meeting or stop any work to answer. There's nothing more important than family. And that's one of my most important takeaways from this war. Everything passes, but we have each other, no matter the circumstances.

***

We had very little communication for several days. On the whole, I'd have to be very lucky to get even the smallest hint from my husband about when they were engaged in active combat over there.

During those days, I hardly knew what to pray for or how to pray. I was exhausted – on the one hand, by not knowing how he was doing; on the other, by knowing what was happening on the front lines in the sector where his unit was deployed. I just hoped he would survive.

Do you know what military wives fear most? Getting calls from numbers they don't recognize. If possible, always send a text message first. Because if your husband hasn't messaged you in a while and then your phone suddenly rings, you immediately go through a whole range of emotions that no one should have to endure. Your whole life – present and future – in all its possible scenarios flashes before your eyes.

One day, I got a phone call like that. My husband said he was wounded and that his phone was gone. Then he hung up.

I sat on my bed with questions swarming in my mind. He was wounded... Will they be able to get him to safety? Will he get medical help? What are his injuries? How bad are they? Will he live? Are his fellow soldiers alive? Where is he now?

My husband doesn't like spending money on himself. He'll gladly buy anything for me and the children, but he is reluctant to buy things for himself. Just before he was wounded, he had bought a new phone, which was vital for his work of flying drones – a skill that was still uncommon at the time. The first thing I did was to find the money to buy him an even better phone. For some reason, it felt very important to do so.

A little later, I called back the number he'd called me from. Another soldier answered and said my husband did "go out" (on a mission). Only later did it dawn on me that since my husband had managed to call me, he must have been in the area with cell phone service – which meant that he had been evacuated.

Later, he called again, this time from Dnipro. I dropped off the children at their grandparents' house and headed out. I learned that my husband had no papers, no money, no car. Their vehicle had been shot up by a tank, and it was only by God's grace that he wasn't critically wounded and managed to get out alive.

While travelling by train from Kyiv to Dnipro, I got another message saying that my husband was being transferred to our city for treatment. Great news indeed! Amid the war, we finally got a little time to be together. Broken and battered – emotionally and physically – but we had each other.

Since my husband was recovering from shell shock, he found it difficult to handle loud sounds. I tried to keep the children quiet around their father, but reining in two whirlwinds was an impossible challenge. I saw how taxing such chaotic moments were on my husband.

My husband had been wounded alongside a fellow soldier – a twenty-three-year-old lad. Even though their car was hit, they made it out under machine-gun fire. This young man also suffered from shell shock. After receiving treatment for just three days, he returned to his duties on the front line, defending our country. However, this time, he lasted only three weeks. I was there when my husband got the news that this young man had been killed and his body could not be recovered. All I could do was to sit with my husband in silence. I still don't know what words could possibly bring solace in moments like these.

What can you say when your husband tells you that he went out at night to try to recover a soldier's body – but it had frozen into the ground? What do you say when, the next morning, he asks you to wash the gloves he wore while trying to pry the body free? I still haven't found the right words. In such moments, I try to just be there, quiet but present. I also go to the funerals of the soldiers in my town. It's the least I can do. It's important to me to remember and honour those who make it possible for me to work, raise our children, and continue living my life.

Grief and happiness intertwine so closely that at times, my mind can't keep up. One minute, I'm feeling happy because it was my husband who taught our kids to ride a bike. The next minute, I'd get the news that someone I knew had been killed.

Some time ago, I wanted to get my hair coloured. I had a head of long, thick hair – that is, until stress took its toll. But I didn't do it because spending money on a cut and colour felt frivolous. Then my husband reminded me that he's over there precisely so I can live out my life. I'm learning to do that – bit by bit.

Despite all this, the year 2022 also brought some great opportunities. The children and I were fortunate to go to Dnipro for a couple of days and spend some time with our husband and father. Travelling by train for seventeen hours one way was totally worth it. Even though our time together was short, we felt like a family again. Such days were rare, but I always tried to take pictures so that the children could remember our time together.

***

In 2023, my husband was transferred to a different unit. That year, I had a respite from worries as my darling defender went to Germany for training and then continued at the training ground.

But then the Ukrainian offensive began. Word spread quickly, so this wasn't unexpected. It's the consequences that were unexpected. Too many losses. Too many hopes shattered – blown to smithereens on minefields. The offensive also revealed the unwillingness of some to get involved – not a reality that people talked about very much.

My husband found a way to keep me from worrying so much – whenever he couldn't contact me, he had a friend send me updates.

Another day goes by with my phone silent. I've waited all day, but there's no word from him or about him. There are many days like this now. At first, I would walk around in a daze, hardly able to breathe, eat, or walk. I'd turn up the ringer volume, hold the phone tight in one hand, and do whatever else I had to with my other hand. Even at night, I would go to bed with my phone clutched tight. I couldn't read, listen to music, or watch anything. My thoughts were so closely intertwined with my prayers that I couldn't tell them apart. On days like that, I didn't drink coffee, put on make-up, text friends, or leave the house unless it was absolutely necessary.

I was on autopilot as I bathed the children and cooked them the simplest possible meals. The smallest action required enormous effort. I constantly scrolled through the news and social media pages of my husband's soldier friends whom I knew. But they, too, were mostly silent. A desperate step would be to call and wait, even for him to decline the call. At least I would know he's alive.

My responsibilities at work increased. That's when I realized that I had to live in spite of everything. There won't be another life. There won't be another today. Nobody else can live this day for me.

On days like that, I make a to-do list of even the simplest of tasks and work through them one by one. Days like that are not the time for creativity – just simple, routine actions, while my thoughts and heart are far away.

I have no complaints against God. Although we're living through hard times, these are the days through which history is being made. God knows that we will persevere. God knows that even if we don't make it, those who come after us will continue the fight. The key is to raise them to be capable and wise.

Over and over again, I repeat my husband's words: "We have chosen our path." If we could start over, would we have made the same choice? We would. All our lives, up to this point, God has been shaping us – through circumstances and people – to be who we now are.

Only now, looking back on my journey, do I begin to see the purpose of past challenges we faced and overcame.

Sometimes happy days happen, as if snuck away from this war. Whenever we have opportunities to meet, it brings so much happiness just to have breakfast together, to wake up in the middle of the night and find my beloved asleep by my side instead of out fighting on the battlefield, and to have him close enough to touch, close enough to see the wrinkles in the corners of his eyes – sure, new ones keep appearing, but each one is beautiful and cherished.

Sometimes, we take a short ride – just a stone's throw from home – in his car, which is crammed with his gear and other things his current life demands. Such days, or sometimes mere hours, are unbearably few, but they are so precious! They are worth any trip and any expense.

I try to hold on to those moments, every single one of them. But they fade, whittled away by loneliness, distance, and the different contexts in which we now spend our days.

In 2023, my husband took his first leave. We went on a car trip abroad to visit his parents. Those were good days – but also challenging ones. We were so out of practice at being together. We had each acquired new habits and new quirks. It was like being newlyweds again – getting to know each other and learning to communicate again. But as soon as we began getting the hang of it, it was time to part. We ended up on the opposite sides of the country, and communication was once again reduced to a bare minimum. The drifting apart began again.

The church ceremony was in Sloviansk. The church where we got married had the vows written in Russian. I translated them and recited them in Ukrainian. I often re-read those vows now, and every word has a new layer of meaning.

The state registration of the marriage took place in Bakhmut, we spent the next few days in Svyatohirsk, and the next few years in Svitlodarsk. Most of these towns are now gone – nothing left but ruins. Yet we are still here.

Some time ago, my husband received a prophecy that he and his wife would clear the thicket so that other people could live there. I'm usually sceptical about such prophecies, but . . . who could have imagined such thickets of people perverted by evil and the desire to destroy? No matter how much we wanted to get away from Donbas, it is still part of our lives.

I've listened to my husband's interviews in the media dozens of times. The first time, I listened especially attentively so that I could understand him better – because in real life, our conversations rarely last longer than five or ten minutes. People who think that officers do nothing are so wide off the mark. Being an officer is a huge responsibility that leaves no time for family.

Now I watch and listen to those interviews again just to hear his voice. I miss him so much, and hearing his voice helps ease my loneliness.

I take screenshots of comments posted by my husband's fellow soldiers. I'm keen to know what they say about him and how much they appreciate him. I remind myself that he's a great commanding officer and that this kind of leadership requires time and effort. Although I didn't think I could be any prouder of him than I already am, knowing this makes me even prouder. I consider him one of the finest people I've known – as a man, as a soldier, and as a Christian. His faithfulness and his choices flow from his trust in God. Sure, nobody's perfect – we all make mistakes. But I'm so proud of the fact that I have nothing to be ashamed about. At a time when so many are looking for ways to avoid fulfilling such a difficult duty, he stepped up and continues to fight to protect us and to protect Ukraine.

***

War is also about loneliness. Yes, I still have a husband. He's brave, he's good, and he's willing to help me out. But the war sets the rules for him. Now, he's incredibly busy and often unreachable. He has pretty much no days off, no breaks.

The first challenge is that you no longer have your spouse to talk about your day. Suddenly, there's no one with whom you can share your successes, failures, disappointments, or whatever happened that day, that week, or that month. Gradually, you even forget how to share. Your thoughts become yours to keep, and the need to talk to someone about your life dissipates. Now you've turned into an introvert.

I was never like this. Now, after more than two years of war and loneliness, even my fellow psychologists tell me that I've become a deeply introverted person. Yes, the woman who once had tons of friends and social groups. I don't know if experts can explain this change. For me, this strange withdrawal into myself is yet another unhappy consequence of the war.

The Lord is the only one with whom I am still able to share all that's on my heart.

I grab every opportunity to see my husband – gladly dropping everything to go to him. Unfortunately, in 2024, my husband's deployment is in a sector and rank that makes it impossible for him to travel to Dnipro and meet us. I can't take kids to the Donetsk region – it's too dangerous. So I go alone. Our visits are very short. Before I have time to get used to being near to him, it's time to part again. But every moment of being together is worth the effort. Even if we're both busy with other things, just being together is special and precious.

Quite often, I have to trek across the country just so we can spend an hour together. In this war, especially in the army, no one is their own master. The front line is constantly shifting, with plans often changing from one minute to the next. You just have to embrace this uncertainty. No one knows how much time together you have left. Whether on the front line or in the rear, life can be cut short in an instant. That's why every second is priceless.

The third year of the full-scale war has brought weariness. Unimaginable weariness. But it has also made us realize that we have each other and that must live out our life to the full, however long or short it may be. We give our best to the children without neglecting our own needs. We ask for help when we need it. We plan time for work, for kids, and also for rest. We carve out precious and tender bonding moments – however brief – with our spouse and children. We treasure these moments. And we share our thoughts – at least on paper.

***

Few people talk about the burden borne by the wives of soldiers on the front lines. This burden is enormous. There comes a point when men are no longer able to function as spiritual leaders of their families. There comes a time when men must focus on other tasks and, therefore, all other responsibilities – from prayers to practical matters – fall to women. Did I want this? No, not really. Do I have a choice here? No, not really.

This new order has become so routine, so normal, that even when my husband is on leave, just hanging around, I'd still do everything myself. He would ask, "Why don't you just ask me?" I have forgotten I could ask for help. I'm used to being strong – although I long desperately to let myself be weak again.

The third year of the full-scale war has also brought an understanding and awareness that we, the wives of soldiers, are stuck in between worlds. We are not in the military, we are not brothers-in-arms to our husbands, but we're no longer civilians, either. We have lost the ability to live an ordinary life. We get deeply upset when people evade the draft and refuse to defend our homeland. It's not that we want anyone to experience first-hand the horrors of the battlefield – it's far too harrowing. But at the same time, we want relief for our loved ones so that we could spend a few days together.

Yes, we realize that our lives will never be the same. The return of our loved one from the war will just be the beginning of a new and difficult journey. Will things ever get easier? Unlikely. I just hope and pray that our children won't have to go through anything like this.

One day, my little Eva cried on the way home from preschool. "Mom, why do other kids get picked up by their fathers?" I explained what's happening, of course, but what can I do to help her deal with such difficult emotions? She is still experiencing them.

My heart breaks every time my little daughter cries at night for her Daddy or my son rewatches videos with Dad again and again, talking to the figure in the video. I can't promise them that everything will be fine, but I can be there for them in these challenging times. We hug a lot more and frequently say "I love you." Alongside their hatred for the "Muscovites" – the Russians – who took away their chance to grow up with Dad and forced them to waste time sitting in shelters, they also need to feel love.

Sometimes, I worry that my husband and I have changed into very different people. We've both been through a lot – and we went through it while very far apart, with barely any opportunities to communicate. Yet I remind myself that it is God who united us. He brought us together from very different families and regions of the country. God knows the future. He knows what our family has to go through. He knew it back then, too. And I believe that his blessing and the love he's given us will give us the strength to follow the path we have chosen. We have wonderful children – amazing little people, with their own views and desires. They know exactly where their Dad is and why he is there. Most importantly, they know that he loves them dearly and misses them so much. I lean on the Lord, asking that he will grant us all strength, wisdom, and patience.

Do I think this could all end differently than we hope? Yes, as a mature adult, I'm well aware that some of us may not survive this way in this war. Although I often feel that everything will turn out all right, my thoughts can be different. I hope for the best, but I live with the understanding that the worst could happen. But I believe that God is always with me – in my deserts, in my joys, and also in the tedious, humdrum routines of day-to-day life.

But I, a newly minted introvert, still lack a healthy community. I keep searching for one. I dream of the day when sermons in our churches will be sound and relevant. We cannot go on pretending that this war does not concern us Protestants . . .

The other day, I was at the funeral of soldiers, men who had done a lot of good, friends who had been killed when an incoming shell hit their dugout. There were about twenty priests at the funeral – but not a single Protestant minister. I thought about this for quite some time. I was taught that Christians should suffer with and bear the burdens of their people. I can't be responsible for what others choose to do – or choose not to do. But I thank God for my path, here in the rear, working with the families of soldiers, while there on the front line, my husband has become one of the best commanding officers. I wish I had a priest with whom I could share all that I'm going through. But I am grateful that I still have God, who understands me completely.

"Relatives and friends come together. It feels like a wedding all over again. Except this time it's a black dress, not white. It's picking out a coffin, not a ring. There's a certificate of death, not marriage. It's still necessary to send out invitations, plan a dinner, choose a place, write a speech . . . 'Until death do us part' echoes faintly." Daria Papushoi (p. 271)

11

Faith in Spite of Everything

Daria Papushoi

Wife of a Fallen Hero, Mother of a Wonderful Boy

I remember us sitting in the car and trying to make the most difficult decision of our lives. The trunk was packed tight with belongings we had amassed over almost five months of married life. The phone kept buzzing with inconceivable news. Somewhere in the distance, another explosion boomed. After that, silence hung heavy.

"I must go."

More silence.

"I'm so afraid, Dasha."

"Afraid? Of what?"

"I'm afraid of the unknown before me. Afraid to leave you and not be right by your side when you need me the most. Afraid for the lives of my mother and sisters. Afraid of making the wrong decision and regretting it for the rest of my life. But if I stay – I'm afraid I'll never forgive myself."

"We'll pull through. If you truly feel that your right place is there, I'm sure that God will take care of us here."

"So that means you'll let me go?"

Still silence. Then, a stifled cry.

"Hardly. And yet, I know that if I love you, I must let you go."

We embrace and hold each other tight.

"Do you remember that time after we got married when we sat in the kitchen drinking tea?"

"I sure do! I remember adding just two teaspoons of sugar in your tea instead of your usual five. But you, hubby dearest, didn't even blink. You just kept looking at me with those lovey-dovey eyes, trying to drink that concoction."

"I didn't want to upset my missus. You worked so hard on that cuppa tea."

A smile brings on a fleeting flood of memories.

"Anyway . . . remember the promise we made to each other that evening?"

"That we would depend on each other but not be dependent?"

"Precisely. That we would put our hope in the Lord, help each other through this life's journey, and accomplish our purpose."

"And you think that time is now?"

"I think so, yes."

"Then I do let you go. With a heavy heart, but I do. Because I know that wherever you are, God will be with you."

"Thank you, darling. It means a lot to me to have your support. Will you pray for me?"

"Of course!"

Hands joined, heads bowed . . .

"Oh Lord, thank you for Pavlo. Thank you for his brave, selfless, humble heart. You have formed him to be remarkably strong. You have brought him through many trials and troubles. You made his feet like those of a deer and trained his hands for battle. You hold his hand and guide his paths. Heavenly Father, be with him wherever he goes. Protect him from evil and bring him home safe and sound. You know that I love him more than life itself, but your love for him is so much greater. I put his life in your loving hands. In Jesus's name, I pray. Amen."

"Amen. Dasha, I love you so much!"

Our Family Story

Prayer runs like a red thread through the whole story of our family. This story is one marked by many challenges and trials, and sprinkled with joy and sorrow, but I believe that it was prayer that helped us get through it all and keep loving God and each other.

I began praying for my future husband when I was a teenager. At a Christian summer camp, I made a promise to God that I would save my heart for the man I would one day call the father of my children. I took this promise so seriously that even Pavlo, my husband, had to work hard to earn that place in my life. Every year at camp, there'd be a workshop on "Relationships before Marriage," which ended with an assignment for all the participants, both boys and girls. Our task was to make a list of qualities and traits we'd like to see in our future spouse. My list was rather elaborate. I wrote down every little detail: love for sweets and hiking, and a passion for mountain camping and stargazing. I prayed for his safety and that his heart would be filled with wisdom, faith, and love.

I also put together a list of qualities that the Bible says a wife should have so that she can, in due season, become an answer to her husband's prayers.

Our family story began in October 2020, while I was serving as a missionary in Mykolaiv, a large city in the south of Ukraine. One Sunday, after the service, a woman came up to me and asked if I would pray for her son, Pavlo, because he was serving in the army and, she felt, needed prayer support. I hadn't yet met Pavlo, but every night, I prayed that God would be with him wherever he went. As I continued working with the local youth, I met Pavlo's younger sister and, later, Pavlo himself. He had a warrior's heart and godly wisdom. At the time, he was enlisted in the army under contract, but two weeks after we met, he was deployed to the Anti-Terrorist Operation in Donbas.

The day before he left, he sent me a text message: "Would you like me to show you a place of power and peace? I know that you have to deal with a lot of people, and it's gotta be exhausting."

An hour later, we were seated on the edge of a cliff. Silence, stars, and a lighthouse beam were our only companions. Pavlo shared stories of his life as a soldier. I reflected on the challenges I faced as a missionary ministering to youth. Such seemingly different walks of life, but we still had something in common: a willingness to be a humble servant with the brave heart of a warrior. We shared our vision for the future, including the way we pictured a family. We talked about mountains and the starry sky. As the conversation ended, I prayed a blessing over Pavlo's deployment. I felt as if I had known him my whole life – a kindred heart if ever there was one. After I got home that evening, I turned to the last page of my diary, the one with my list of qualities. I smiled and thought: "He does love mountains and sweets."

We didn't know that night how much our lives would intertwine, what trials our relationship would face, or how that lighthouse would become a place filled with so many memories.

During the time Pavlo was deployed, I often went to that lighthouse alone. I prayed for his needs, big or small, asking for strength, resilience, and courage. And it did become a place of power and peace for me. Here, I could feel God that much closer.

Although we were physically apart, Pavlo and I spent a lot of time together. I printed out his assignment schedule so that I could tag along, albeit virtually, and brighten his humdrum soldiering routine. At some time during the day, we'd each read a bit from a Bible reading plan from the YouVersion Bible app. In the evening, we'd discuss what we'd read and share prayer requests. I'd listen closely to all his stories and, at the end of the month, send him a letter capturing the highlights of his month:

12.01.2021

Druzhkivka, Donetsk.

A day in the life of a soldier

Well, now I'm sick. We've been outside all day packing up the equipment. I'm on my last legs, but at least I don't have back trouble. My phone gets too cold to work, so I have to warm it up in my inside pocket. I tried to warm up some water in the sun – it had got literally ice-cold overnight. I didn't think my sore throat would do well with something that cold. I took some paracetamol – that'll help. Hopefully, this will be resolved without complications. I received a text from Dasha, one with her favourite hashtag: "Guess what's this!" The accompanying photo shows a strange green fruit that looks a bit like a kiwi. Where does she find this stuff? "It's feijoa. Supposedly immune-boosting. Tastes like a mix of kiwi, pear, pineapple, and . . . soap. You have to try it!" She's funny, always trying to feed me. I love her various hashtags – they take my mind off things and brighten the mundane life of a soldier. We're reading our twelfth plan, "7 Laws of Love." I have never read so much in my life. I feel amazing! At the end of the day, we share an insight we particularly liked: "Love thrives where love is rooted in commitment." While I was on duty, we talked about the reading plan and how our day went. I think I'm starting to like being on duty despite the bitter cold I have to weather. The time now is just past midnight, so I'm a bit loopy. I got the second shift duty today, so I better catch some sleep before getting up in two hours. As is now our tradition, we'll share our prayer requests and a virtual hug. And I get back a dear sweet reply: "Good night, brave soldier. I'm waiting for you at home."

What a wonderful day this was! Thank you, God.

So we rejoiced together and wept together. As we couldn't see each other face to face, we learned to see and feel each other's hearts. God used this time to lay a firm foundation for the storms and trials of life ahead.

After Pavlo returned from his tour, almost every weekend we would take an evening walk together down the all-too-familiar path to the lighthouse and sit on the edge of the cliff. This was our place of power and peace. Those were some of our happiest, most carefree days. Eventually, Pavlo asked me to marry him. A few months later, on that very spot, I stood in front of him once again, this time wearing my wedding dress. "For better or for worse," echoed over the hills. "I do," we both confirmed.

We continued to come to the lighthouse in the evenings and share our dreams and plans for the future over a cup of fruit tea. But just like that October evening when I first heard of Pavlo, we had no idea what trials and tribulations awaited us.

Five months later, war would come to Ukraine. We would be sitting in the car, trying to make the most difficult decision of our lives.

Why? or What For?

The day after the mobilization announcement, my husband joined the 79th Air Assault Brigade. His mother, younger sister, and I sheltered in the basement of our house for a while before moving to the church's bomb shelter.

A cold basement. Blaring air-raid siren. Missile threat alert. Loud explosions. Children crying. People around are so different but scared just the same. I'm waiting for my love to call.

A bomb shelter. Blanket on the cement floor. Pixelated uniform. Frigid air. More than two hundred souls awaiting orders. My love is struggling to get phone reception.

"Hey! Can you hear me?"

"Yes, dear, I can hear you. It's so good to hear your voice! Are you all right?"

"I'm fine. I just miss you all a lot. Are you safe?"

"Yes, we're in the basement of the church. There are a lot of people here – your mom and sister, too. Don't worry about us."

"I'm being sent today with a few other guys to the fields to dig trenches. Please pray for our safety and for my health. My lungs are still bothering me."

"Why did they pick you, of all the two hundred people? Why does it have to be you? You're still sick! I don't understand . . . why?"

"Dasha, it's fine. Didn't you put me in God's hands? If so, don't ask *why* – ask *what for*."

Praying that evening was quite a struggle: Do you not hear my prayers? Does the cry of my heart not reach you, Father? Why do you stay silent? Where is your protection, your care, your answer? Where are you when I need you so much?

That night was rough. Early morning, at around 6:00 a.m., the city awoke to a faint rumble followed by an explosion. Russian missiles hit the barracks at the permanent base of the 79th Air Assault Brigade. At the time of the enemy attack, about two hundred soldiers were on the premises. Some were killed in their sleep.

It was the same barracks from which Pavlo had called yesterday . . .

Another call from my love.

"Dasha, don't you worry, I'm all right. It's terrible about the guys. There were so many of them there."

I could hardly hold back my tears.

"I was angry with God yesterday . . ."

"Why?"

"Because he doesn't hear my prayers and doesn't properly care for you."

"Do you take it back now?"

"Yes, I do."

"Remember this, because it's true: when God allows something 'bad' to happen in your life, he is actually protecting you from the worst thing that could have happened."

"Because he is good. He's been so good to us. Always."

"Precisely."

"I'm so glad you're fine!"

"I gotta run, lo . . ."

The connection was lost.

"I love you, too. Love you more than anything! Be safe!"

Thirty Seconds of Life

The hardest part of being a military family is living in two different worlds. His world is full of daily losses and trials. Death surrounds him on all sides, nipping at his heels every moment, but he wants to live. Your world is full of life – people around you are busy with everyday routines, planning, dreaming, laughing, and rejoicing – but you feel dead inside. Maybe that's why you wish life would speed up and the days would pass faster – so that you don't feel the pain and devastation. Meanwhile, he truly appreciates every minute because each moment could be his last.

> Donetsk. It's late at night. Yet another shelling. There were six of us there. A drone was hovering over us. We couldn't hear the artillery fire, only the explosions. We had to keep moving to survive. Having figured out that there's a thirty-second window between the shot and the explosion, I'd hit the ground for cover at the

twenty-eighth second. I counted out loud so those behind and in front of me could keep up. If I were lucky enough to survive, I'd get up and live another thirty seconds. And so it went on for three and a half hours. Through it all, I prayed and kept thinking of Psalm 23: "Even though I walk through the valley of the shadow of death, I will fear no evil, for you are with me; your rod and your staff, they comfort me" (ESV). Those thirty seconds of life were so precious as I was still alive; I still had a bit of time, for God has kept me safe . . .

During those three and a half hours, he could have died 420 times, but God kept him safe 420 times!

Almost every day, if I was able to get in touch with him, he would end the call by saying, "Just don't stop praying for me, please!" Because there, in the face of death, no one doubts the importance and necessity of prayer.

A Believer and a Soldier

Pavlo was probably the only believer among his fellow soldiers. Among the people we knew, very few believers were soldiers. Our family's decision caused a significant backlash from some of the churches and charities I worked with. Fortunately, our church honoured all those who stood up to defend Ukraine, supporting them both in prayer and action.

Should believers go to war and take up arms? I believe this is a personal decision, which should be settled strictly between a believer and God. But every time I'm asked that question, I remember a story that my husband shared at the beginning of the war:

There was a pastor serving in the infantry unit in the Marinka sector. Many people knew about him because it's not every day that you see a pastor with a machine gun, fighting side by side with his fellow soldiers, digging trenches, and sharing his last chunk of bread. But that pastor is remembered best for his actions during an assault, where he used his body to shield four of his fellow soldiers and, ultimately, took a fatal hit. At his funeral, the men recalled that the pastor had often told them about Jesus, who had given his life for them, and shared that they only fully understand this sacrifice after the pastor's death.

One of his fellow soldiers said, "We often talked about God, prayer, and death. When we asked him what assurance we'd have if we believed in his God, he offered a poignant explanation":

Suppose there are two soldiers serving in the same brigade – a believer and a non-believer. In a sense, they are on equal footing: both can die at any time. Prayer and faith in God do not guarantee that they will survive. But the essential difference between them is that the believer goes through all difficulties and trials with God, and death is only the beginning for him, while the unbeliever goes through life alone, and death is the end for him. Therefore, by believing in my God, you lose absolutely nothing. And, as old man Pascal once said: If there is no God and I believe in him, I have lost nothing. But if there is a God and I don't believe in him, I lose everything. That is pretty much it.

Advice for a Military Spouse

Being a military wife is no easy feat. Unfortunately, many women still underestimate the importance of their role. The truth is, a wife's delicate shoulders bear tremendous responsibility: to motivate and inspire, to offer wings and hope, to support and listen, to love deeply, and to help in making difficult decisions. And above all, to pray for him – because the fervent prayer of a loving wife avails much.

Below is my little "Note to a Military Wife" about her responsibilities:

- Make digital copies of your husband's documents and, if possible, note down passwords for the most important items such as his phone, bank cards, and so on.
- Get contact information for at least one of his fellow soldiers or officers so that you can always get in touch with your husband.
- Don't demand certain emotional reactions, and avoid triggering emotions that could negatively impact his focus – being emotionless and cool-headed on the battlefield is an important key to survival.
- Avoid involving him in mundane everyday problems that you can solve without his input. He is currently living a very different life and can't afford to be pulled in two different directions.
- Remind him frequently how proud you are of his decision to defend the country! That decision was not easy for him to make and stick to – especially when so many around him have quit. He is your hero, your defender, and your role model! He remains there for the sake of you and your family.

- Share your small victories with him (for example, I learned this, I did that, I was able to figure out this other thing), and, if necessary, remind him how irreplaceable he is in your life.
- Don't demand that he share with you everything that is happening at the front line. He's doing everything he can to ensure his own safety as well as yours. Be grateful for the information he shares, and trust him for what he cannot share.
- Take care of him. Be aware of his needs and try to meet them – buy him comfortable socks, a warm uniform, and yummy treats. You're a team – let him feel that!
- Pray for him constantly. A wife's prayers are powerful! Let him know that you're fighting this battle together as one: he has his line to hold and you have yours.
- Write to him often, letting him know how much you love him. He needs to hear this every day! It's much harder for men to love long-distance, so they are more likely to feel guilty. Don't let him doubt that he is the best man for you and that you love him more with every passing day.
- Listen to him, learn about his new hobbies and, if necessary, take the time to research all that military jargon you don't understand. Speak his language, and take an interest in his role and duty because this is now his way of life.
- Don't dump your dark mood or tears on him, and don't play games with him. If you have family, friends, or someone you can talk to, share those negative emotions with them. Then pass on the warmth and support you receive to him.
- Replace "It's gonna be all right" with "It's gonna be hard, but we'll make it through together."
- Share details of your day-to-day life and involve your husband in what's happening in your life. His life is not only in danger but also constricted and regimented, so think of ways in which you can help to spice it up a little.
- Learn about PTSD and read up on ways you can help him get back to normal life when he returns.
- Take care of yourself for his sake. If necessary, ask those around you for help. Stay safe – come home before dark, and shelter in the basement when shellings occur.

- Take proper care of yourself, continue to live life to the fullest, and embrace positive emotions. Remember that a happy wife makes a happy husband.
- Praise him frequently! His every victory, however small, is won by sweat and blood, and praise from a beloved wife is like a double victory.
- Always be on his side. Guard your heart and mind against rumours and negative comments about your spouse and your relationship.
- Give him tips to help him love you the way you need him to love you. His mind and thoughts are currently occupied with survival, so instead of holding on to unspoken expectations or resentment, help both him and yourself by direct and honest communication.

Wait for him, no matter how long it takes. And remember this: if you have someone to wait for, someone to worry about, and someone who keeps you up at night, you are the most fortunate person in the world!

"An excellent wife who can find? She is far more precious than jewels. The heart of her husband trusts in her, and he will have no lack of gain. She does him good, and not harm, all the days of her life" (Prov 31:10–12 ESV).

Sorrowful News, Powerful Prayer

One year and eight months since the beginning of the full-scale invasion – that's how long my fight and endless prayers for my husband's life lasted. Waiting for him to return from the war alive was my only desire, my reason for waking up each morning and falling asleep at night, my motivation to hang in there and not lose heart, not lose hope, and fight . . . to the end. It feels like you are living, but it's like a dream. You work and volunteer as a form of diversion. You try to appreciate every minute because you understand that you only have one life, but at the same time, you wish that time would fly a hundred or even a thousand times faster so that this nightmare would finally end.

During this period, we had the opportunity to see each other four times. The final occasion was in Dnipro, where Pavlo was undergoing a military medical examination to approve his transfer to Mykolaiv. After that, he returned to the front line, waiting for his transfer order. I was supposed to welcome him home sometime in October.

Later that month, I found out that I was pregnant – we had a baby on the way! I was overjoyed because we had longed to have children and a big family ever since we started seeing each other. But it was only the next day that I could bring myself to share this news with my husband as I felt a strange premonition of inevitable pain. For some time, my health had prevented us from having children, so I knew that this was nothing short of a miracle! Yet at the same time, I felt as though this new life budding in me was given in exchange for another . . .

Pushing aside unnerving thoughts, I began to get ready for my husband's homecoming, decorating the house and baking his favourite home-made cake. I could hardly believe that after a year and eight months, I would finally see him back home.

A few days later, I received terrible news:

> He was taken to a hospital in the city of Dnipro. He is in a coma, in critical condition. A drone hit the car he and another soldier were in. They were on a mission. The other soldier survived but sustained numerous injuries. Pavlo collapsed almost immediately because shrapnel penetrated his skull. His chances of survival are slim but never zero.

Dumbstruck silence . . .

Prayer is not the word to describe my wails and groans that rose to the heavens that night. My broken heart was too heavy . . . but I had to keep my emotions in check for the sake of the new life growing inside me.

Knowing the power of prayer, I asked my friends and acquaintances to pray for Pavlo. My prayer request was shared all over Ukraine and far beyond its borders. People wrote from almost every corner of the world. Churches organized prayer chains so that prayers for Pavlo could continue day and night.

- Church in Poland is praying!
- Church in Cleveland is praying!
- We're praying here in Texas!

Canada, the US, Europe – people sent messages with their prayers. Some had never prayed before and asked me to teach them how to pray. Friends and strangers, believers and non-believers alike – it felt as if the entire world, all living beings, stood strong with me. I barely had time to cry because I was constantly receiving texts and calls of support.

Once again, God was closer than ever.

"So, Where Is Your God?"

"So, where is your God?" "Half the world prayed for a miracle, yet tragedy struck. Why?" "What's the point of prayer then if God doesn't hear?"

That day, I was asked many such questions. That day, I, too, had lots of questions for God.

I ran through nearly the entire hospital, looking for my husband in the intensive care units. I was sure he was not listed because of some clerical error. I bought ten pairs of shoe covers to help keep the ICU clean. I had brought him the ultrasound scans of our baby. I had packed a blanket to sit by his side day and night, waiting for him to wake up. I was ready for any diagnosis, any condition, any challenge ... But I was definitely not ready to hear that my beloved was no longer listed among the living. He had died at 8:00 a.m., without ever coming out of his coma. He died just a few days before returning home. He died at a time when half the world was praying for a miracle ...

> You have to go home now. You have a lot of paperwork to do.
> Please accept my condolences. Take care of the little one.

With jelly legs and misty eyes, I walked back down the same hallway I'd rushed through just fifteen minutes earlier. Not much had changed: an older gentleman was still eating his poppy seed bun, a mother and daughter duo were still waiting to be seen, and the nurse who had sold me those shoe covers smiled at me ... But this time, it felt as though I was in a dream – the kind of dream you long to wake up from and never see again.

I stopped just outside the hospital entrance. My mind refused to embrace reality, my thoughts were jumbled, and all I could think was, "My God, *why*? Why? I can't believe it! I don't want to believe this! Why ..."

Meanwhile, people around the world were continuing to pray and send words of support: "Dasha, we're here for you! God will work his miracles!" "Praying for Pavlo with faith in his healing!" "Our church is praying, waiting for good news!"

How could I tell all these people that praying was no use now? Or rather, how could I ask them to pray now, more than before, despite everything? How could I explain to an unbeliever why God did not hear and answer his first-ever sincere prayer? How could I defend God and his sovereignty – and did he even need me to come to his defence at all?

All these questions sprang up within my heart, their weight pressing down heavily on me.

I tried to think back to my husband's words at the beginning of the war. He was the one who taught me never to ask God "Why?" He taught me to believe without seeing, even in the most difficult circumstances. He taught me to replace my "Why?" with "What for?" Because God is faithful. He has been faithful to us. Always...

But this time, it was extremely difficult to make that switch. This time, everything around me seemed to be crying out with me: Why? Why, God? Because, unlike other hardships and trials of life, I knew there was no way to bring back the life that had been lost.

As I stood at the entrance to the hospital, I needed a *miracle*.

A miracle to get through all the stress and pain that awaited me and not let it all affect the child I was carrying.

A miracle to have the fortitude to support my family and friends, even while I needed support myself.

A miracle to let my husband go – right there, at the entrance to the hospital.

A miracle to hold on to my faith in the power of prayer and my faith in God, trusting that death and life are in his hands.

That day, the miracle that half the world had been praying for – the miracle intended for my husband – happened to me instead!

He's Home Now

Coming home makes it feel like this whole thing was just a bad dream. It feels more like I'm just waiting for him to come home... And maybe he *is* home.

The familiar scent of his clothes still lingers in our room.

An eyeful of all that gear – bought with donated money, carefully packed, and sent with love to keep him warm and safe.

The neat stacks of letters – he saved every single one.

Photos that he probably looked at before drifting off to sleep each night.

An ultrasound picture of our unborn baby.

A bloodied bulletproof vest.

A bloodied phone.

A next-of-kin notification of death.

He's home... or is he home?

The mind once again rejects the idea of loss because waiting for him is my familiar routine. "He will come back... he *has* to come back. He promised!"

Relatives and friends gather. It feels like a wedding all over again.

Except this time, it's a black dress, not white.

It's picking out a coffin, not a ring.

There's a certificate of death, not a marriage certificate.

It's still necessary to send out invitations, plan a dinner, choose a place, write a speech...

"Until death do us part" echoes faintly.

Once again, the heart beats wildly, awaiting the moment of our meeting.

The same loving eyes seek his face – except this time, he doesn't smile back.

It's not the first kiss – it's the last.

The warm embrace cedes to a chilling touch.

It's the last time his name is lifted up in prayer.

He no longer needs our prayers.

He is home now.

Testimony without Triumph

That day, standing at the front of the church, I had a hard time starting my testimony. I had thought about how to say this: "Hello, my name is Dasha. Hundreds of people around the world prayed for my husband's healing, but none of those prayers have been answered." Maybe I could begin, "Hello, my name is Dasha. Thank you for praying for the miracle of my husband's healing – unfortunately, there was no miracle."

I realized that I had never heard someone get up at church and share a testimony about pain and loss that ended like this: "I prayed and had faith, but I have not been healed by God. Yet I continue to be God's faithful servant because my faith and commitment to God are not contingent on what this God gives me."

Too often, testimonies are about triumphs, victories, fulfilled hopes, and answered prayers. Rarely are they about painful loss and continued faith despite the pain.

Many churches have created a kind of "success culture." If you love God, pray, read the Bible, go to church, engage in ministry, and avoid sin, you will experience blessings in your life, and God will be near. But if you have illness, pain, and trials in your life, it means that you need to examine your heart for sin and readjust your relationship with God. It seems like a kind of transaction. Where did we find such a God? Maybe the Bible portrays him incorrectly? Or maybe you have misplaced faith?

If the reason for your faith is miracles and a carefree life, then your faith has no roots and will not be able to withstand the storms of life.

Authentic faith does not depend on circumstances. Genuine love for God is unconditional and selfless.

An attack killed the wife and daughter of a soldier. The missile hit the house and left nothing but rubble. During the funeral, the soldier approached the priest with a question: "Well, where is your God?"

The priest replied, "My God is with me. I don't know where yours is."

A Tale of Two Wolves

Grief wields a powerful instrument called "power over thoughts." It skilfully uses this tool for its own purposes, filling the human mind and sending down its roots deep inside, holding tightly to the past and painting the future in every shade of sorrow. And if you don't master it, grief will take you over completely.

The pain does not go away – you just have to learn to live with it.

Healing is possible. What's not possible is getting your old life back.

The devil exists, and his mission is to bury you in your own thoughts.

When I was a child, I heard a story that I still use almost daily as I wrestle with my thoughts, "A tale of two wolves":

> Once upon a time, an old man shared a profound insight with his grandson.
>
> "You see, there is a constant battle going on inside every person. This struggle is very similar to the fight between two wolves. One wolf represents evil: envy, jealousy, regret, selfishness, greed, lies ... The other wolf represents good: peace, love, hope, care, kindness, loyalty, truth," said the old man.
>
> The grandson, moved deeply by his grandfather's words, thought for a moment and then asked, "Grandad! Which wolf wins in the end? The evil wolf or the good wolf?"
>
> The old man replied with a knowing smile: "The one you feed."

The better you know God, the easier it is to distinguish between thoughts that are of him and thoughts that come from the adversary. Then you can invite the former into your heart and allow them to take root, while uprooting the latter thoughts like weeds and keeping them from growing. This is daily, painstaking labour, invisible to others. It is a fierce battle that you wage with your own thoughts every second of every day. Each day, you celebrate small victories, step by step, falling and getting up, time and time again.

But you are not alone on this journey. God is still with you.

Healing Project

Time went by, but the prayers didn't stop. All those people who prayed for Pavlo and still believed in the power of prayer continued to pray for me and the baby. I truly believe that those prayers were the reason that my pregnancy went smoothly despite all the stress and struggles.

I didn't have time to mourn and weep. Instead, I turned my attention to getting our home ready to welcome my son. The house needed major repairs, and time was running out. Before he died, my husband had sent me a detailed plan of all the necessary repairs, but my state of health made it impossible for me to do anything. Friends and the church came to my aid. Every day, someone contributed their time and energy to the task: friends and strangers, believers and non-believers, brothers and colleagues. Some even came from other cities to contribute to this project. Some helped with their labour, some gave financially, and others shared advice or helpful contacts. The house was filled with music, laughter, fervent prayers, and conversations that soothed my soul. And from early in the morning until late at night, the work continued in full swing . . .

Similarly, work was taking place in my heart and in the hearts of all who came to my home. God used this time to teach me to accept help and allow others to serve and bless me – so that I wouldn't allow the devil to permeate my thoughts and my mind; so that, in the midst of my own pain, I could relate to the pain of others and offer a listening ear; so that I could feel his boundless love for me in the deepest parts of my heart; so that I could allow him to heal my heart; and so that I could become an instrument for righteousness in his hands.

I remember sitting on the floor of my room after an exhausting day and noticing an old hammer in the corner. Over the years, it had done so much work in this house! Although shabby and cracked in several places, the hammer shone in the hands of its master and did so much good. It could have stayed on the shelf in its original packaging and avoided being beaten by life. It could have worked hard to avoid those blows and preserve its original appearance and shape. But then, there would have been little point in its existence. I bowed my head in prayer: "Thank you, Father, for using me for your glory. Thank you for every scar, every trial, and every heartache. All these have made me stronger in one way or another. Help me not to compare myself to other hammers and envy their newness and shine. Help me always to be an instrument of righteousness in your hands. Amen."

Within a few months, the house was completely transformed. A week after the renovations were complete, this house welcomed a brand new life.

Hello there, Son!

Throughout my pregnancy, I saw God's hand at work, caring for me and my baby. Despite my past health issues, my vital signs and all my tests were normal, and the baby was developing right on target. The doctors were always amazed, and they all said the same thing: "It's a real miracle!"

The labour and delivery were no less of a blessing. A mere two hours passed between my checking into the hospital and finally holding my son!

People continued to pray, and I continued to see miracles in my life.

On my son's birthday, I wrote him a short letter to commemorate the journey we had been on together:

> Hello there, Son!
>
> It might be a while before you can actually read this, but trust me, when you do, you'll be amazed. Your whole journey, from conception to birth, was a miracle! You had no idea what a light you would bring into this world. I think you still don't fully know it . . .
>
> Hundreds, maybe thousands, of people were praying for you, for your life. The doctors didn't think your existence was even possible. The circumstances at the time had them thinking you might not make it. But they didn't know that your life was in the hands of God himself! They didn't know that the miracle prayed for your father would be passed on to you . . .
>
> Your dad gave you everything he had, to his last breath, and his prayers are still at work in your life. His friends continue to care for you. People from all over the world whom you haven't even met send you gifts and write that they've been waiting for you to be born and continue to keep you in their prayers. I suppose that means you have your own army of prayer warriors. Imagine that! Looks like from the day you were born, you are a warrior, just like your father.
>
> You are so blessed to have real friends. Your dad always said that friends are a treasure that money can't buy. Well, that means that you were born the richest person ever! Friends and family members can't wait to tell you about your father. I can't wait, either, because your dad was an incredible man.
>
> You have made me the happiest person in the world . . . for the second time. Thanks to you, the love between your dad and me lives on. It will keep watch over you for the rest of your life,

both from heaven and from down here on earth. You can be sure that this love will never fade or end!

Your name has a special meaning: Timothy means "one who honours God." Honour him, Son, and you will see many more miracles in your life.

much love

your smitten Mom

I already have one family tradition with Timothy: every morning before breakfast, I pray with him for his future wife and bless her day. When he grows up, we'll make a list together so that he, as a future husband, can be the answer to the prayers of his future sweetheart.

Life with God: Before and After

Has my relationship with God changed? I can confidently say that it has. It has become much deeper and stronger. I still run to him in both my joys and my sorrows. But now, my relationship with him is less about me and more about him. My conversations with him are filled with more silence. I no longer try to impress him or win his approval because I know that he loves me unconditionally. I have stopped defending and justifying him because he doesn't need me to do so. I have stopped expecting him to fulfil all my wishes. And even though I still sometimes struggle to understand his will, I no longer ask him "Why?" or even "What for?" – instead, I just want him to be near when those questions arise.

I realized that I actually knew him too little and not learned enough about him. What is he like? The Bible says that the limits of the Almighty are higher than the heavens and deeper than Sheol (see Job 11:7–8). His fullness cannot be fathomed.

As someone has said "Life with God is not immunity from difficulties, but peace in difficulties."[1]

I continue to pray. I continue to believe in miracles.

"Even though I walk through the valley of the shadow of death, I will fear no evil, for you are with me; your rod and your staff, they comfort me" (Ps 23:4 ESV).

---

1. Sometimes attributed, probably wrongly, to C. S. Lewis. See https://essentialcslewis.com/2018/02/03/ccslq-43-immunity-from-difficulties/.

"I encountered you in a queue for canned food in Chernihiv. I saw you in a children's camp in Kherson. You were also present at the meetings with the families of the victims. I built a new house in a destroyed village – and it turned out that you now live in it. Well, hello, God, you are with me once again." Dmytro Tyshchenko (p. 292)

12

Gospel in a Yellow Box

Dmytro Tyshchenko

Leader, Mercy Ministries, Ukraine for Christ; Pastor, New Life Church, Kyiv, Ukraine

Losing God

Before the full-scale invasion, the biggest challenge to our faith was the age old question: "where is God when we suffer?" This question assumes that God exists; what needs expounding is whether he is near and why he lets us suffer. But in wartime, there's no room for God. No one here asks where God is or why he is letting all this happen. He's just not here.

I can imagine God being present in a hospital by the bedside of an ill person. There's a cross on the wall, and a New Testament – courtesy of the Gideons – sits on a shelf. That feels right and proper because we're accustomed to thinking of God when we are in a church, a hospital, or a cemetery. He must feel right at home there. But not in war. There is no God in that place of cruelty, atrocities, blood, dirt, and constant propaganda lies. It's hard to imagine war as a place for a human being, let alone God. War is a time of chaos and darkness, ruled by bloodthirsty predators.

So, when the full-scale war began, I lost that sense of God's presence. It was a bit like that moment in the fairy tale *Cinderella* when the clock strikes midnight and Cinderella's carriage turns back into a pumpkin. All that was once lofty, spiritual, and beautiful turned grey, dull, and profane; the dream world collapsed, revealing an ugly reality. The Bible no longer seemed like a relevant religious book. Sunday services felt more like refugee networking events. Back then, there were many people who felt like us in the churches of Lviv.

Prayer held out longer than any other spiritual practice that the war undermined. Perhaps that was because we were compelled to pray without ceasing: pray to get out of Kyiv, pray to find shelter on the way to Lviv because traffic jams meant travelling well into the night; pray that the car wouldn't break down during a twenty-hour trip in terrible traffic; pray that the queue at the petrol station would move faster; pray that we could find a place to rent in Lviv; and, needless to say, pray that we wouldn't get caught in a shelling.

My ability to preach has suffered even more. This was absolutely devastating because preaching had always given meaning to my life. But the war challenged everything – not just my daily activities but also my sense of purpose. My familiar life fell apart, and I had to adjust to a different life: a different city, a different house, a different way of living. And, most importantly, I had to learn to live out a different purpose.

Life before War

We had been living in Kyiv for six years before the full-scale invasion began. I was working as a leader in a Christian organization. Our small leadership team ran a student movement that operated across the country, spanning about twenty cities. We had sixty people on staff and hundreds of volunteers and were represented, to some degree, in every major higher education institution in Ukraine.

My workplace was a nice modern office in Kyiv, and my work entailed travel to many big cities. Many of my colleagues were young thinkers, driven by a calling and desire to change the world. My wife worked in another office of the same mission organization. My youngest son attended an excellent private school. Our church – which was large and well-known in Kyiv – was doing well. My long-time dream of becoming a pastor had finally come true. At forty-two, I felt like I was at the top of my game. Although COVID-19 did hinder the success of some of our projects, overall, everything was great.

I had ample human and financial resources. We were developing modern approaches to ministry among young people. One of my projects on self-discovery had been picked up for translation and use in other countries. I was involved in the branding process, website development, and spreading fresh ideas about the dialogue between the church and today's youth. I regularly spoke at various Christian youth conferences and taught a course on practical evangelism at several seminaries.

Our large national student projects – the "Infinity" winter conferences and "Speakout" summer conferences that attracted hundreds of students from all over the country – inspired me greatly. We worked together with colleagues in the US and the EU because our mission was part of a global organization. Since our student movement in Ukraine was recognized as one of the most prominent, I had opportunities to speak at international conferences and share our insights and experiences with other student organization leaders. We had already made plans to hold major youth conferences in Ukraine in the summer and autumn of 2024, featuring international partners from all over the world.

But on 24 February 2022, all this came to an end. Life was forever split into "before" and "after." With the first explosions of Russian missiles striking Kyiv at 5:00 a.m., all my successes and achievements dissolved into nothing more than a mist of pleasant memories.

Westwards

That day, I experienced numbing fear and panic attacks for the first time in my life. The mission organization, like a true US corporation, had been preparing us for war, putting in place protocols for evacuation. I followed the messages in our group chats, tracking the departure of most of our staff's families as they left Kyiv and headed westwards. Some had left immediately and had already reached safer regions of our country. I was left distraught, staring at the red lines on the still-running traffic map app, the realization that we were effectively trapped by traffic jams slowly sinking in – not that we had any place to go since my mother was in Berdiansk and my wife's mother was in the Sumy region, both places that were even closer to the advancing Russian troops.

Ironically, it was the Russian KA-52 "Alligator" attack helicopters that snapped me out of my petrified state. About thirty of them, grim and menacing, flew over our rental house in the Kyiv suburbs. I found out later that they were carrying the landing party that attacked the military airfield in Hostomel, another suburb of Kyiv.

That terrifying "air show" prompted my swift decision to get out of Kyiv immediately. But where to go and how to get there was still a challenge, with night fast approaching and the roads still congested with vehicles. During those first few hours of the war, the sense of God's absence hadn't yet registered; on the contrary, his divine intervention seemed obvious. We found options for where to go and, miraculously, a place to stay for the night – a village near the Kyiv–Chop highway, which connects the capital to Chop, Ukraine's westernmost Ukrainian city and home of border crossings to Hungary and Slovakia. The village where we stayed overnight was later occupied by "orcs"[1] – yes,

---

1. A pejorative used by Ukrainians to refer to Russian troops. The word is borrowed from Tolkien's *Lord of the Rings*, where "orc" refers to a fictitious race of brutal monsters.

during the early months of the war, the choice names we used for the Russians could still be found in dictionaries.

One of my most striking memories of that harrowing road to Lviv involved pets. Dozens of families making a stop at a petrol station let their pets out of their cars. Cats, dogs, hamsters, and other animals rested alongside children at that petrol station. The scene was like a mashup of images of the millennial kingdom taken from a Jehovah's Witness magazine or footage from an apocalyptic film.

I also remember a coffee queue – full of drama and empty of hope. It was hopeless because the coffee machines at that fancy petrol station ran out of water, coffee beans, and milk. Who would have thought that it would be easier to get a full tank of fuel than a cup of coffee?

At one point, I thought we were finally starting to move again, but not for long. We had to inch towards Lviv for many hours in a never-ending traffic jam that felt more like a gridlock. The traffic jams stretched over hundreds of kilometres. The roadsides were lined with broken or abandoned cars, and some people were even driving along the oncoming lanes. This was only day two of the war, just a small drop in the sea of people leaving their homes and fleeing westwards. And it was even more difficult for those who didn't have a car or were heading out of Kyiv in the other direction.

A Different Lviv

Lviv felt very, very different – perhaps because it really was different now, shaped by a completely different set of circumstances. The existential crisis intensified with our arrival not as tourists but as refugees. Seeking shelter from war in a city where we had once spent our vacations destroyed our fond memories. Lviv's romantic atmosphere had vanished – now, instead of looking for a hotel, we were searching for decent accommodation to rent for less than $1,000 a month.

The residents of Lviv were very conscientious, sometimes overly so. Everyone dreamed of catching a "separatist." On our first Sunday there, in the parking lot near the church, one of our employees – who had evacuated from Kyiv but was originally from Mariupol and was driving a van with Donetsk licence plates – had his tyres deflated by locals who then called the police. We also faced a rather amusing situation in the METRO cash and carry. My wife was using her phone to take photos of canned stew to send to the owner of a catering company in Kyiv. This company was feeding up to five thousand people a day – Territorial Defence troops, children in the Okhmatdyt children's hospital, and volunteers – and we were bringing them food supplies from Lviv. During one of our regular shopping trips, a well meaning retired couple saw my wife taking pictures of the groceries and created an uproar, convinced that this was some kind of espionage. On another occasion, the residents of the building where we had miraculously found a decent apartment to live sternly questioned the landlord about why his new tenants were not sheltering in the basement during air raids.

Having said all this, I'd be remiss if I didn't mention the incredible volunteer efforts of Lviv's residents. The city transformed into a huge humanitarian hub, working around the clock to welcome tens of thousands of refugees arriving by train from Kharkiv, Zaporizhzhia, Dnipro, and Kyiv. Students from our movement also joined these efforts – some made sandwiches, others met arrivals at the train station, those who had cars were on duty at the railway station to drive refugees to the border or to local shelters, and others helped to clear out old basements and set up bomb shelters.

Church and Chinchillas

Churches were quickly converting their facilities into shelters. I vividly recall the first time I attended church after evacuating. The friends who had given us shelter were part of a small evangelical congregation that met in a rented space. This congregation had a sister church in Poland, which helped them to buy necessary supplies quickly – quite a feat at the time – and they had used sleeping bags and air mattresses to turn the main worship hall and all the Sunday school classrooms into a refugee shelter.

I decided to help out and eventually became a night manager of sorts. People kept arriving and had to be settled. Sometimes, volunteers would bring us several families off a 2:00 a.m. train for a quick rest before taking them to the Polish border at dawn. That's why volunteers were constantly present at the shelter.

One night, I helped settle five families from Irpin and Brovary, two towns in the Kyiv metropolitan area. They related how difficult it had been for them to just get to the Kyiv railway station and described their struggle to get on a train because the schedule was out of whack and so many people were trying to board. Their journey had been long and hard. One of the girls had brought her several cats along with her. Confined to their carriers the entire trip from Kyiv to Lviv, those poor creatures had to do their business in there as well. Distressed by the whole ordeal, they darted out and scattered as soon as she let them out.

There was also a large family from Kharkiv – adults, children, and five chinchillas in a cardboard box. They were allocated a Sunday school classroom to themselves, and the atmosphere was, well, pungent! For whatever reason, this family couldn't decide where to go next and ended up staying in the church shelter for two whole weeks. Although this was a breach of the shelter's rules, no one had the heart to kick them out.

This church community gave their all for this cause. Some of their members with experience in counselling offered spiritual and emotional support to the refugees. One such case was a mother of six, middle-aged but quite immature. She arrived at the shelter with her six children and struggled to figure out her next move. The women from the church took good care of her and her children, offering emotional support. Since she had never been abroad, they also assisted her with the paperwork necessary for border crossing. However, after a while, she began to exploit their kindness. This went on for a few weeks, but the volunteers remained unruffled and, eventually, helped this large family get to Poland.

My fondest memory is of a time when the church readily made the decision to cancel Sunday services because there were so many refugees in the shelter that it was impossible to free up the worship hall for even a few hours. Tired and sorrow-stricken Ukrainians from the south and east found places to sleep – even on the stage, alongside a cross and a drum set, while cats and chinchillas scampered about Sunday school classrooms. During those days, I had no desire to go to church to pray, listen to sermons, or sing. But this kind of worship appealed to me. This flexibility for the sake of charity functioned as a test of authenticity for God's church.

First Sermon

First, I had an internal debate about the need to preach. I am a pastor, and a pastor must speak to the flock, especially in trying times. The next issue I had to wrestle with was relevance. It made no sense to stand up before a congregation of people who had left their homes behind but had nothing to look forward to and offer tired clichés. I had always considered relevance and timeliness important for a sermon, but in the spring of 2022, these qualities were absolutely essential.

At that time, thousands of Russian-speaking refugees were trying to figure out life in the Ukrainian-speaking western parts of the country. It was a challenge for everyone involved. Lviv residents were stressed by hearing Russian spoken everywhere; refugees from Mariupol and Kharkiv felt out of place in the local culture. That's why my very first sermon after the full-scale invasion was titled "How Not to Lose Yourself in Troubled Times." I recognized that my audience was twofold: people fleeing the war and people taking in those refugees. Although both groups faced different challenges, both were experiencing the shattering of their familiar worlds.

I include below some excerpts from that sermon because it was an important stage in my recognition of a new reality and the renewed sense of God's presence in my life.

This is what I said to the refugees:

> "Now those who were scattered went about preaching the word" (Acts 8:4 ESV). Every single person brings something to the world. We can easily see this in the example of the church. As we relocate, in that move, we bring not just stuff we were able to pack but also culture, habits, language, and a world view ... When Europeans arrived in North America, they brought not only new faith but also new viruses. We can also trace the influence of certain nations on certain regions. Lviv is still marked by the legacy of the time the region was part of Poland and Austria-Hungary. German settlers left an indelible mark on the southern regions of Ukraine where I'm from. Those settlers built not only factories but also churches. Lutherans and Mennonites contributed to the emergence and spread of evangelical Christianity in Ukraine in the late nineteenth century.
>
> Wherever we go, we bring our identity, whatever is at the core of our being. Russian invaders did that, too. They brought into our towns and villages their ingrained values: drunkenness, theft, destruction, persecution, violence, and death.
>
> What do we bring as we come?
>
> Luke describes an incredible story of the church spreading beyond Jerusalem. Moreover, it happened not because of a missionary strategy set out by the apostles but after the stoning of Stephen and heavy persecution of Christians in Judea. People were fleeing persecution, and that's quite different from travelling for business or pleasure. That leaves you feeling quite helpless. But the early Christians rediscovered themselves in the gospel and found the ability to give. If our inner world is filled with the gospel and Jesus, if it's brimming with the hope of resurrection, then we will

hold on to it in the darkest hour. This faith will remain with us; this faith will be evident.

Personally, I have not had any trouble from refugees yet, but I understand that your church has encountered many challenges in interacting with different people. I especially remember one colourful guy (maybe he is here today) who lived in the church and walked around in nothing but a woman's plush robe, asking people if they have a smoke.

Let me tell you a little about myself. I'm not at home here, either. Even Lviv, the city I often long for and find so romantic, looks sad and depressed now. Some people seem irritated. And I understand why they react this way to me or to others.

My world lies in ruins, albeit not in a way like for the residents of Mariupol. All the projects I've been working on for years and which have finally begun to come to fruition – they are now irrelevant or downright impossible. Instead of organizing conferences, interviewing famous theologians, and travelling around the world to deliver lectures, I get to go to a wholesale market for canned stew and then sort it in my friend's garage.

What inspires me in this story of Christian refugees who fled Jerusalem is Philip. He did not lose himself in his grief. He understood that there is a purpose even in persecution and that Samaria had changed. "Philip went down to the city of Samaria and proclaimed to them the Christ. And the crowds with one accord paid attention to what was being said by Philip, when they heard him and saw the signs that he did. For unclean spirits, crying out with a loud voice, came out of many who had them, and many who were paralyzed or lame were healed. So there was much joy in that city" (Acts 8:5–8 ESV).

The next part of my sermon was directed towards those who were welcoming the refugees:

"Do not neglect to show hospitality to strangers, for thereby some have entertained angels unawares" (Heb 13:2 ESV).

"Rejoice in hope, be patient in tribulation, be constant in prayer. Contribute to the needs of the saints and seek to show hospitality" (Rom 12:12–13 ESV).

Back in those days, the fate of refugees and travellers was tragic. It's still a sorrowful thing today, but back then, people could die of cold and hunger if nobody would take them in to spend the night. There were no social service agencies, no notion of refugee rights. If you were a foreigner, anyone could wrong you. That is why in the old days of the patriarchs and later in the law, guidelines were laid down regarding the treatment of strangers.

Guests may come not only bringing problems but also bearing blessings, just as it happened with Abraham. This might be hard to believe because a stranger in our home sooner or later becomes a fount of trouble. As the saying goes, "A guest is like a bone stuck in your throat" or "Guests are leaving, thank God for that." This is how our typical selfish attitude towards other people plays out. That's why the Lord gives special commandments on this matter.

However, hospitality is not just about guests and refugees. Above all else, hospitality is about the ability to accept the other. In fact, tensions rise because visitors hailing from far away might as well be outright aliens to the locals. It's challenging to welcome and embrace a guest of a different culture. Some displaced persons from the east of Ukraine find it difficult to understand the local dialects of those from the west. And vice versa: the Russian language spoken by Kharkiv residents can greatly annoy Lviv residents.

Personally, I try to speak Ukrainian everywhere I go. But who am I kidding? My accent is so thick that everyone can immediately tell I'm not local.

Accepting – welcoming and embracing – the other does not mean agreeing. It does mean respect. And it is a sacrifice. God embraces us – even as we're far from him. The gospel taught the world to accept commoners, slaves, women, and children as equals. In Christ Jesus, "there is neither Jew nor Greek."

Perhaps it was easier for the believers. We leaned on the words of Jesus, paradoxical though they were: "For whoever would save his life will lose it, but whoever loses his life for my sake will save it" (Luke 9:24 ESV). And these words brought us understanding: losses still carry a purpose.

We also sought to find joy and comfort in serving our neighbours because it is more blessed to give than to receive.

Two Garages and Twelve Minibuses

I began this story by talking about the feeling of God's absence during the war. Dmytro Shandra, a young Kyiv poet turned combat medic, put it well: "There is no God in Donbas. He left for Poland via the Way Programme."[2]

After 24 February, I had to do some God-searching again because his presence in my life was no longer a given. I have already mentioned how I found a new way to attend church in a building that had been turned into a shelter for displaced people. But it was volunteering that played a key role in bringing God back.

Everyone was trying to stay busy, to do something useful and stay sane. Figuring out logistics was an excellent way to do that. For example, we had to find a seller abroad, buy communication equipment, and deliver it to the besieged Sievierodonetsk. What a quest that was . . . The brand's official distributor informed us that they were sold out and that the next delivery would be in six months. We had a whole team working on this. Some coordinated the process in Poland. Some handled the border crossing to Ukraine because such equipment couldn't be brought in without special paperwork and, as it turned out, without special connections either. My task was to deliver a $50,000 shipment from Lviv to Sievierodonetsk – and for this, I needed reliable transport.

Some of our workers owned passenger minibuses, which they used to evacuate people and deliver humanitarian aid to localities near the front lines. I realized that I, too, needed to get a minibus in order to actively support my country. That idea presented two challenges: first, where to find the money; second, how to buy and bring a minibus across the border. At the time, the used car market had been seriously picked over, and bringing in a new vehicle from abroad – say, from Germany – was incredibly difficult because men were not allowed to leave Ukraine and the customs offices were closed.

We needed a way that was at least semi-legal to bring minibuses to Ukraine. I contacted our partners in Switzerland and asked if they could buy the vehicle in Switzerland and drive it to Ukraine. At that time, I was still collecting donations to purchase just one minibus. But then a miracle happened: my private commitment grew into a large project that brought together two organizations – Ukraine for Christ and Campus Crusade for Christ. From March to May

---

2. On the first day of the full-scale war, 24 February 2022, martial law was introduced in Ukraine, suspending the right to leave the country for men of conscription age (18–60). The "Way Programme" (*Shlyakh*) – a system of electronic permits – was introduced to allow male volunteers to legally travel outside Ukraine for the purpose of transporting military equipment for the armed forces, medical supplies, and humanitarian aid. Sometimes, men who received permission to cross the border remained abroad and did not return to Ukraine.

2022, our Swiss partners bought and delivered twelve blue Opel Vivaro minibuses to Ukraine – well, one broke down on the way, so we actually received eleven vehicles. The buses were mostly in good condition, with low mileage. It seemed symbolic that they had previously "served" in the Swiss army – but only for non-combat missions such as transporting personnel over short distances. Their powerful diesel engines, with turbos still operational, saved the lives of our volunteers many times during their trips to the front lines. I remember how we revved up one of those buses to 180 kilometres per hour when fleeing from a Russian "Grad" shelling near Lysychansk.

When our Swiss friends bought the first four minibuses, I asked them to do two things: first, to load each one with the supplies that were needed at the front lines; and second, to place stickers with "The Four" symbols on the rear windows. "The Four" is the gospel in symbols, a long-standing resource of our ministry, originally designed by our Swiss partners and inspired by Bill Bright's landmark booklet, *The Four Spiritual Laws*.

At the time, I didn't realize that this marked the beginning of a new chapter for our mission. From that time, eleven identical blue minibuses with "The Four" stickers would be delivering humanitarian aid and evacuating people across Ukraine.

When we received the first four minibuses – filled to the brim with the supplies that were most urgently needed at the time – another issue arose: Where would we store it all? A friend of ours in Lviv had a workshop in a garage co-operative. This large, warm garage served as our first warehouse for humanitarian aid. Sometimes, important things begin with what may seem like mere coincidences. Later, we rented another garage next door, and that became our first official warehouse. But even after our humanitarian initiative moved to Kyiv – into a large industrial building capable of accommodating trucks – the garage in Lviv continued to operate as our western branch.

"For I Was Hungry and You Gave Me Food" (Matthew 25:35)

I have spent most of my life preaching the gospel to college-aged young people. I know what the good news is and how people receive it. My audience was mostly university students who led a fairly normal life. We talked about growth, self-awareness, emotional intelligence, and a coherent world view. Occasionally, some students needed more practical help, but this was rare and limited in extent. For the most part, our support was at the level of mentoring. And if a person was entirely uninterested in the spiritual aspect of our movement, sooner or later we parted ways because our goal had always been to help future leaders turn to Christ. However, after the beginning of the full-scale war, I became less interested in the intellectual and philosophical aspects of religious beliefs. I felt I had no right to simply talk to the needy about the love of Jesus without offering practical help.

On one occasion, we were leading a convoy of five minibuses, taking refugees from Nizhyn to Lviv and then to the Polish border. There were mothers with small children in my minibus. After several hours of travelling, when we stopped at a petrol station for coffee, I realized that we should also feed our passengers since they probably wouldn't be able to buy anything for themselves. I bought coffee and hot dogs for everyone. People were grateful, saying that their children hadn't had meat for a while. At that moment, I realized that getting these families to a safe place, putting them up for the night, and feeding them *was* the gospel and that, for now, that was all that was needed.

Sometimes, we distributed food kits while under shelling. On one occasion, a local pastor gathered a fairly large crowd of people eager to receive humanitarian aid. He suggested that we share God's word and pray for them. This was a residential area not far from Antonivskyi Bridge on the outskirts of Kherson. We could hear the distinct booms of artillery firing in the distance and then the unmistakable sound of another round of counter-battery fire – an artillery duel between Ukrainian forces on the west bank of the Dnipro River and Russian forces on the occupied east bank. So I simply said a few words about God's care, which is displayed through the volunteers who regularly bring in aid to the locals, and reminded the people that they were not forgotten – either by us in Kyiv or by believers in other countries, who were sending money to help Ukrainians get through this horrific time. It was just a three-minute message. Then we sent the people on their way.

As I see it, the war radically changed everything. Some people became disillusioned with God; others, conversely, finally turned to him. Some preachers started calling for repentance even more earnestly than before, seizing on the fact that needy people are ready to listen to anything for a can of meat stew. I found it extremely difficult to look needy people in the eye and tell them that God loves them. So, I limited my outreach efforts considerably. Now, I focus mainly on humanitarian projects, hoping to connect with God through his hungry and distraught children.

Yellow Is the Colour of Light and Joy

By April 2022, we had figured out all the places in Lviv – as well as in Kraków and Budapest – where we could purchase food in bulk and then deliver it to the needy. Almost everything was available in the wholesale market – but the terms were cash only. I remember one Roma man who gave us a substantial discount on vegetables when he found out that we were volunteers delivering aid to Kyiv, which was at the time was near the front line.

Cards were still accepted at the METRO cash and carry, but shopping there was a challenge due to ongoing air strikes and the resulting store closures during air-raid alerts. One day, after scouring the store for several hours and filling huge trolleys with all the necessary items, my wife and I were on our way to the checkout when the air-raid siren went off again – and the store shut down. It was already evening, and our blue minibus was scheduled to leave for Kyiv at 6:00 a.m. the next day.

As requests and opportunities mounted, our volunteer efforts needed to be better organized. That's when we came up with the idea of having food kits in branded boxes. While we weren't the first to realize that it was easier to transport and distribute food in small boxes, we adopted a distinctive strategy based on the concept of "The Four." We printed these symbols on the boxes and included booklets explaining their meaning. A person would receive not just one box but four over the course of a month. This support group strategy was designed to last four weeks, with each symbol representing part of the gospel. Once people received all four boxes, they could put the whole puzzle together. For the churches, this was a good opportunity to foster casual fellowship over a cup of coffee in small groups. This approach also eliminated the problem of some churches using humanitarian aid to manipulate people by distributing the food kits only after the Sunday sermon, thereby effectively pressuring the needy to attend their services.

But why are our food boxes yellow? Very often, these kits end up in the most depressing and gloomy places – such as a destroyed village in the Kharkiv region, where the shops have been closed for weeks. Then comes a blue bus full of yellow boxes. One day, I received a video of a volunteer wearing a bulletproof vest carrying one of our packages into a dark basement where a family with children had been living for several weeks. The box contained not just pasta and meat stew but also coffee, tea, candy, and biscuits. The children were overjoyed. In the darkness and hopelessness of that basement, the yellow box stood out like a ray of light. I pray that these people will take a decision to move to a safe place and, someday, rejoice not only in a beautiful package with good food but also in the word of God. But there is a time for everything.

Well, Hello There, God!

If I may expand on the metaphor of God leaving the hellish Donbas for safe Poland, I would add that he came back immediately – and that he didn't return empty-handed.

God came back to Lviv, driving one of those eleven blue minibuses. God came back to Sievierodonetsk with fifty excellent radios and a repeater that helped my friend's unit break out of an encirclement. God came back to me in the design of the yellow box – and over one hundred thousand of those boxes were distributed across Ukraine. God was present in a makeshift chapel in Lysychansk during a communion service we held for headquarters. There were explosions all around us, and a well-known military commander cursed out loud – but God is not frightened off by swearing.

I encountered you in a queue for canned food in Chernihiv. I saw you in a children's camp in Kherson. You were also present at the meetings with the families of the victims. I built a new house in a destroyed village – and it turned out that you now live in it. Well, hello, God, you are with me once again.

> Then the righteous will answer him, saying, "Lord, when did we see you hungry and feed you, or thirsty and give you drink? And when did we see you a stranger and welcome you, or naked and clothe you? And when did we see you sick or in prison and visit you?" And the King will answer them, "Truly, I say to you, as you did it to one of the least of these my brothers, you did it to me."
>
> Matt 25:37–40 (ESV)

Restoration and Our Future

In May 2023, we brought mattresses and yellow food kits to a small village in the Kherson region. There was not a single house left standing. The village had been completely destroyed because of its location on the line of contact. It was here that the Armed Forces of Ukraine had stopped the enemy on the outskirts of Mykolaiv.

At first, there were no shops open, so we brought food kits. Later, groceries became available, but since many houses had been left standing for months with damaged roofs, everything inside – including the furniture and other items – was ruined. People were returning to their homes, but they had nothing to sleep on. That's why we brought mattresses. One woman, after we carried a mattress into what was left of her house, ran after our minibus, begging us to help her rebuild her house. Essentially, it was a shed that had been damaged by shelling. The events of that day got me thinking: Who needs a box of food if they have no place to cook it? Who needs a mattress if they have no place to put it? I also realized that this woman and her fifteen-year-old granddaughter had no future.

It was an extremely difficult case. Valia (name changed to protect privacy) was raising her granddaughter, Lisa (name changed), alone. Her daughter's – that is, Lisa's mother's – parental rights had been terminated due to alcohol abuse. Valia also had an adult son, but after being shot through the spine by a Russian sniper during the ATO[3] and ending up in a wheelchair for life, he had started drinking and squandered all his benefits. Valia and Lisa had once lived in a nice house, but it had been completely destroyed – all that remained was a pile of rubbish. Some friends had sold her a very old and tiny house on loan, but then its roof was smashed by Grad rockets, the ceiling caved in, one of the walls collapsed, and, of course, there were no utilities. So Valia and Lisa moved in with their neighbours.

That trip made me realize that we needed a more comprehensive approach if we wanted to help in people's recovery and restoration. That's when I decided to start a rebuilding project. Fast-forward to summer's end – we had restored or built four houses. The first house we built was for Valia. We also partnered with a student movement team in Kyiv, who raised money to purchase a smartphone and laptop for Lisa so that she could continue her education online, which was the only option available in that region due to imminent danger. This team even worked out a customized integration and socialization plan for Lisa to spend a few weeks in Kyiv – learning to be a barista, experiencing life in a big city, and exploring options at various universities, with a view to further studies. Unfortunately, Lisa was hospitalized and couldn't attend.

Restoration is not only about buildings – it's also about people. That's why our mercy ministry adopted the following slogan: "Restoration for Ukraine and Ukrainians."

I now have a greater appreciation for the Gospel stories where Jesus healed people and proclaimed that the kingdom of God was drawing near and that this world destroyed by sin will be restored. The apostle John compares the gospel to the light that God separated from darkness at the beginning of creation: "The light shines in the darkness, and the darkness has not overcome it" (John 1:5). The darkness of war – brought to us by these savages from the North – is engulfing not only cities and villages but also people's souls. Despair echoes

---

3. The Anti-Terrorist Operation (ATO) was initiated in Ukraine in the spring of 2014 to repel Russian aggression in the Donbas region.

across destroyed homes and over the graves of fallen soldiers. Now more than ever, the church must act to bring God's comfort and healing to Ukraine. We used to go out in the streets, sing songs and proclaim the gospel in the form of biblical narratives and ideas. But writings and sermons have no power unless the Lord is behind them, working miracles and transforming our fallen world into the kingdom of God. For Valia and her granddaughter, the gospel became real in the form of a rebuilt house. The light overcame darkness when their old mud-brick house, battered by missiles, was made whole.

Today, sociologists and other experts are only just beginning to study the terrible consequences of this war for Ukraine. Millions of people are in need of restoration. I believe that Ukrainians have already recognized the dire need for radical changes, both political and societal. Our mental health is anchored in the hope of victory and change. Therefore, it is impossible to envision Ukraine's future without restoration. I hope this war will help the church to grow in maturity. Our theology must focus on the concept of comprehensive restoration, in which the gospel is not reduced to an ideology but proclaimed and revealed through practical and social aspects. It is essential to turn from judgemental and preachy practices to constructive and humanitarian ones. The church must once again reform itself and become a community that welcomes all kinds of people and contributes to their recovery – a community for the millions of Ukrainians ravaged by war.

Bottom Line

From February to May 2022, our family lived in Lviv. Those three months seem reminiscent of the three days the Saviour spent in the tomb – a special time of transition from death to resurrection, from decline to restoration. Those three months changed me forever.

In early June 2022, we returned to Kyiv to launch a project to help the displaced. It had a simple name: "Yellow Boxes." We aspired to put together and distribute ten thousand food kits marked with "The Four" symbols. Our garage in Lviv was too small to handle a project of this scale, so we rented a three-hundred-square-metre warehouse in Kyiv, which had all the equipment necessary to assemble and store our kits.

God performed a miracle. This project became a distinct mercy ministry of the Ukraine for Christ Mission (known worldwide as Campus Crusade for Christ or Cru). Today, our team consists of seven staff members and dozens of volunteers. More than one hundred thousand yellow boxes have already been distributed. We also began making Christmas-themed kits and special kits for troops – and have distributed twenty-five thousand of these so far.

Our warehouse has become a volunteer hub, where volunteers from all over Ukraine – and sometimes even from other countries – gather every week. These are people of varying ages and from all walks of life: students, youth from church groups, internally displaced persons, veterans, widows, chaplains, activists and representatives of volunteer organizations. Quite often, people who have received our yellow boxes or Christmas parcels come and offer their help. For some displaced people and widows, volunteering at the warehouse has become a form of therapy.

Besides producing and distributing the food kits, we hold workshops to train moderators for support groups that use our programme. We regularly travel to the front lines to help both troops and civilians.

We have also started accepting shipments of humanitarian relief from our partners in Germany, the Netherlands, and the UK – these include clothes, mattresses, blankets, medical equipment, generators, personal care products, and much more. This cooperation has enabled us to expand our humanitarian efforts across a wide range of projects.

We are rebuilding destroyed homes in the Kherson region, as well as helping the army, police, firefighters, universities, secondary schools, orphanages, hospitals, and shelters for women who have experienced violence at home or during the Russian occupation. We work with about 250 churches and non-profit organizations across the country. And it all started when a few internally displaced people packed one hundred food kits in a rented garage in Lviv . . .

When I think about the future, two things help me hold on to hope. First, the unchanging character of God. If God remains active in my life even during the war, even when I do not feel his presence and lose the desire to commune with him, then no new upheaval can undo his love for me. Second, I hope that my theology and practical ministry will always be ready to adapt and face new challenges so that I can stay grounded and be truly helpful.

Langham Literature and its imprints are a ministry of Langham Partnership.

Langham Partnership is a global fellowship working in pursuit of the vision God entrusted to its founder John Stott –

to facilitate the growth of the church in maturity and Christ-likeness through raising the standards of biblical preaching and teaching.

Our vision is to see churches in the Majority World equipped for mission and growing to maturity in Christ through the ministry of pastors and leaders who believe, teach and live by the word of God.

Our mission is to strengthen the ministry of the word of God through:
- nurturing national movements for biblical preaching
- fostering the creation and distribution of evangelical literature
- enhancing evangelical theological education

especially in countries where churches are under-resourced.

Our ministry

Langham Preaching partners with national leaders to nurture indigenous biblical preaching movements for pastors and lay preachers all around the world. With the support of a team of trainers from many countries, a multi-level programme of seminars provides practical training, and is followed by a programme for training local facilitators. Local preachers' groups and national and regional networks ensure continuity and ongoing development, seeking to build vigorous movements committed to Bible exposition.

Langham Literature provides Majority World preachers, scholars and seminary libraries with evangelical books and electronic resources through publishing and distribution, grants and discounts. The programme also fosters the creation of indigenous evangelical books in many languages, through writer's grants, strengthening local evangelical publishing houses, and investment in major regional literature projects, such as one volume Bible commentaries like *The Africa Bible Commentary* and *The South Asia Bible Commentary*.

Langham Scholars provides financial support for evangelical doctoral students from the Majority World so that, when they return home, they may train pastors and other Christian leaders with sound, biblical and theological teaching. This programme equips those who equip others. Langham Scholars also works in partnership with Majority World seminaries in strengthening evangelical theological education. A growing number of Langham Scholars study in high quality doctoral programmes in the Majority World itself. As well as teaching the next generation of pastors, graduated Langham Scholars exercise significant influence through their writing and leadership.

To learn more about Langham Partnership and the work we do visit **langham.org**

www.ingramcontent.com/pod-product-compliance
Lightning Source LLC
Chambersburg PA
CBHW070753230426
43665CB00017B/2345